D1271903

The Burning of His Majesty's Schooner *Gaspee*

Journal of the American Revolution Books highlight the latest research on new or lesser-known topics of the revolutionary era. The *Journal of the American Revolution* is an online resource and annual volume that provides educational, peer-reviewed articles by professional historians and experts in American Revolution studies, and is edited and managed by Todd Andrlik and Don N. Hagist.

Other Titles in the Series

Grand Forage 1778: The Battleground Around New York City
by Todd W. Braisted

The Road to Concord: How Four Stolen Cannon Ignited the Revolutionary War
by J. L. Bell

The Invasion of Virginia 1781
by Michael Cecere

A JOURNAL OF THE AMERICAN REVOLUTION BOOK

THE BURNING

OF *HIS MAJESTY'S*

SCHOONER

GASPEE

AN ATTACK ON CROWN RULE
BEFORE THE
AMERICAN REVOLUTION

STEVEN PARK

WESTHOLME
Yardley

Westholme Publishing, LLC
904 Edgewood Road
Yardley, Pennsylvania 19067
Visit our Web site at www.westholmepublishing.com

First Printing November 2016
10 9 8 7 6 5 4 3 2 1
ISBN: 978-1-59416-267-1
Also available as an eBook.

Printed in the United States of America

CONTENTS

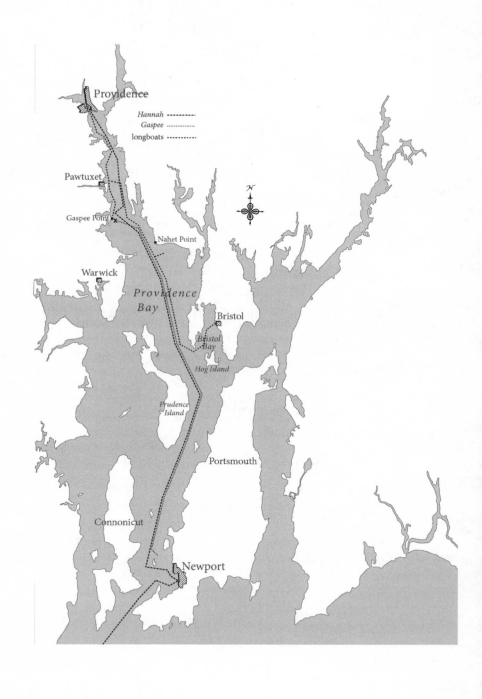

Providence

Hannah ----------
Gaspee ....
longboats ----------

Pawtuxet

Gaspee Point

Nahet Point

Warwick

*Providence
Bay*

Bristol

*Bristol
Bay*

Hog Island

*Prudence
Island*

Portsmouth

Connonicut

Newport

INTRODUCTION

THIS BOOK EXAMINES IN DETAIL A SINGLE EPISODE IN ONE SMALL British colony, an episode that unfolded over an eighteen-month period. The actors in this narrative lived in the expansive and diverse Atlantic world. The predominantly English-speaking, white, Protestant men who monopolize this narrative lived in a maritime culture[1] where diverse people of African descent, Native Americans, and Francophones moved freely (and some not so freely) conducting their business, raising their families, and meeting in their houses of worship. The British schooner *Gaspee* was boarded off the coast of Rhode Island by men of relatively high station in the colony but assisted by others, several of whom were black. The only colonist to give a deposition in the *Gaspee* investigation was an African American man named Aaron Biggs. When another colonist, Stephen Gulley, headed to Newport to tell his story, he heard reports that there were Indians on the road with pistols who would thwart his attempt to "turn informer." The maritime culture of colonial Rhode Island was a diverse and well-connected world.

British America in 1771–1772 was relatively calm in the wake of the repeal of most of the provisions of the 1767 Townshend Acts. Most inflammatory rhetoric of the 1760s had subsided, and merchants returned to the business of making profits. But Rhode Island merchants would not quickly forget some recent unruly behavior when a mob formed around one of the *Gaspee*'s sister schooners, the *St. John*. Only eight years earlier agitated colonials attacked some of the *St. John*'s crew, threatened to burn the vessel, and fired at this schooner from Newport's battery. The gunner, who wisely fired wide shots, was reprimanded by colonial leaders for his poor marksmanship. A similar event occurred in 1769 when a Newport mob succeeded in burning and destroying the *Liberty*, formerly the property of radical Boston Whig John Hancock, but subsequently pressed into the unpopular Royal Customs Service.

One reason that Rhode Islanders reacted so strongly to interference in their smuggling trade was that colonial British America could not produce enough molasses to keep their economy going. So Providence merchants traded extensively with the French-speaking peoples of the West Indies during times of peace and war. Officials in London could only see this as treason, and with the renewed emphasis on traditional imperial mercantilism after 1764, Rhode Island's maritime behavior seemed piratical. Rhode Island's economy was highly dependent upon the larger Atlantic world, and the molasses and slave trade. Thirty years earlier Governor Ward had reported to the Board of Trade:

> Navigation is one main pillar on which this government is supported at present. . . . We have now above one hundred and twenty sail of vessels belonging to the inhabitants of this colony, all constantly employed in trade; some on the coast of Africa, others in the neighboring colonies, many in the West Indies, and a few in Europe.[2]

Referring to the 1760s, naval historian Neil R. Stout argued that Rhode Island was unique among the colonies:

> The resistance that the navy and the customs service met in Rhode Island was not typical of the other northern colonies. The very life of Rhode Island depended upon the molasses trade, which was one reason why its citizens rose up in a violent and united op-

position that other colonies mustered only for the Stamp Act crisis.[3]

This study focuses primarily on the events in a single colony, surrounding the fate of a single schooner, and the failures of a single commission. Because Rhode Island was unique among the colonies, a study of this colony runs the risk of being idiosyncratic. But when Rhode Island is considered in the larger context of the scholarship of Atlantic history, this study can contribute to the growing knowledge of the regions bordering the vast Atlantic basin.

One

Trading with the Enemy

ENGLAND WAS AT WAR WITH FRANCE THREE TIMES DURING THE first six decades of the eighteenth century. In fact, between 1739 and 1763, the nations enjoyed only six years of peace. Therefore, the English colonies of North America found ways, legally and illegally, to trade with French possessions in the Caribbean during peace and war.[1] English colonial governors were empowered to issue a "flag of truce," a pass under which vessels could visit French ports to exchange prisoners. This loophole was widely abused; frequently a group of prisoners was returned one at a time in order to gain access to French trade. Indeed, Sometimes these vessels carried no prisoners at all. Some "prisoners" were merely French-speaking colonists who made the trip both ways. In March 1761, prisoner exchange became the duty of the Royal Navy, ending the convenient "flag of truce" smuggling.[2] Massachusetts governor William Shirley wrote to the Board of Trade in 1748, indicating that of the sixty vessels that had left New England for the French Caribbean islands over the previous eighteen months, the lion's share hailed from Rhode Island. During King George's War, Shirley believed that these French possessions would have surrendered without access to this crucial supply line.[3] Even Rhode Island's governor Stephen Hopkins admitted that during the first four years of the Seven Years' War, thirty-two Rhode Island vessels sailed to French ports under flags of truce. Many transported lumber and British dry goods that helped to fit out French privateers and also aided island communities—delaying their surrender to besieging British forces.[4] The Board of Trade made an official inquiry in 1759 regarding the illegal trade with the enemy that took place between the North American colonies and the French and Spanish islands. The Board of Commissioners was not surprised that it occurred; they merely remarked that they were unable to prevent Ireland from providing beef to the French army—and Ireland was closer to England and much more strictly governed. In early 1760, the Privy Council reported to the king that a serious trade problem in the Empire was occurring between the Spanish colonial port of Monte Cristi in the West Indies and the independent charter colonies of Connecticut and Rhode Island.[5] The report's scope went far beyond issues of trade regulations and smuggling; it recommended voiding these colonial charters, making them royal colonies and thereby more directly subject to imperial control.[6] In addition to direct trade, indirect trade with the enemy was done through neutral ports. The colonies of Pennsylvania and Rhode Island were infamous for their illegal wartime trade between 1756 and 1763, during the Seven Years' War (known as the French and Indian War in North America).

At the close of the Seven Years' War, George Grenville became First Minister and the head of the Treasury Department. Grenville was horrified by the size of England's debt: £137 million of debt cost the government 5 million per year in interest at a time when the government only collected 8 million annually in revenue.[7] Sir William Meredith, addressing Parliament, said, "That if necessity gave a right to tax America, the state of our finances at the close of the last war fully justified the Stamp Act."[8] Looking for a way to solve three different problems—England's debt, colonial smuggling, and freeing the colonial judiciary from popular pressure[9]—Grenville turned to the Customs Commissioners. In March and April 1763, while still the First Lord of the Admiralty, Grenville sponsored the act[10] which made the Royal Navy an integral part of the Customs Service. This expanded the "Hovering Act" passed under George I and gave the navy a new mission in North America now that hostilities with France had ceased. Sea officers carried two commissions, one from the Admiralty and one from the Treasury.[11] Many sea officers did not want to return to England where their inactive status would demote them to half-pay, a system of semi-retirement. Still smarting from what many officers considered colonial "trade with the enemy," they were pleased to stay at sea in peacetime to help the customs commissioners improve their collections. The sea officers, like the customs collectors, kept a percentage of what they seized. Grenville now had the means at his disposal to raise revenue in the colonies, curtail smuggling, and pay judicial salaries. But he had to reform entrenched customs laws and practices that had been in place for nearly a century.

AFTER the restoration of Charles II in 1660, Parliament renewed the Navigation Act[12] which governed trade within the British Empire, with modifications, into the nineteenth century.[13]

Previous laws had protected coastal trade in the British Isles; this law was designed to protect the British shipping industry from foreign competition in the colonies. Colonial goods had to be shipped in English vessels, with an English shipmaster, and three-fourths of the crew had to be English or His Majesty's subjects in the colonies. A large, well-trained merchant marine gave the Royal Navy a reserve of seamen from which it could draw during times of war. By the 1770s the basic law had been altered by more than 150 statutes, executive orders, legal opinions, and judicial decisions.[14]

In 1673 Parliament passed an act to close loopholes in the law.[15] In terms of the American Colonies, the most important part of this act was the placement of customs collectors and officials in colonial ports. By 1696, those collectors had the Imperial Acts[16] to give them the enforcement powers they needed and Vice-Admiralty Courts where colonial cases could be tried without a jury.[17] Also, in that same year, William III set up the Board of Trade under the Treasury Department, which lasted until 1782.[18] But most customs collectors remained in their comfortable homes in England and delegated their duties to underpaid deputies. These deputies were easily bribed. The long period before 1764 is often referred to by historians as a time of "salutary neglect," to indicate the lax enforcement of the Navigation Acts.

When measures were taken in 1763 to enforce the old 1733 Molasses Act, the Rhode Island Assembly acted quickly. They passed the Rhode Island Remonstrance in January 1764 and forwarded it to the Lords Commissioners of Trade and Plantations. This was the first official protest from the colonies against the new, tighter enforcement policies. Rhode Island imported 14,000 hogsheads of molasses a year, of which only 2,500 came from within the British Empire.[19] Rhode Island's economy was so dependent on foreign molasses that the British Islands alone could not provide enough molasses to last even one year.[20] One historian noted that:

> In 1764 Rhode Island estimated its annual molasses imports at 1,150,000 gallons, but its average annual imports from 1768 to 1772, according to customs house figures, were less than 500,000 gallons. During the same five-year period, Rhode Island's exports of molasses and rum were so large as to leave little doubt that the customs house figures were far short of true imports.[21]

The 1696 Act also created ten courts of vice-admiralty in North America. Before 1764 the only significant change to this structure was the addition of a Rhode Island court in 1758. Prior to that time Rhode Island's assembly had petitioned for many years to have its own court, distinct from Massachusetts. Providence merchants saw to it that the "sympathetic" Judge John Andrews, a local official who would interpret rules in a more accommodating fashion, served on their bench.[22] In 1764, imperial reforms placed Judge William Spry on the bench of a "super court" in Halifax that had jurisdiction over the entire Eastern Seaboard from Newfoundland to Florida. In actual practice, though, this had little impact on colonial trade patterns. Only in 1767, when the Townshend Acts created four regional vice-admiralty courts (Halifax, Boston, Philadelphia, and Charleston), did merchants truly feel the pinch of more rigorous enforcement. Rhode Island lost its court and once again its merchants were under the authority of Boston[23] only nine years after they had secured a quasi-independence.[24] To implement and administer all of these reforms, the Royal Navy needed more coasting vessels.

Admiral Lord Alexander Colville, the reluctant new head of the North American command in Halifax, purchased six Marblehead sloops and schooners[25] to add to his fleet so as to assist in the suppression of French smuggling in the St. Lawrence River area. This purchase brought the total North American Squadron to twenty vessels manned by 2,380 officers and men.[26] These new vessels were commissioned with Canadian place names (*St. John, St. Lawrence, Chaleur, Hope, Magdalen,* and *Gaspee*), to recognize the recent British acquisition of new territory in Lower Canada.[27] Expecting that French smugglers would be more hostile than English ones, Colville equipped these fast vessels with eight guns each. Additionally, since the French retained certain fishing rights in the area,[28] Colville needed vessels that could keep the English, French, Irish, and American fishermen a safe distance from each other. The Admiralty believed that these fore-and-aft rigged sloops and schooners were ideal for customs service because they could stay at sea longer into the autumn and deploy earlier in the spring than a traditional man-of-war. The laying-up process on larger vessels was time-consuming and labor intensive. Since winter was the prime smuggling season, this was an important consideration. Also, since search and seizure of suspected illegal cargo was required to take place within nine statute miles of the coast, vessels must be nimble, with a shallow draft to work into the small bays, inlets, and rivers of the seaboard.[29] In contrast to large, heavily manned, and expensive square-rigged vessels, small and relatively inexpensive vessels could vastly aid in revenue collection. Indeed, these vessels could virtually pay for themselves.[30] While the Admiralty did not release funds for more schooners until 1775, captains of frigates frequently purchased small boats at their own expense to launch into bays and inlets. These sea officers reasoned that small boats would pay for themselves with increased profits from seizures.[31]

These vessels ran into trouble almost immediately. Already in Newport on June 30, 1764, Lieutenant Thomas Hill of the *St. John* seized ninety-three hogsheads of sugar from the *Basto* from Monte Cristi. Fearing that his vessel would be sailed to Halifax for condemnation and sale, the owner had Lieutenant Hill arrested, and won a restraining order from Newport Vice-Admiralty judge John Andrews so that the *Basto* would be prosecuted locally.[32] In the meantime, Customs Collector Robinson re-seized the vessel, claiming that Hill's customs deputation had not been properly sworn in and documented in Halifax.[33] Hill went overland to Boston to take up the matter with the Surveyor General, John Temple. While awaiting the outcome in this dispute, the *St. John* sent one of its boats to the wharf in Newport to capture a deserter. This man had left the vessel several days earlier in plain sight and made no attempt to hide. Seeing a mob forming, the *St. John* fired an unshotted swivel gun[34] to warn its boat to return immediately. Failing to reverse course in time, the officer of the boat, Mr. Doyle, was taken prisoner by the mob, and most of the boat's crew was injured under a hail of stones. The mob wanted the *St. John*'s pilot, and even threatened to burn the schooner itself if the crew did not cooperate.

The *St. John* sent another boat for advice to the larger *Squirrel* anchored nearby, while the mob approached them in a sloop. But since the *St. John* was ready to defend herself, the mob backed down. Captain Smith of the *Squirrel* went to the battery on Goat Island to instruct them that he had ordered the *St. John* to weigh anchor and that it would be unwise to fire upon a British warship. Members of the mob assaulted him and he was fortunate to get away from them at all. The battery at Goat Island fired eight shots at the *St. John* before it anchored under the safety of the stern of the *Squirrel*. One shot went through the mainsail. Daniel Vaughan, the main gunner on Goat Island, aimed his shots wide. Later he was reprimanded by the colonial council[35] for not following his order to sink the *St. John* if it tried to leave the harbor. When the battery fired one more shot, very close to the *Squirrel*, the sloop turned its broadside on the battery and the mob backed down. Captain Smith, of the *Squirrel*, admitted that Vaughan had stopped firing just in time; the *St. John* was seconds away from giving a full broadside to Newport's battery. Mr. Doyle was released the following morning.[36]

When the captain and the lieutenant later went ashore to ask the governor under what authority the gunner had fired upon them, he assured them that the gunner had orders from two council members. Apparently the *St. John* was harboring three thieves (suspected of stealing some pigs and chickens). A peace officer[37] had approached the vessel seeking their arrest. When this officer was turned away, the mob cried out for justice. The captain went ashore, it seems, to assure them that he would turn over the thieves to the local authorities and that they should not fire upon one of the king's vessels.

In the spring of 1769 another vessel, the *Liberty*, entered the Customs Service after being confiscated from prominent Boston merchant John Hancock. Its new master, William Reid, enjoyed considerable success enforcing the Navigation Acts on Long Island Sound and in Narragansett Bay. On 17 July, Reid brought two prizes into Newport harbor, but the customs collector could not immediately find grounds for their condemnation. When the New London merchant Joseph Packwood, master of one of the seized vessels, went aboard to gather personal effects, some of the crew of the *Liberty* challenged his motives. Words were exchanged and some (possibly inebriated) crew members fired one of the *Liberty*'s deck swivels point blank at the master's face.[38] But the gun misfired and the skipper got away. With this whole series of events occurring at a very public pier, a group of angry colonists gathered, captured Reid, and insisted that he order his crew off of *Liberty*. This mob, led by Joseph Packwood and another New London merchant, Nathaniel Shaw, sailed their two prizes away and scuttled the *Liberty*.[39] With its mast cut and hull leaking, the *Liberty* drifted ashore; the tide carried it to Goat Island where the vessel was set on fire by persons unknown. The customs commissioners, in vain, offered a £100 reward for information leading to an arrest.[40] The matter came before the Privy Council in December but they took no action.[41] The *Liberty* entered government service as the consequence of political conflict and left the same way.

THE Admiralty began the *Gaspee*'s payroll for officers and crew on December 20, 1763. Colville purchased the vessel in Halifax for £420 and it was re-fitted in the careening yard[42] for naval and revenue service. Measuring only forty-nine feet in length with eight small guns, the *Gaspee* was a modest vessel, even by eighteenth-century standards.[43] The paybooks show that they began sea victualling on June 22, 1764. Lieutenant Thomas Allen was the *Gaspee*'s first commander, and he was supposed to have a complement of thirty men.[44] Given the high rate of desertions along the North American coast, the legal and social difficulties associated with impressments, and the need to man prizes and seizures, many commanders complained that their vessels were undermanned at any given time.

Under the command of Lieutenant Thomas Allen, the *Gaspee* patrolled the waters between Philadelphia and Halifax, Nova Scotia. Halifax served as the headquarters for the North American squadron until 1770, when the Admiralty relocated it to Boston to help curb what they perceived to be increasing lawlessness emanating from that port. Vessels had to put in to Halifax for maintenance, as it had the only government careening yard in North America. Allen's charge was twofold: he was to support larger vessels of the Royal Navy in their duties in naval operations and support the customs service in suppressing illicit trade. With only eight guns and a small arms chest, the *Gaspee* was not equipped for rigorous naval warfare; its purpose was to interdict merchant vessels.

Smuggling in violation of the Navigation Acts was not unique to Britain's North American colonies. In the British Isles, it was not unusual for merchant vessels to carry cannon and use them against customs service vessels. Merchant sailors and Royal Navy personnel injured and even killed each other almost routinely in conflicts during the late eighteenth and early nineteenth centuries.[45]

By December 1764, Allen had had dramatic encounters with all four of the biggest human challenges facing sea officers on the Eastern Seaboard: desertion, impressments, enforcement of customs, and colonial resistance. Inclement weather forced the *Gaspee* out of its normal cruising grounds and into the Casco Bay area of Maine. Seeing vessels failing to process their cargos through the customs house in Falmouth, Maine, Allen made several seizures. While Allen tried to get the customs collector to prosecute them, several crewmembers from the *Gaspee* fled, as did one of the seized ships. With his vessel now undermanned, Allen pressed several merchant sailors to fill these vacancies. A mob kidnapped Allen and forced him to release his new recruits. After releasing his impressments under duress, Allen's kidnappers sent him back to Halifax empty-handed, with no prizes, all of which cost him nine men.[46]

In 1765, the *Gaspee* appeared again during a well-known colonial uprising. When Andrew Oliver resigned his position as stamp distributor in the face of a Boston mob, Governor Francis Bernard asked Captain Thomas Bishop of the *Fortune* to intercept the stamp ships and steer them toward Castle William, where the stamps could be safely stored. The *Gaspee* and the *Jamaica* were ordered to Boston to aid Bishop in his mission. Ultimately, it was the *Gaspee* that had the dubious task of intercepting the *John Galley* with the hated stamps on board for New England's distributors.[47]

Sometime in 1767 or 1768 the *Gaspee* was refitted from a one-masted sloop to a two-masted schooner. Indeed, Lieutenant Allen sometimes called the *Gaspee* a schooner and sometimes a sloop, even in the same report.[48] It appears from some loose letters that many of the sloops from the *Gaspee* class were being refitted into schooners in the Halifax yard during this time.[49] A schooner had more sail area, making it potentially faster, though it still required only a small crew. The *Gaspee* made a number of seizures in Long Island Sound during the spring of 1768.[50] In April, the Admiralty ordered Lieutenant William Dudingston to the *Gaspee*; five months later he took command.[51]

When twenty-nine-year-old William Dudingston took command of the *Gaspee* in September 1768, he had been in the Royal Navy for nine years, although this was his first command.[52] In June 1769 and again in July 1771, he sailed the *Gaspee* from Philadelphia. One historian relayed an account of Dudingston physically maltreating a Philadelphia man who later sued him in civil court.[53] An examination of the *Gaspee*'s surviving log books reminds the reader that life on

an eighteenth-century naval vessel was physically and mentally difficult. The command structure of the vessel was hierarchical, and discipline was harsh and violent. The threat of physical force was never
far away. James Dundas, Dudingston's Master, kept his own journal.
He recorded crew members being punished with twelve lashes for
theft, drawing a knife on the master, drunkenness, disobedience to
command, and contempt for a superior officer.[54]

The *Gaspee* had visited Rhode Island in 1765, 1767, and 1769.
Rhode Islanders had opportunity to read in the *Newport Mercury*
about the new commander's misdeeds in Philadelphia.[55] Allegedly,
Dudingston had beaten up an unarmed fisherman near Chester, Pennsylvania, for no good reason. At this time, if a sea officer gained a
reputation in a particular area, his Admiral would move him to a
new station in order give him a "fresh start." Colonial newspapers
got better at reporting the deeds and misdeeds of customs and sea
officers in other colonies, making such transfers less effective.

When Admiral John Montagu took command of the North American Squadron in Boston in August 1771, he made it clear that he
was more concerned with smuggling in New England than in
Canada. Montagu knew Rhode Island's reputation for smuggling and
trading with the enemy, especially the reputations of captains Abraham Whipple and George Hopkins, and the John Brown family.[56]
Shortly after the *Gaspee*'s arrival in Newport in January 1772, Rhode
Islanders accused the crew of stealing livestock and firewood from
local farmers.[57] Although most secondary sources place the *Gaspee*
in Rhode Island beginning in March 1772, Admiral Montagu "Order'd the *Gaspee* Schooner to Rhode Island, to remain upon the station until further orders" on January 25, 1772.[58] It appears that
Dudingston was able to follow his orders even in the middle of winter
because less than a month later, on February 17,[59] the *Gaspee* seized
a cargo from the sloop *Fortune* of twelve hogsheads of West India
rum belonging to Jacob Greene, some Jamaica spirits, and brown
sugar belonging to Nathaniel Greene, Jr. & Co,[60] and sent it to
Boston.[61] Dudingston could not have known that this one seizure
would embroil him, his crew, and his schooner in one of the most
significant events of the American colonial era.

Already sensing trouble, on February 22, Dudingston wrote to the Commissioners of Customs in Boston asking for guidance dealing with a sloop from St. Martin. He believed that this vessel had been "lightened" and was meeting two smaller boats near the flats off Greenwich Point. When Dudingston sent two boats to investigate, someone fired a musket[62] and the smugglers yelled to warn others on shore. Dundas, the *Gaspee*'s master, and the boat's crew seized the sloop and some rum that did not have the required papers.[63] Dudingston, concerned about the exact legal course of action to take in this instance (when a vessel had no manifest describing its cargo), wrote to the customs commissioners in Boston asking for guidance. He did not consult his commanding officer, Admiral Montagu, but Montagu heard about his troubles nonetheless. Not wanting to leave the *Gaspee* alone in Narragansett Bay, on February 24, 1772, Montagu, "order'd Captain Linzee of the *Beaver*[64] to Rhode Island . . . — to remain until further orders."[65] Later, in April, Montagu warned Captain Linzee (or Lyndsey) that it was his duty to protect the *Gaspee* from a possible reprisal.

On March 9, Vice-Admiralty justice Robert Auchmuty set the court date for March 24 for the *Fortune* case, and the rum belonging to Jacob Greene[66] would be condemned in Boston.[67]

A caustic correspondence began on March 21, when Deputy Governor Darius Sessions[68] in Providence wrote to Governor Joseph Wanton[69] in Newport indicating that the "gentlemen of this town" complained that a schooner has "much disturbed our navigation."[70] Rhode Island chief justice Stephen Hopkins agreed with Sessions that the common custom of the colony dictated that the commander of this schooner should show his orders to the governor and actually swear an oath regarding his commission in the governor's presence.[71] As if expecting a politically charged outcome, Sessions made reference in his letter to the *Liberty*[72] incident from three years earlier where a customs vessel was burned by a mob in Newport. The next day, when Wanton sent a message to Dudingston asking him to show his credentials, the governor pretended not to know him or that the *Gaspee* was a Royal Naval vessel. Wanton addressed his letter to the "Commanding Officer of a Schooner near Brenton's Point."[73] Dudingston replied by sending a subordinate officer in his place.

On March 24, 1772, Lieutenant Dudingston sent a packet of letters to Admiral Montagu. These letters contained a heated passage in which Dudingston insisted that he did present his naval orders and customs deputation to the governor of the colony (which was considered customary if not actually legally required).[74] The lieutenant claimed he only stopped short of showing the governor his private orders and correspondence from the admiral. He warned Montagu that many local citizens were inflamed by what they read in the newspapers, and there was talk of fitting out an armed vessel to resist seizures of merchant vessels.[75]

But Rhode Island's business and merchant interests were not especially alarmed by the occasional seizure of goods. It was the bypassing of the Rhode Island Vice-Admiralty Court and even the common-law courts that drew the most ire from Rhode Islanders. It seemed that for certain merchants—those who the sea officers believed had traded with the enemy in the last war—their vessels would be sent to Boston for condemnation.

On April 8, Admiral Montagu sent a letter to Governor Wanton that demonstrated his unconditional support for the lieutenant, who was "strictly complying with my orders." Montagu said that the "letters [Wanton sent Dudingston] were of such a nature" that he was "at a loss at what answer to give them, and ashamed to find that they come from one of His Majesty's governors."[76] Indeed, merchants were irritated by the fact that the *Gaspee* stopped every small vessel on Narragansett Bay. This, however, was precisely the way to interdict eighteenth-century smuggling. Smugglers had to transfer goods to increasingly smaller vessels that could avoid the customs house and well-traveled piers and wharves. The Sugar Act of 1764 allowed for the stopping of coastwise and local traffic, even within a single colony.[77] Montagu, already belligerent, did little to veil his contempt for the government of Rhode Island and what he perceived to be a thriving illicit trade. In fact, he seemed pleased with Dudingston's ability to disrupt their trade and promised to hang as pirates anyone who "rescued" a seizure that the *Gaspee* sent to Boston. He specifically warned that the sheriff should not try to board His Majesty's schooner.[78]

Whether based solely upon Dudingston's letter or perhaps other sources as well, Montagu wrote on April 18:

> ... and from the encouragement they receive from their governor they are worked up to committ almost acts of piracy. . . but [Dudingston] very properly refuses to show him [Wanton] my private orders. Which I presume he had no right to see. . . I am going to send the *Beaver* to protect the Schooner [*Gaspee*].[79]

On 8 May, Wanton wrote back to Montagu indicating that Dudingston never showed his orders to him, so he was unable to determine if he was a pirate or not. He expressed dismay that a commander would lie to his superior officer. He also assured him that any talk of arming a vessel to resist the *Gaspee* was "without foundation."[80] Shocked by the tone of Montagu's letter, Wanton asked for and received the Rhode Island General Assembly's approval to forward it to the secretary of state, the Earl of Hillsborough. He also assured the admiral that he would send the sheriff anytime, anywhere in the colony as he saw fit. The questions of jurisdiction and the limits of authority touched upon in this correspondence were much bigger and graver than these men could solve; indeed these issues were among those that brought about the end of the first British Empire.

While Admiral Montagu did not conceal his distaste for Rhode Island's merchants and government, his lack of manners and refinement were also well-known. John Adams "heard many anecdotes from a young gentleman in my office of Admiral Montagu's manners."[81] Apparently, the admiral's genteel birth but boorish behavior were widely recognized and seen as disagreeable.[82]

Admiral Montagu, in his journal entry on May 18, 1772, indicated that he warned Captain Linzee of the *Beaver* (who had some similar experiences to Dudingston with the local people and the civil magistrate) to have as little communication and contact with the local population as possible. He advised against going ashore and also warned him "to prevent any piratical attempt being made upon the *Beaver*."[83] Several days later Dudingston tried to salvage his reputation with Admiral Montagu by recalling his first relatively cordial meeting with Governor Wanton and claiming that the governor never actually asked to see his orders. He asserted that his authority was never questioned, until he seized Greene's sloop.[84] Dudingston thought this whole exchange was blown out of proportion, since Greene was a man of means and could travel to Boston as easily as Newport for his court hearing, and would certainly purchase the *Fortune* back without opposition, "in the manner they have been used to."[85] Typically, the former owner would offer the only bid when his vessel was sold at auction.

Two

The *Gaspee* Incident

FEWER THAN THREE WEEKS LATER, ON JUNE 9, 1772, THE *Gaspee*, without a local pilot on board, parted company with the *Beaver* at noon.[1] Commander Linzee recorded in the *Beaver*'s log, "At noon spoke His Majesty's Schooner *Gaspee* at Point Judith bearing SW 6 leagues."[2] Shortly thereafter Captain Benjamin Lindsey[3] of the packet *Hannah*, seeing the *Gaspee* alone, left Newport (with very little or no cargo) for Providence. Dudingston, with the faster vessel, ordered full sail and was gaining on Lindsey. Sitting higher in the water than the *Gaspee*, the *Hannah* was able to travel over Namquid Point near Warwick, where the *Gaspee* ran aground at 3 or 4 o'clock in the afternoon. The water was only a foot deep on one side of the *Gaspee* and two feet deep on the other. Dudingston took advantage of the exposure by having the crew scrape the bottom. They worked for several hours, and also used the vessel's anchor and winch to try to dislodge the schooner from the spit. Ephraim Bowen, who would be among the colonials who boarded the stricken vessel, would later claim that the *Hannah* lured the *Gaspee* to shallow waters.[4] Indeed, Lindsey worked for John Brown and reported the *Gaspee*'s misfortune to Brown soon after it happened, when he arrived at Fenner's wharf, across from James Sabin's tavern, in Providence.

Dudingston, for his part, told a different version of the story. He claimed that the lack of a local pilot and his ignorance about these waters caused the grounding. He was on his way to Providence to retrieve some men sent down from Boston, and while anchored off Namquid Spit to take some soundings, the *Gaspee* touched bottom when the tide fell. At this time, the schooner carried only nineteen men on board, partly due to the fact that five men had recently taken a seized vessel to Boston.[5]

The presence of the *Hannah*, Dudingston claimed, was mere co-incidence.[6] Dudingston's self-serving account is not entirely credible, since if they merely touched bottom, and they already had an anchor out, they should have been able to free themselves. Regardless, Dudingston reiterated this version, when it was certainly in his interest to protect Linzee's reputation and his own in light of the warnings they had about potential danger brewing in Rhode Island.[7]

Ephraim Bowen declared that the tide had been ebbing for two hours at the time that the *Gaspee* ran aground; John Brown concluded that the *Gaspee* would float again by 3:00 AM. Some people believed that Brown was aboard the *Hannah*, as he had some experience with Namquid Point, having run aground there himself with his brother Moses[8] twelve years earlier.[9]

Thirty-six-year-old John Brown called for eight longboats, each carrying five pairs of oars requiring ten rowers, to assemble at Fenner's Wharf.[10] Brown put his employee Abraham Whipple in charge of the operation. At age 39, Whipple was an accomplished seaman[11] and the brother-in-law of Chief Justice Stephen Hopkins. Daniel Pearce beat a drum along Main Street to call the raiders to Sabin's Tavern.[12] Some men cast bullets in the kitchen of the tavern, and the raiders departed from Providence around 10:00 PM. Relatively fit men would have had no trouble rowing against the tidal current to get to Namquid Point in two hours' time. If another longboat had joined them from Bristol, it had a greater distance to travel, but the advantage of rowing with the tide. One anonymous source reported that the men blackened their faces and hands.[13] Brown put a sea captain in charge of the tiller of each boat. Obviously, they could not hope to do anything until nightfall, and the month of June gave them the longest days of the year. Coming out of Providence, they would have to row against a flooding tide and muffle their oars and oarlocks in order to approach the *Gaspee* undetected. The raiders would want to arrive after the moon had set, which indeed they did.[14]

In the darkness on June 10, 1772, Bartholomew Cheevers, the *Gaspee*'s deck sentinel on watch at the time, spotted what he thought was just a pile of rocks, so he reported nothing. [15] At 12:45 AM, he hailed the approaching longboats asking them to identify themselves. Dudingston came on deck, clad in his nightshirt, and repeated the call. Cheevers claimed that he tried to fire his musket but it misfired repeatedly. The commander called for light on the deck but had no success. He called for more small arms, but the arms chest was locked and the keys were down in his cabin.

Surely Dudingston must have had some concern about the readiness of his crew. He did not have the added protection of the *Beaver*. He had only nineteen men on board at the time. Indeed, he was on his way to Providence to pick up more men coming down from Boston. The men he had were below decks in their nightclothes, and tired from scraping the hull. The schooner's small arms chest was locked and the lanterns were not lit on deck.

Abraham Whipple raised his voice, identified himself as the sheriff of Kent County,[16] and declared he was in possession of a warrant for Dudingston's arrest.[17] Dudingston hollered back that the sheriff should return at a more appropriate hour.[18] When men tried to board near the starboard forward shrouds, Dudingston struck someone with his sword and cut him. Then he called for all men on deck. *Gaspee* midshipman William Dickinson claimed that the men in the boats gave "three cheers" and that the *Gaspee* deck lookouts then fired upon the boats with muskets.[19] The men in the boats—Dickinson estimated half a dozen—returned musket fire, and the *Gaspee* lookouts responded with pistols. Already the raiding party was too close for the *Gaspee* to use its larger cannon; besides, the attackers approached directly at the bow. Ephraim Bowen claimed that he gave his gun to Joseph Bucklin, who proceeded to fire only one shot, which hit Dudingston in the left arm and groin.[20] A minute later they boarded without further opposition over the starboard bow and quarter, not the more accessible stern. This indicates that the *Gaspee* was still listing significantly to starboard. *Gaspee* midshipman Dickinson estimated that thirty or forty men (out of 150–200 total)[21] boarded and overwhelmed the British schooner's crew. With their commander down, the crew was forced to surrender. The Rhode Islanders calling themselves the "captain" and the "head sheriff" gave their word that the *Gaspee* crew would not be harmed.

The raiding party seemed specifically interested in Dudingston and the pilot, Mr. Sylvanus Daggett.[22] Local pilots who helped Royal Navy and customs vessels navigate the shallow waters that were utilized by smugglers were not popular among merchants and seafarers. While the raiders had brought doctors with them, they did not immediately tend Dudingston's wounds. Perhaps they expected to treat members of the raiding party only. Whipple and Brown allowed Dudingston to bleed on the deck, and later claimed that they thought he had been shot by his own men. Still not certain whether to let the lieutenant live or not, they made him beg for his life. They had Dickinson tied up in one of the boats for a half hour before he was summoned back onto the *Gaspee* to carry the lieutenant below. Apparently Whipple and Brown later rethought their actions and asked the commander if he had a surgeon on board. When he said that he had none, the raiders brought Dr. John Mawney up from the stern of one of the boats. Dudingston apparently wanted Dickinson to help them find material and make bandages. Dickinson went below and showed the "ringleaders of the mob" the officers' commissions, orders, and instructions, which the raiders took. This, of course, also gave the officers the much-needed artificial light to see the faces of their adversaries for later identification. Some of the papers went into the raiders' pockets; others went over the side and may or may not have made it into the boats. Regardless, the "ringleaders" saw Dudingston's commissions and deputations, and therefore could not claim that they thought Dudingston was acting without orders. Dickinson also claimed that he saw a "negro" (his word) holding Dudingston's sword.[23] Peter May, a *Gaspee* mariner, testified that the raiders wanted remuneration for Jacob Greene's seized rum. They would take Dudingston's personal effects in exchange and return him to the schooner.[24]

The wounded Dudingston and his crew were herded aboard the raiders' boats. While the *Gaspee* officers and crew were still angry, or afraid, or both, something unexpected happened. The dark, now moonless night sky of Narragansett Bay suddenly filled with a bright light as the schooner, which had been their home and fortress, burst into flames. Was it set aflame intentionally? Was it an accident? They watched from the boats as they were rowed quietly away; when the flames finally reached the powder magazine buried deep in the hull for protection, a dramatic explosion occurred that must have been heard for miles around. Light and sound filled the normally quiet coast, and Rhode Islanders were awakened from their slumber. There was very little of the *Gaspee* left to salvage. The *Gaspee* crew could see other longboats returning to Cranston and Providence.[25] Ephraim Bowen, in his later recollection of events that night, claimed that it was the leaders of the raid who returned to burn the vessel, not some rogue element.[26]

The raiding party took the *Gaspee* officers and crew ashore a couple of miles north of Namquid Point in Pawtuxet—at first the crew feared that they were being left on an island, but they were mistaken. Lieutenant Dudingston was carried and placed on a blanket but later was taken to the house of Joseph Rhodes.

Within three days, on June 12, Dudingston had recovered sufficiently to send off a brief letter to Admiral Montagu. He expressed some doubt that he would survive his wounds, optimism that he could identify some of his attackers and have them convicted, and the fact that the schooner and its stores were completely lost, though his men got off with mere bruises from wooden handspikes.[27] Dudingston indicated that one of the raiders may have been killed and buried privately, quietly on shore.[28] He also would have agreed with the opinion of Captain John Linzee of the *Beaver* when he stated that no one could have predicted an attack, since the *Gaspee* lay aground so far from "any principal Town."[29] Dudingston and his crew could not have hoped to make an adequate defense of the vessel in their nightclothes. While Linzee defended Dudingston by saying that no one could have predicted an attack, the correspondence from the previous three months, and lack of preparedness on the 9th and 10th of June, did not reflect favorably on his leadership.

The news traveled fast. Although Newport's Reverend Ezra Stiles did not record the *Gaspee* in his diary until June 11,[30] Boston merchant John Rowe[31] already knew about it from Admiral Montagu on the 10th.[32] At daybreak, only hours after the fire and explosion, Deputy Governor Darius Sessions and Vice-Admiralty judge John Andrews[33] were the first magistrates to arrive in Pawtuxet.[34] Although Andrews lived in Cranston, he had spent the night with friends in Providence and heard men talking in the street outside his window about some trouble in the bay. On his way to Sessions's house, he saw Daniel Jenckes, Esq., chief justice of the common pleas in the county of Providence. Jenckes urged Sessions and Andrews to find the individuals guilty of this treachery, so that the whole colony would not be punished for the deeds of a few.[35] Andrews accompanied Sessions, not as a judge, but to secure any salvageable stores from the vessel.[36] He hired Daniel Vaughan to retrieve iron fittings from the wreck and Samuel Aborn to recover the anchors, guns, and other stores to keep them safely in a warehouse until further notice.[37] There was probably not much to salvage and whatever Vaughan did find has been lost to history.

When Sessions and Andrews arrived they found Dudingston, as might be expected, in an agitated state. Dudingston refused to give a statement to Sessions, indicating that he was still recovering from his wounds and that he must first report to Admiral Montagu. He did, however, reluctantly allow Sessions to interview Bartholomew Cheevers, seaman; John Johnson, boatswain; and William Caple, seaman. Their affidavits told a fairly consistent story. Sessions seemed most interested in whether they could identify any of the raiders or not. Dudingston took no assistance from Sessions other than to ask him that his men be delivered to the admiral in Boston or to the *Beaver* in Newport. Dudingston did not want to be moved. Sessions called upon Dr. Henry Sterling to follow up on the lieutenant's medical treatment. William Checkley, a customs officer in Providence,[38] also traveled to see the lieutenant, and found that he would not receive any assistance. Dudingston was unwilling to trust anyone the morning after the raid. He preferred to die with his version of the story rather than to have someone else distort it. Checkley found that the sheriff had already arrested Dudingston and served him with a writ for the seizure of Jacob Greene's rum.[39] Midshipman William Dickinson was able to travel quickly to Boston, and answered questions before Massachusetts governor Thomas Hutchinson and Admiral Montagu.

When Montagu forwarded Dickinson's testimony to Philip Stephens, the secretary to the admiralty, the admiral stated that "the Inhabitants of Rhode Island in general, are a set of lawless, piratical people, and whose whole business is that of smuggling and defrauding the king of his duties, I cannot expect any satisfaction from that letter [referring to Dickinson's testimony]."[40] He praised Dudingston's diligence and character and recommended him for merit, should he survive his wounds.[41] This whole unpleasant ordeal and the loss of his vessel did not hurt his career; Dudingston retired from the service decades later as a rear admiral.

Massachusetts governor Hutchinson wrote to the Earl of Hillsborough:

> From schooner's being dogged, I apprehended something tragical . . . the constitution [of Rhode Island] makes the governor subservient to designs of illicit traders . . . If some measures are not taken in England . . . it will encourage the neighbouring colonies to persevere in their opposition to the laws of trade.[42]

By June 12, Rhode Island governor Joseph Wanton, at the urging of the deputy governor, posted a reward of "one hundred pounds sterling money of Great Britain" to "discover the perpetrators of the said villainy, to be paid immediately upon the conviction."[43] Two hundred copies of a proclamation were posted throughout the colony. Ignoring the previous debate regarding the vessel's civilian versus military status,[44] the proclamation referred to the *Gaspee* as "His Majesty's armed Schooner *Gaspee*."[45] The colony's General Assembly was not scheduled to meet again until August, so the burden of acting quickly in the wake of this crisis fell on the executives. Given the events of the previous three months, and the assurances the governor had given the admiral that the *Gaspee* was in no danger, it was imperative that the governor and deputy governor appear zealous in pursuing the perpetrators of this villainy. When Governor Wanton wrote his summary of the events to the Earl of Hillsborough on the 16th, his letter was nearly 1,200 words long. First, he summarized the raid on the *Gaspee*, cataloging the events known up to that point. Wanton dedicated his remaining six hundred words to explaining his grievances, and how much the legitimate trade of the colony suffered due to the presence of the *Beaver* and the *Gaspee*.[46] Given the tone of this letter, Hillsborough certainly did not see Wanton as a reliable and zealous investigator. But Wanton was an elected governor, so he could not appoint a new royal governor as a replacement. Hillsborough was obligated to rely to Wanton, even making him the head of the Royal Commission of Inquiry. Perhaps this one factor, more than any other, doomed the commission to failure.

By July 8, Admiral Montagu had the testimony of a man variously described as a "free negro," "mulatto lad," or an "indentured servant" named Aaron Biggs (sometimes Briggs),[47] age 18, of Prudence Island.[48] Biggs claimed he was out on Narragansett Bay the night of June 9 and spoke a longboat that had allegedly left from Bristol under the leadership of Simeon Potter.[49] Biggs named John Brown, Joseph Brown, and Dr. Weeks of Warwick as being among the raiders.[50] Unlike Ephraim Bowen's narrative, Biggs's account claimed that John Brown shot the lieutenant. He recalled that there were seventeen longboats total, and that he himself was in the longboat that carried Dudingston ashore. Biggs swore that he gave this statement without duress and with no promise of reward.[51] Montagu thought this testimony reliable because Biggs's statements corroborated what was already known from other sources.[52] Considering the powerful, influential people Biggs claimed to have seen that evening, he fled to the British navy for protection. Montagu encouraged Governor Wanton to question Simeon Potter and John Brown in the presence of Lieutenant Dudingston, who could readily identify them. He also urged Wanton to send "a proper person" aboard the *Swan*[53] to take Biggs's sworn statement. The following week, on July 16, Biggs gave a deposition to Charles Bardin, justice of the peace.[54]

In the meantime, Governor Wanton took three affidavits from four different people to discredit Biggs. Samuel Thurston, Samuel Tompkins, and two slave men called Somerset and Jack, appeared before Governor Wanton on the 10th and 11th of July. They indicated that Biggs was on Prudence Island all night on June 9 and that the only boat he could have used was in such poor repair at that time that it would not have floated.[55] The two slaves claimed that they shared a bed with Biggs up until July 2, when he escaped to a British man-of-war. Biggs, they said, had made no mention of the *Gaspee* incident to them. One year later it was revealed that Biggs was not an eyewitness to the events and apparently was "coached"[56] about the events by seaman Patrick Earle aboard the *Beaver* in the first week of July.[57] Earle, for his part, swore under oath that he recognized Biggs as the man who helped him at the bow oar to row Dudingston ashore and that he even gave him some chewing tobacco.[58] Biggs's testimony was crucial because he was able to do what nobody on the *Gaspee* could do: name names. This was why Sessions was eager to interview crew members. As there had been enough light in the *Gaspee*'s cabin at the time of the raid, if a few of the ringleaders were brought before Dudingston, or even Midshipman Dickinson, they should have been able to identify them. Consistent with its behavior in previous situations like this, the London government wanted the ringleaders; others could be pardoned.

On July 22, Governor Wanton wrote a frustrated letter to Admiral Montagu expressing his disbelief that the British navy and Captain Linzee would not turn Aaron Biggs over to the sheriff, who had a warrant. He even offered to return Biggs to the *Beaver* after questioning, rather than to a local jail.[59] In this same letter, Wanton argued that the *Gaspee* was so far up the Providence River, almost thirty miles from the open sea, that the local authorities had the "*only* [emphasis mine] power and jurisdiction. . . *infra corpus comitatus*[60]. . . the Admiral hath no jurisdiction."[61] In fact, local sheriffs had arrest warrants in the past for British sea officers, who then simply avoided going ashore. This raid forced Dudingston on to dry land.

On July 23, Newport customs collector Charles Dudley wrote to Admiral Montagu that "the government of this colony bears no resemblance to any other government under the Crown of England." He expressed his belief that "the attack upon the *Gaspee* was not the effect of sudden passion and resentment but cool deliberation and forethought. . . it had been long determined she should be destroyed."[62] Given the speed and efficiency with which the schooner was taken, and the optimal tide and moon conditions, some planning or even rehearsal might have taken place. Yet ultimately, in the absence of evidence to the contrary, the commission found that the attack was spontaneous, merely taking advantage of the schooner's vulnerable state on Namquid Spit.

Apparently, when the news of the *Gaspee* attack reached the English press, it received little notice.[63] The printer of the *Kentish Gazette* believed that the government was embarrassed by the *Gaspee* incident and that influential merchants valued profits over love of country.[64]

On July 16, Rhode Island attorney general Henry Marchant, about to return home from an extended stay in England, heard about the destruction of the schooner as he sat in the New England Coffee House in London.[65] Marchant's mission to get the treasury to reimburse the colony for expenses incurred during the Seven Years' War had been marred by the behavior of colonists during the Stamp Act riots. Certainly, this additional civil disturbance doomed any chance of Marchant seeing any funds from the London government.[66]

At the Admiralty in London, Philip Stephens sent copies, and sometimes merely extracts, of Montagu's letters to the Earl of Hillsborough. Hillsborough inquired of Solicitor General Edward Thurlow and Attorney General Alexander Wedderburn whether the "principals" could be tried in England.[67] Admiral Montagu was directed to travel from Boston to Rhode Island to discover the perpetrators and to offer a £500 reward in His Majesty's name, a far greater amount than was offered by local authorities.[68] Without waiting for a reply from the attorney and solicitor generals, Hillsborough sent a copy of the Dockyard Act with his correspondence on August 7.[69] Hillsborough's administration displayed a new seriousness about prosecuting persons who vandalized His Majesty's naval property.[70] Yet Hillsborough acted hastily, on impulse, by sending off a copy of the act so suddenly.[71] Relying only on correspondence from Montagu, Dudingston, and Wanton, he demonstrated no confidence in the colony's ability to bring any of the perpetrators to justice. By August 14, only eight days after first learning of the *Gaspee* raid, for reasons unrelated to the incident, Hillsborough resigned, and Lord Dartmouth was appointed the new secretary of state and head of the American department.[72] Many contemporaries and later historians have considered Dartmouth more moderate in his views toward the American colonies and less likely to "rule with an iron fist."[73] Yet even with Hillsborough removed from the department, the ministry continued to demonstrate their lack of confidence in the colonial government.[74] On August 26, the King's Proclamation was issued that offered a £500 reward for information leading to the arrest and conviction of any person involved in the *Gaspee* raid and an additional £500 for the persons called "Head Sheriff" or "Captain."[75] There would be no pardon for the "ringleaders" or the person(s) who injured Dudingston. Lieutenant General Thomas Gage was ordered to provide sufficient funds to Admiral Montagu to cover the reward.[76] The Crown also ordered Gage to provide protection for the Royal Commission to conduct its work.[77] This commission was the Crown's formal inquiry. They were empowered, only by working through the governor of Rhode Island and its courts, to send defendants and their witnesses to Admiral Montagu for transport to England for trial.

The King signed the *Commission of Inquiry into Burning of* Gaspee on September 2 at Westminster.[78] Two days later Lord Dartmouth informed General Gage, Governor Wanton, Governor William Tryon of New York, Governor Thomas Hutchinson of Massachusetts, Governor William Franklin of New Jersey, Chief Justices Daniel Horsmanden of New York, Frederick Smythe of New Jersey, and Peter Oliver of Massachusetts that the attack on Dudingston, the plunder of the vessel, the piracy, and the arson would all be treated as a "whole transaction." Therefore, the offenders were guilty of high treason, levying war against the king. Dartmouth indicated that Wanton was to turn prisoners and their witnesses over to Mon-

tagu for transport to England.[79] If the commissioners ran into difficulty, the ministry ordered Gage to provide the necessary men to put
down any disturbances and riots. Given the legal and political struc-
tures in place in Rhode Island, local sheriffs and local courts would
ultimately have to arrest and indict suspects. However unlikely, only
then could they be handed over to the admiral. Many Rhode Islanders, for their part, still believed that the commission of inquiry
had much greater powers than it did. In addition, many thought that
the Dockyard Act was passed in reaction to the *Gaspee* raid and that
it was going to be used against them.

In the colonies, the "friends of government" and the "liberty people" waited anxiously to hear the response from the Crown officials
in England. Governor Hutchinson summed up the mood in Massachusetts:

> People in this province, both friends and enemies to government,
> are in great expectations from the late affair at Rhode Island, of
> the burning of the king's schooner; and they consider the manner
> in which the news of it will be received in England, and the meas-
> ure to be taken, as decisive. If it is passed over without a full in-
> quiry and due resentment, our liberty people will think they may
> with impunity commit any acts of violence, be they ever so atro-
> cious, and the friends to government will despond and give up all
> hopes of being able to withstand the faction.[80]

If Newport pastor Ezra Stiles[81] was correct, that most colonists
did not consider the burning of the *Gaspee* a treasonable offense, and
if Newport customs officer Charles Dudley was right that it was
planned and premeditated, then Rhode Island residents must have
wondered what caused such a harsh reaction from Whitehall. But
given Hutchinson's comments, what reaction could they expect? Certainly the Admiralty might send more armed sloops and schooners.
Montagu suggested to Philip Stephens, the secretary of the Admiralty,
that the small arms on a schooner might not be sufficient protection
in the event of an attack.[82] Dartmouth then wrote to the Lords of the
Admiralty, "I am commanded by the King to signify to your Lord-

ships. . . a larger number of the vessels under his [Montagu's] command and some of superior force should be placed on that station" to stop Rhode Island's illicit trade.[83] The number of seizures in fact went up drastically in Rhode Island after June 1772.[84]

The burning of the *Gaspee* marked an escalation of colonial resistance on the water. The final commission report claimed that the raiders were emboldened by the lack of repercussions from the burning of the *Liberty* customs vessel by a Newport mob in 1769. Chief Justice Smythe thought that maritime resistance went back further, to the firing on the *St. John* from Fort George in July 1764.[85] But the destruction of the *Gaspee* was not merely an attack on a royal official, or a mere confiscated customs vessel; it was one of His Majesty's own. Colonial opinion notwithstanding, surely this was an act of treason, and perhaps even the start of a war.

Three

Three Thousand Miles
to Be Hanged

LOOKING BACK ON THAT FATEFUL EVENING OF JUNE 9, 1772, THE Rhode Island deputy governor, Darius Sessions, remembered hearing about a dozen boys playing with a drum in the street outside his Providence home. The moon was bright, so he could see them clearly; they appeared to be ten to fourteen years old. They meant no harm and were amusing themselves, so he said nothing. When Sessions retired for the night, the only vessels belonging to His Majesty that he knew about were in Newport, some thirty miles away. One can imagine his surprise when a neighbor burst into his house the following morning to tell him that the armed schooner *Gaspee* was on fire near Pawtuxet, only six miles south in the Providence River. Myriad possibilities must have raced through Sessions's mind: was it a maritime accident, foul play, a mutiny or an impressment riot, or even possibly a bold act of piracy? The deputy governor must have wondered if local residents or possibly a foreign government were responsible. But Britain had been at peace with its enemies for almost a decade. Lacking an explanation, Sessions soon found the vice-admiralty judge, John Andrews, and together they hurried off to Pawtuxet to investigate. Thus began an unfolding of events, well-known to contemporaries, but largely forgotten today. Boston Patriot Samuel Adams wrote of the *Gaspee* six months later in a letter to Darius Sessions that, "Such an Event as this will assuredly go down to future Ages in the page of History."[1]

The fact that a Royal Navy vessel was patrolling the waters in the far northern reaches of Narragansett Bay during peacetime was a function of three factors. The British ministry in Whitehall knew that Rhode Island merchants and shipmasters engaged in significant smuggling, especially with French, Spanish, and Dutch possessions in the Caribbean. Secondly, England's taxpayers were straining under a wartime debt accrued over the last several decades. By some estimates, British taxpayers were paying ten times more in taxes than their colonial counterparts.[2] A more rigorous enforcement of the Navigation Acts, those laws that regulated trade within the Empire, could increase the flow of revenues into the Treasury. And lastly, sea officers[3] of the Royal Navy were, after 1763, deputized to act as customs collectors to supplement the customs apparatus already in place in the colonies.

Lieutenant William Dudingston may have been ordered to Pennsylvania and Rhode Island in the late 1760s and early 1770s because of his reputation for zeal in the enforcement of customs laws.[4] The system rewarded the assertive officer with a lucrative portion from the sale of seized goods.

In September 1773, Benjamin Franklin, writing of the *Gaspee* Affair, offered satirical advice to the ministry on the proper management of colonial trade:

> XV. Convert the brave honest Officers of your Navy into pimping Tide-waiters and Colony Officers of the Customs. Let those who in Time of War fought gallantly in Defence of the Commerce of their Countrymen, in Peace be taught to prey upon it. Let them learn to be corrupted by great and real Smugglers; but (to shew their Diligence) scour with armed Boats every Bay, Harbour, River, Creek, Cove or Nook throughout the Coast of your colonies, stop and detain every Coaster, every Wood-boat, every Fisherman, tum-

ble their Cargoes, and even their Ballast, inside out and upside down; and if a Penn'orth of Pins if found un-entered, let the Whole be seized and confiscated. Thus shall the Trade of your Colonists suffer more from their Friends in Time of Peace, than it did from their Enemies in War. Then let these Boats Crews land upon every Farm in their Way, rob the Orchards, steal the Pigs and Poultry, and insult the Inhabitants. If the injured and exasperated Farmers, unable to procure other Justice, should attack the Agressors, drub them and burn their Boats, you are to call this *High Treason* and *Rebellion*, order Fleets and Armies into their Country, and threaten to carry all the Offenders three thousand Miles to be hang'd, drawn and quartered.[5] *O! this will work admirably!*[6]

Any analysis of what came to be called the "*Gaspee* Affair," the firing upon the *St. John*, and the burning of the *Liberty* must examine four intersecting components of eighteenth-century British law and politics: first, Royal Commissions of Inquiry, going back to Norman times; second, the establishment of treason laws and, later, the manner of conducting treason trials; third, the role of customs officials in port communities; and last, the role of the crowd and the sheriff in enforcing local laws and customs. This was the context in which the colonists petitioned for redress, the Privy Council in London made its decisions, and the royal commissioners in Newport made their report. All provided for complex, and sometimes competing, interpretations and applications of imperial and Rhode Island laws, customs, and actual practice.

WHEN the Privy Council met in London on August 20, 1772, to discuss how to proceed in response to the attack on the *Gaspee*, its members could survey an abundance of documents. They were most interested in why the attorney and solicitor generals had dismissed the use of the Dockyard Act and why American Department undersecretary John Pownall believed that a royal commission was the best option.[7]

Pownall brought to their attention the use of royal commissions in Antigua, Virginia, and New Jersey; the imprisonment of Sir Edmond Andros in Boston; a treason case from Barbados; and the transportation of pirates to England for trial.[8] While it would be difficult to set up a court of oyer and terminer[9] where courts already existed, royal commissions did not present such a problem. Pownall's research also tells us about his view of the Atlantic world and the context of colonial British America. He cited cases from the British West Indies and Canada seamlessly along with those from colonies that later became the United States.[10] The case precedent provided by Pownall which follows here is presented not chronologically, but thematically.

Royal Commissions existed long before Parliament, legislative machinery, and modern bureaucratic government. The scholars Hugh Clokie and J. William Robinson considered the Domesday survey (1080–1086) to be the first Royal Commission of Inquiry.[11] For a commission to be considered a Royal Commission of Inquiry, it had to be appointed by the Crown, and its commission had to be passed under the seal and carry the signature of the English monarch. Traditionally, the commissioners were not paid, but drawn from the aristocracy, although they could submit their traveling expenses to the Treasury.[12] They were not a standing committee, but gathered for a period of time to study and investigate particular social or legislative problems, disturbances or riots, or alleged abuses by the government or government officials. A Royal Commission of Inquiry was intended as an "occasional" instrument of the government. Their findings would be published in their final report, but then the commissioners went their separate ways and their combined wisdom was scattered. Not being tied to any particular party, faction, department, or branch of the government, the commission was supposed to be impartial and nonpartisan.

The Inquest of Sheriffs in 1176 was an example of barons named as royal commissioners to investigate abuses and injustices alleged against particular sheriffs and local officials. The Magna Carta, at the beginning of the thirteenth century and the rise of Parliament at the end, can both be seen as measures taken by the barons to put checks on the growing use and power of royal commissions.

The Tudors and the Stuarts enlarged royal prerogative in many areas of English life, including the use of commissions.[13] The Commission on Enclosures (1517) was considered the first truly "modern" commission to study a social problem. The skyrocketing number of commissions under the Tudors and Stuarts in the sixteenth and seventeenth centuries, though, was necessitated chiefly by changes in religious belief and practice. Strong Puritan reactions against the High Commission and the Star Chamber curtailed the use of royal commissions in the seventeenth century. The Star Chamber, while initially instituted in London to prosecute politically well-connected individuals where a local court might fail, later became associated with secretive, behind-the-scenes deal making. But commissions did not disappear entirely; the success of the parliamentary faction assured that Parliament would play a role in approving commissions (and commissioners) under the "Great Seal of England." Puritan leaders effectively utilized committees, a practice that went back to the fourteenth century in both houses of Parliament. After the Glorious Revolution, monarchs were extremely reluctant to appoint a royal commission that did not have wide parliamentary and public support. Commissions, then, were clearly for inquiry and research purposes; they did not have judicial decision-making powers. Subsequently, the eighteenth century was the institutional nadir for royal commissions.

To fill this void, parliamentary committees made a comeback in the eighteenth century. According to Clokie and Robinson, "Hundreds of select committees were set up during the eighteenth century for the purpose of considering both public and private legislation, the enclosure of common lands, administrative questions, the determination of disputed elections, etc."[14] This period, they argued, was one of profound parliamentary conservatism. While bitter partisanship, tribalism, and cliques abounded, changes and proposals for legislative or administrative changes were modest. Since Parliament contemplated no drastic reforms, the need for royal commissions waned. Not until the Victorian period of the nineteenth century did royal commissions enjoy a resurgence.

Prior to his meeting on August 20, 1772, with the Privy Council in London, Undersecretary John Pownall did some research, and in his report he cited three North American precedents for royal commissions: cases in Virginia, Antigua, and New Jersey. He also found instances where persons were transported to London for trial, as in the case of Dominion of New England governor Sir Edmund Andros. Pownall also cited the case of a West Indian merchant tried in London for treason.

Pownall's first and most dramatic investigation examined Bacon's Rebellion in Virginia in 1676–77.[15] Rebel leader Nathaniel Bacon had already been dead for four months when the first two royal commissioners, Francis Moryson and Sir John Berry, arrived in Virginia in January 1677 with 200 troops. Colonel Herbert Jeffreys landed shortly thereafter with an additional 1000 men. He was authorized to serve as lieutenant governor while Governor Sir William Berkeley went to England, although it was unclear exactly when Berkeley was supposed to leave. By April 1677, tensions between the commissioners and the governor were so strained that Jeffreys proclaimed himself governor of the Colony of Virginia even prior to Berkeley's departure.

The commissioners were supposed to remain subordinate to Governor Berkeley. Berkeley was to seek the commissioners' advice on Indian negotiations and the lowering of the Burgesses' salaries. Other than those two specific tasks, the commissioners were primarily on a fact-finding mission to record grievances and report to King Charles II.[16] The commissioners collected many post-rebellion grievances, some county-wide and others personal. There were very few pre-rebellion grievances and no real charges of corruption or graft. When the commissioners tried to settle grievances they overstepped the bounds of their authority, since their charge was only to report to the Crown.

In an unsettled situation with slow communication, the officials who drew up the charge of the commissioners could not know if Berkeley might be in exile or even deceased by the time the commissioners arrived in Virginia. Therefore they empowered Jeffreys to succeed Berkeley in the event that Bacon had taken charge of the colony. Once the commissioners arrived in Virginia, acting upon information that was several months old, they portrayed themselves as there to help crush the rebellion, offer pardons, and arrest Bacon.[17] Indeed,

Berkeley had already quelled the rebellion, although Jamestown, Virginia's capital, lay in ruins. The governor had not asked for troops, and having to house and feed such a large British force in the wake of the plundering of the rebels was more than the small provincial government could bear. The commissioners insisted upon issuing the King's Proclamation of Pardon, as it was written, which only gave more encouragement to Berkeley's opponents. Far from being subordinate assistants to the governor, the commissioners were creating almost as many problems for him as Bacon had. The relationship between the commissioners and the governor continued to deteriorate through February and March as the royal visitors collected, and in some cases, tried to settle, the grievances of former rebels while largely ignoring those of Loyalists.[18]

By May 1677, Governor Berkeley decided that he must travel to England to give his own account to the king, and defend his actions in light of the commissioners' report. Worn out from putting down the rebellion, his conflicts with the commissioners, and the long trans-Atlantic trip, Berkeley died at age 72 before he got an audience with the king.[19] The historian Wilcomb Washburn, defending the governor, found only one positive contribution by the commission: the commissioners had brokered a peace with the tributary Indians who had been dislocated by Bacon.[20]

The "Royal Commission to Investigate Bacon's Rebellion" displayed several criteria typified by a royal commission. They were investigating a social disturbance apparently caused by a social problem(s). There were allegations of abuses by government and government officials. There were questions about oppressive leadership and the legal problems created by confiscating property during and immediately after the rebellion. These were the kinds of conditions royal commissions had investigated in the past. Also, the royal commissioners were empowered to hold Bacon's trial either in the vicinage or in England. While many colonials may have believed that a trial across the sea would be their undoing, royal officials frequently welcomed them as the only means to an impartial trial. Unfortunately, Pownall's extensive appendices were lost, so we do not know his conclusions.

The second example that Undersecretary Pownall reported to the Privy Council was a case of insurrection, government corruption, and the assassination of the governor of Antigua in 1711–12. The residents of Antigua had constantly feared a French invasion during Queen Anne's War, and they were harassed by French privateers. Colonel Daniel Parke[21] went to Antigua as governor of the Leeward Islands in July 1706. Parke, who grew up in Virginia and served on the council there, had left his wife and two daughters, sailed to England, and joined the army. His heroic performance at the Battle of Blenheim earned him an audience with Queen Anne, who gave him the governorship of the Leeward Islands. Parke had been hoping for the governorship of Virginia and was never able to hide his disappointment.[22]

When Parke arrived at Antigua in 1706, he found an island economy with an enormous disparity in wealth. Parke openly resented the power of the planter class and their control of the islands' political and legal apparatus. He complained that the rich could not be found guilty of anything; they were acquitted of felonies and even murder.[23] Unfortunately, while he experienced some early success with limited reforms, Parke did not have the background or skill to master this difficult governorship. After several attempts on his life and many complaints to Queen Anne, the ministry ordered Parke to return to England to answer the accusations. His opponents read this order as a recall and they believed that he had lost his governorship. Ultimately, when Parke did not leave his post, the loyalty of army officers and troops wavered, and he was assassinated in December 1710. A lieutenant-general administered the affairs of the colony until a new governor could be sent.

The Privy Council sent Colonel Walter Douglas the following April to serve as the governor of the Leeward Islands and to inquire into the death of Colonel Parke.[24] The commissioners were instructed to send between three and six ringleaders and the army officers who failed to support Parke to England for trial. Douglas was also directed to offer a general pardon to the population of the islands at large. Upon arrival, Douglas reported that sympathy for the rebels was still strong and that for the present it was inadvisable to issue the pardon and set up the commission of inquiry.[25] In fact, he did not issue the pardon until February 1712. It came out later that Douglas had taken bribes from many powerful planters in order to be included in the general pardon and not among the "ringleaders." The Privy Council handed down a sentence of five years of confinement and a £500 fine for former Governor Douglas.

Pownall's most current example presented to the Privy Council involved another small northern colony, New Jersey. Throughout the 1740s, frontier settlers and more prosperous farmers struggled over land rights with the proprietary land owners in the western counties of New Jersey. According to New Jersey historian Morris Schonbach, "In 1749, it was estimated that fully one-third of the population of Essex County was rioting."[26] New Jersey in the 1740s was troubled by repeated jail breaks, grand juries that failed to indict, trial juries that failed to convict, assassination attempts, and extra-legal committees that formed to protect the rights of squatters. Governor Lewis Morris "called the riots almost 'high treason' and said that such occurrences were but 'too likely to end in Rebellion and throwing off his Majesty's Authority; if timely Measures be not taken to check the Intemperance of a too licentious Multitude.'"[27]

The board of the Southern Department (which oversaw southern England, Wales, Ireland, and the American colonies) met in July 1749 to discuss the unrest in New Jersey so that they could report to the Privy Council. They studied the council's response to Bacon's Rebellion seventy-three years earlier. Three ideas emerged: send over a new governor whose salary was paid by the home government and supply him with enough troops to suppress any lawlessness; borrow military forces from New York; or reunite New York and New Jersey under one governor.[28] The underlying belief of the board was that the government of the colony needed a greater measure of independence from the people.[29] New Jersey governor Jonathan Belcher replied that these solutions still did not get at the heart of the problem; land disputes and taxation issues should be heard by an unbiased tribunal. The land proprietors had skillfully kept this from happening. They would pursue matters with the London government until they believed that the formation of a commission of investigation was imminent, and then they would retreat. Belcher never got the commission of inquiry he desired, and these disputes continued throughout the French and Indian War and into the War for American Independence, although the added presence of British regulars had a dampening effect on the riots.[30]

Despite the failures of these royal commissions of inquiry, they seem to follow a pattern: first, there was a general pardon for a large percentage of the offenders, followed by an effort to "round up" a small number of "ringleaders."[31] The commissioners that went to Antigua were even told how many ringleaders to find. Given the general beliefs of "top-down" politics and the hierarchy of social responsibility, there seemed to be a belief on the part of the Privy Council that most of the Crown's subjects would want to be loyal. Many elites believed that there must be extreme social conditions or oppressive local magistrates abusing their power to cause British subjects to behave otherwise. A royal commission of inquiry, officials hoped, would discover the conditions under which loyal subjects could be driven to such extremes. But not wanting to seem "soft" on riotous or murderous behavior, they would make an example of a few of the leadership.[32]

UNDERSECRETARY Pownall provided the council with two other case precedents relevant to the *Gaspee* although they did not involve royal commissions of inquiry. In 1689, with the collapse of the Dominion of New England following the Glorious Revolution and ascension of William and Mary to the throne, former governor Sir Edmund Andros's imprisoned government petitioned the Privy Council for a hearing in England. Having antagonized powerful colonists and the local militia, the former governor did not believe that he could get a fair trial in Boston. Twice Andros escaped jail in women's clothing, one time getting as far as Rhode Island. Ultimately, he did get to England where a London trial dropped the charges against him, and the very next day Andros was sent to Kensington Palace to kiss the new king's hand.[33] The episode did not even hurt his career, because shortly thereafter Andros returned to North America to govern the colony of Virginia. Although Pownall's notes have not survived, it seems that he cited Andros's case as a successful example of a royally appointed official traveling to London for an "impartial" trial.[34]

It is clearer why Pownall chose a case from the West Indies in 1712. Governor Lord A. Hamilton of Jamaica imprisoned a merchant and supercargo from Barbados, David Creagh, when he arrived in Port-Royal. Hamilton claimed that Creagh was guilty of trading with the Queen's enemies.[35] What started out as a seizure and condemnation by the Admiralty court, upon further investigation and counsel, turned into a charge of high treason. Creagh's sloop traded slaves and dry goods for indigo from the French settlements in Hispaniola. Hamilton's attorney general advised him that Creagh could only be tried for such a crime in England, and he was sent out, with two accusers, on the *Jersey*.[36]

Pownall had done his research well, and he was able to present the Privy Council with adequate precedent for both a royal commission of inquiry and for a trial in England for crimes committed in the colonies. While pirates could be taken to England for trial, the ringleaders of the *Gaspee* raid could not be charged with piracy. But the charge of treason seemed to fit the case more closely.[37] The Privy Council did not need a detailed report on treason laws and precedent; Parliament had recently re-visited the topic in the 1768–69 session and updated their treason law to include British colonials. In the late 1760s they had considered transporting some of Boston's radicals to London for trial.[38] But this controversial legislation did not pass unanimously; Rockingham Whig and opposition spokesman Edmund Burke[39] railed against the extension of the treason law before Parliament in his *Speech on American Resolutions* on May 9, 1770.[40]

Under Edward III in 1351, the law of treason was subdivided into seven categories. The historian James Hurst wrote, "The most important were to 'compass or imagine the death of our lord the King in his realm,' to 'levy war against our lord the King in his realm,' or 'to adhere to his enemies, giving them aid and comfort.'"[41]

The other categories dealt with counterfeiting money and seals as well as defiling the king's wife, eldest daughter, or the nursemaid to the heir.[42] These provisions were designed to protect the king's property and the lineage of the royal family. Within a few decades, the Great Rebellion in Kent in 1381 and the insurrection in Oxfordshire in 1398 demonstrated that the Crown still required more inclusive legal definitions to tackle popular uprisings. Juries also needed clarification in their instructions for distinguishing between felony and treason. Act 33 in the law of treason under Henry VIII allowed for treason trials to be moved out of the local county or shire to London.[43] This was quickly repealed for English and Welsh subjects. Reluctant to hold trials for Irish or French traitors among a large crowd of fellow Catholics, Henry VIII moved their trials to Westminster before the King's Bench under Act 35.[44]

Due to these "ancient" laws, the Privy Council decided that the *Gaspee* ringleaders could be tried in Rhode Island or in London. This decision gave the Patriot press its greatest rallying cry. These laws were passed before there were any English colonists in North America. American colonists, it seemed, did not truly have the same rights as other Englishmen. The possibility of a trial outside of the vicinage demonstrated more clearly than any other single factor in the *Gaspee* affair that the American colonists could be treated the same as the Irish.

In December 1772 and January 1773 the editors of the *Providence Gazette* and the *Newport Mercury* reminded readers of the legal difficulties surrounding a treason trial in London.[45] The Rhode Island General Assembly had endorsed the Virginia Resolves in 1769,[46] which stated:

> RESOLVED, That all Trials for Treason, Misprision of Treason, or for any Felony of Crime whatsoever, committed and done in this his Majesty's said Colony and Dominion, by any Person or Persons residing therein, ought of Right to be had, and conducted in and before his Majesty's Court, held within the said Colony, according to the fixed and known Court of Proceeding. . . .[47]

Rhode Island's newspapers also reminded readers of Massachusetts's resistance to the royal commission sent to, as they said, "subvert its liberties" in 1664. Massachusetts officials had to hide their charter to protect their right to elect their own governor. The commission had brought troops and had secret orders to conduct military operations against the Dutch in New Netherlands. The 1664 commissioners enforced a loyalty oath and the new navigation laws.[48] After the restoration of Charles II in 1660, the Crown took territory from the Dutch and named it after Charles's brother James, the Duke of York, making New York a royal colony answering directly to the monarchy. Unlike the other Puritan colony in Connecticut which enjoyed greater autonomy, Massachusetts felt threatened following the Restoration.

In 1772, after initially misreporting the identities of the commissioners, the *Providence Gazette* and the *Newport Mercury* later reported that Rhode Island's own elected Governor Wanton was going to head the *Gaspee* commission of inquiry. Both newspapers reprinted the March 1, 1663, Rhode Island law that stated, "No Freeman shall be taken, or imprisoned, or deprived of his Freehold, or Liberty, or free Custom, or be outlawed, or exiled, or condemned, but by the lawful Judgment of his Peers, or by the Law of this Colony."[49] *Newport Mercury* editor John Carter aided in republishing and advertising Henry Care's *English Liberties* during the *Gaspee* affair and later during the Tea Act crisis. Excerpts from this book frequently appeared in the *Providence Gazette* as well as the Newport paper. They emphasized the right to a trial by jury.[50] Newspaper stories also provided graphic descriptions of drawing and quartering to emphasize the brutal means by which the London government administered capital punishment to treason convicts.

Newspapers in other colonies picked up the stories of the royal commission and the idea of a treason trial outside the vicinage. These stories were reprinted so many times, and were so far removed from the original source, that Richard Henry Lee wrote to Samuel Adams on February 4, 1773, to ask him for further details.[51] Lee and Adams had not yet met; this was their first direct correspondence.[52] The *Gaspee* commission had such a profound effect on Virginia's Patriots that Thomas Jefferson looked back on the *Gaspee* commission's powers as the event that woke them up during the "lull."[53] He was alarmed, as were most Patriots, by the threat of a trial in England.

This prompted a meeting at Raleigh Tavern, to which Jefferson attributed the forming of the Virginia Committee of Correspondence—in order to get "first hand" accounts of events from other colonies.[54] Contemporary reactions in the colonies demonstrate that colonists were not overly dismayed by the actions of the *Gaspee* raiders, though the threat of a treason trial in England aroused widespread concern. Contemporary reactions in England showed that officials were not so surprised by the attack on Dudingston, but the seizing and burning of the schooner outraged them. To understand the context in which all parties responded to the *Gaspee* episode, one must examine similar instances of attacks on customs officials, sea officers, writs for their arrest, and the burning of vessels.

In 1718 Nathaniel Kay, the customs collector for Rhode Island, discovered five hogsheads of smuggled claret hidden in a "Backhouse." Kay left the wine under the guard of the sheriff and went searching for a cart in order to move the barrels to a secure location. Upon his return he found the wine's owner and a small group of people there acting "in a Riotous manner,"[55] destroying the hogsheads with axes and threatening the officers should they try to intervene. Regarding compliance with the Act of Trade, historian Thomas C. Barrow indicated "one of the basic truths of the customs officers' situation: obstruction, not cooperation, was usually to be expected from the local colonial authorities."[56] Kay knew he would get no satisfaction in the Rhode Island provincial courts. Even the Admiralty courts had been made impotent by colonial adversaries. Kay inquired whether a case like this could be tried in Westminster Hall, and indeed the Act of 1696 (section 7) allowed for a trial in England. But the impracticality of transporting evidence and witnesses made this option less desirable. Another forty years would pass before Parliament would truly address the problems created by colonial nullification of the powers of the Admiralty courts.

In December 1723, the *William and Mary,* a trading ship from Bristol, England, appeared to have landed some smuggled goods north of Boston. Two witnesses from the crew gave testimony for the Crown. But the customs officials and witnesses were beaten nearly to death and only survived by the intervention of the sheriff. Following this incident, Governor Samuel Shute requested 200 troops be sent to Boston to help control the recent riots and disorders.

In both of these examples, the colonial governor backed the efforts of the customs officials. Kay reported that in his case "the Governour gave his utmost Assistance."[57] But congenial relations between customs officials and their governors were not always the case.

In October 1724, the *Fame* sailed into Philadelphia with smuggled goods. John Moore, the customs collector, placed four tidewaiters (men who board and inspect incoming vessels in a port or harbor) on board to guard the vessel.[58] Sixty to seventy people stormed the vessel in disguise, cut it loose, and two waiters jumped overboard. The other two were locked below and therefore did not witness the relocation of the forbidden cargo. Lieutenant Governor William Keith employed a long series of delaying tactics and administrative procrastination in order to frustrate Moore in his duties. Keith was not alone in his resistance. South Carolina governor Charles Craven would commandeer seized vessels and send them out on trumped-up missions. He claimed this seized property as his own and threatened to shoot anyone who got near it. In one case Governor Craven ordered the fort in Charleston to fire upon the customs yacht, and in another case, a man-of-war.[59]

Colonial assemblies, as well as governors, could make the duties of the customs collector almost impossible to implement. Nathaniel Kay complained that officers were frequently arrested for collecting their legal fees. In 1710, the Rhode Island Assembly adopted a set of unusually low fees. They passed an act allowing justices of the peace to issue warrants to arrest customs collectors and naval officers by charging them with collecting too much in fees.[60] Rhode Island shipmasters were known for weighing anchor with the customs officials or tidewaiters on board and threatening to take them on a long voyage if they persisted in their search for illicit cargo.

The customs commissioners and the Board of Trade heard hours of testimony and read sheaves of reports about the need to reform the system, literally since its inception in 1696. When the system was truly reformed, in 1763 and 1764, the tenor and the pace of colonial resistance solidified. The London Customs Board expected some merchant resistance in Rhode Island, and when Admiral Colville arrived in America he ordered the twenty-gun *Squirrel* to spend the winter of 1763/64 in Newport. The Surveyor General of Customs, John Temple, was making an inspection trip to Rhode Island in January 1764, and he used this visit as a chance to set an example of what Rhode Islanders might expect with a more rigid enforcement of customs. Temple attempted to get colonial officials more actively involved in customs enforcement. The General Assembly, anticipating conflict, forbade the Governor from administering any oaths to customs officials without their permission. Frustrated and angered by Rhode Island's resistance, Temple seized an incoming vessel named the *Rhoda*, but the ship and its cargo of molasses escaped to sea two days later. Temple was humiliated into having to offer a £50 reward for its recapture, but to no avail.[61]

Rhode Islanders could tell by the summer of 1764 that they were being targeted by the customs service and navy. As mentioned earlier, in April the *Squirrel*, under Captain Richard Smith, finally arrived in Newport, having experienced weather and communication problems. In May the honest and extremely diligent new customs collector, John Robinson, arrived.[62] The following month, June 1764, the *St. John*, one of the *Gaspee*'s sister ships, arrived in Narragansett Bay under the leadership of Lieutenant Thomas Hill.[63] Another customs dispute, eight years before the *Gaspee* Affair, but so very similar, mirrored the events: a hostile mob, confrontation with sea officers, threatening the pilot, and threatening to burn the vessel. From a Rhode Island perspective, the London government sent too many people and ships into Rhode Island too quickly, as would soon be evident.

By the time the Privy Council inquired into the *St. John* incident, Governor Stephen Hopkins was no longer in office. The new governor, Samuel Ward, claimed that he had no knowledge about the incident in Newport and the matter was dropped. Commanders Hill and Smith did not even get the satisfaction of a seized vessel, as John Temple sided with Collector Robinson in the dispute over the *Basto*. By giving customs deputations to sea officers, Whitehall had drastically raised the stakes for colonial resistance to the customs service. Customs collectors had experienced violence and threats, and customs yachts had run into numerous problems with smugglers since 1696. But after 1764, violence aimed at customs enforcement shifted from solely civilian agents to include military targets. If colonial governors and assemblies failed to follow up on attacks on military officers and vessels in service, it would be harder for the Privy Council to drop these matters as they had in the past with civilian targets. This was, perhaps, a great unintended consequence of deputizing sea officers for customs service. The London government could no longer view colonial resistance as mere "lawlessness" or "insolence"; now it was treason.

Attention to the incidents with the *St. John* and the *Rhoda* give the impression that resistance occurred only in Rhode Island in 1764. But in July, Lieutenant Thomas Laugharne of the armed sloop *Chaleur* (another sister ship of the *Gaspee*) pressed five men from incoming vessels at Sandy Hook, New Jersey.[64] The next time he went ashore Laugharne was captured by a mob and forced to release the men. The impressed men requested that the mob burn the *Chaleur*'s boat in front of New York City Hall, which they did.[65] The mob disappeared before the mayor could arrive, so only two men were detained. A grand jury found that everyone "forgot" everything and dropped the incident within two weeks.[66]

But the year 1764 included more than just shooting and burning. Merchants in New York demonstrated how little legal protection sea officers possessed in the colonies under their customs deputations. Captain John Brown of the sloop-of-war *Hawke* seized the *New York* headed for Perth Amboy from Haiti. Brown received very little assistance from the New York customs house or the vice-admiralty court. On April 27, he was arrested and charged in a £10,500 damage suit. Unable to leave New York, the *Hawke* spent the summer tied up. New York's merchants liked having the *Hawke* in port where it could not inspect cargo or seize vessels. Soon it became apparent that Brown was not going to get a speedy trial. In November his superior officer ordered him to sea. The owners of the *New York* had Brown incarcerated for trying to flee the city. Ultimately, the Royal

Navy assigned another officer to the *Hawke* and it was at that point, nine months later, that Brown was released and resumed his command.[67] Considering cases such as this, many sea officers of the North American squadron could see why Admiral Colville encouraged them to take seizures directly to the new vice-admiralty court in Halifax, though for logistical reasons few actually did so. Rhode Island saw the first test case, not with a sea officer, but rather with a customs collector.

John Robinson,[68] the customs collector at Newport, perhaps following the events in New York, was the first person to have the necessary support to put the new court in Halifax to the test. Robinson, being an Englishman, was not as vulnerable to popular pressure as colonial collectors; he never hesitated to use the Royal Navy to protect his seizures, his staff, or his person.[69] He received a cool reception upon arrival in Newport in May 1764, when the governor refused to swear him into his new office. Robinson did not resort to the Halifax Vice-Admiralty Court right away; instead he gave the local court a chance to prove itself. In March 1765, Comptroller of Customs John Nicoll in Newport joined Robinson in prosecuting what they thought should be an easy case. The naval vessel *Maidstone* seized the brig *Wainscott* and the sloop *Nelly*, whose shipmasters were notorious for ignoring molasses regulations. But Vice-Admiralty judge Andrews[70] blocked the customs collectors so successfully that they wrote to the commissioners of customs to complain. The commissioners of the treasury ordered the governor to investigate. Not only did Andrews release both vessels, he sued Robinson for complaining to the commissioners and the governor. This case dragged on for years until all parties lost interest in it, effectively giving a victory to those who would defy the collectors.[71]

In April 1765, Robinson became suspicious of the small amount of molasses reported by the *Polly* arriving from Suriname. He caught up with the *Polly* in Dighton, Massachusetts, and seized the vessel. Not having enough men to sail it back to Newport, he left two of his men in charge of the *Polly* while he returned to Rhode Island to recruit a crew. In Robinson's absence, a mob liberated the cargo and furnishings off of the *Polly*. In the commotion, the vessel was allowed to run aground. When Robinson arrived back in Dighton with armed marines, a warrant awaited him from the *Polly*'s owner with a £3,000 damage suit, and Robinson spent the next two nights in the Taunton jail.

Massachusetts surveyor general John Temple secured Robinson's release and with the assistance of the man-of-war *Maidstone*, re-floated and re-seized the almost empty sloop and returned with it to Newport. Eight hogsheads were recovered, enough to proceed with the condemnation of the vessel. Temple, in the middle of a power struggle with Massachusetts governor Bernard, used the *Polly* as a chance to send a prize to Judge Spry in the Halifax Vice-Admiralty Court.[72] While the sloop stayed in Newport harbor for more than a year under the protection of the naval vessel *Cygnet*, Temple forwarded the necessary documentation to Halifax. Captain Leslie of the *Cygnet* reported to Rhode Island governor Ward that he heard rumors that a mob was planning to capture Fort George[73] and threaten his vessel in order to force the release of the *Polly*. Leslie threatened full retaliation should Fort George fall into the hands of a mob; yet none of these fears materialized.[74] The *Polly* was sold at a public auction in June 1766.[75] The *Polly* may have been the first true test case for the right to trial in the vicinage. Robinson was reluctant to utilize the Halifax Vice-Admiralty Court option again.

Only a few months after these events in Newport, the *Maidstone* was attacked. Given the timing of the raid, one would expect that it was related either to its role in re-seizing the *Polly* or in enforcing the Stamp Act. But, as in the case of the *Chaleur*, the *Maidstone* episode appears to be a case of impressment. In June 1765, Captain Charles Antrobus pressed the entire crew of a brigantine in Newport harbor. In retaliation, at 9:00 PM, just as night fell, a mob dragged the *Maidstone*'s boat up to the common and burned it.[76] Governor Ward seemed reluctant to prosecute, reporting, "The best information I can get, no person of the least note was concerned in the riot; the persons who committed the crime, consisting altogether of the dregs of the people, and a number of boys and negros."[77] Residents were distressed because Captain Antrobus had given his word to the sheriff that he would not press in Newport.[78] Press gangs kept vessels away from the town, causing a shortage of firewood and driving up seamen's wages.[79]

The next case that has bearing on the context of the *Gaspee* episode came two years later in far away South Carolina. The means by which the mob was mobilized tells us something about the use of the drum by eighteenth-century colonial militias. On May 23, 1767, Captain James Hawker of the *Sardoine*, a sea officer with a reputation for strict enforcement, encountered a colonial mob in Charleston. Hawker's men were beaten and forced overboard when trying to inspect a vessel. Hawker personally sailed over in a dramatic fashion (British flag in hand) to insist on seeing the ship's papers. He considered himself victorious, but was horrified to find the militia beating to arms—not to quell the mob, but to gather one.[80]

Two years after that, back in Rhode Island on May 18, 1769, a mob abused Jesse Saville, a tidewaiter in the employment of William Checkley in the Providence customs house. The Boston customs commissioners offered a £50 reward for information about the perpetrators. But the only information they could get was that Saville was off duty at the time and should not have been lurking around the wharf. After being moved to the Gloucester, Massachusetts, customs house, Saville was again abused, this time tarred and feathered in March 1770. Asleep in bed, he was dragged four miles down to the harbor. A lantern was placed in his hand while he was pushed around town in a cart, with the crowd proclaiming that he was a spy and an informer.[81] Again in 1771, he was stripped, bound, tarred and feathered.[82] Thereafter Saville disappears from the historical record.

In 1769, Rhode Islanders saw the most dramatic destruction of a vessel in government service to date in the burning of the *Liberty*. Even the *Liberty*'s entrance into government service was marked with turmoil and violence. The provocatively named sloop belonged to the Boston Whig merchant John Hancock. In May 1768, *Liberty* docked in Boston with 127 pipes of wine from Madeira aboard.[83] Nathaniel Barnard, master of the *Liberty*, declared only 25 pipes at the customs house. Customs officials waited a month until the *Romney* arrived to seize the *Liberty* and to have marines tow it away from the dock. Only when the sloop was anchored by the *Romney* could they prevent a "rescue." Seeing the approaching marines, and perhaps fearing a press, a mob formed along the pier. As the customs officials walked away from the pier, the angry colonists followed them and pelted them with paving stones and brickbats. Several riotous groups visited the houses of customs officials and damaged some property, but no one was seriously injured. The officials fled to the safety of the *Romney* and later to Castle William.[84] Collector Joseph Harrison's pleasure yacht was dragged out to the town common and burned before an estimated crowd of 500 to 1000 people.[85] John Adams defended John Hancock before Judge Robert Auchmuty's vice-admiralty court and the commissioners dropped their case, again showing the weakness of royal authority in Massachusetts.[86]

At the time of the *Gaspee* attack, the most recent disturbance in Newport had occurred in April 1771, when Collector Charles Dudley[87] was beaten up on a wharf. Newport's reverend Ezra Stiles claimed that the collector's father obtained the position for his son through his influence as an Episcopal clergyman. Customs enforcement, Stiles explained, had become highly politicized. Vessels whose owners were associated with non-importation or the Sons of Liberty would be detained and the masters required to swear numerous oaths. The vessels of merchants who were friends of the current administration, Stiles claimed, were allowed to pass the customs house without notice. [88]

While one could cite additional cases of attacks on customs officers, sea officers, and vessels, the cases described here were those best known to Rhode Islanders as of June 1772. Clearly customs officers, tidewaiters, and their yachts had been the targets of various attacks and threats since the inception of the service three generations earlier.[89]

WHILE some of the pre-*Gaspee* violence was destructive, and people were badly injured, only the King Street riot, dubbed the "Boston Massacre" by Patriots, produced fatalities before April 1775.[90] No British or government officials were killed. Colonials, for the most part, tried to "go through proper channels" to seek redress through their local officials. For example, many sheriffs worked with sea officers to set limits for the type of impressments that they would allow. Sheriffs and mobs confronted sea officers only when they believed that their agreements had been breached.

On the night of the raid on the *Gaspee*, Lieutenant Dudingston did not protest, "Why are you here?" or "I have never heard of a case of a sheriff approaching one of His Majesty's vessels with an arrest warrant." Dudingston merely replied that they should return at a more appropriate hour. The *Gaspee* raiding party was following a known formula, a script or agenda of increasing resistance when ordinary channels of redress failed. Dudingston's response leads us to believe that he was aware of this formula. Eight years earlier a peace officer approached the *St. John* with an arrest warrant for three people on board accused of stealing some livestock. When he was turned away, a mob approached the vessel to seek justice. But, unlike the *Gaspee*, the *St. John* was able to protect herself from being boarded by angry colonists, as the *Squirrel* was nearby.

Historian Pauline Maier described the actions of colonial mobs as *extra-institutional*, rather than *anti-institutional*. Frequently, colonial magistrates led crowds or gave tacit approval for moderate mob activity. They could enforce laws when the sheriff alone could not. They acted only after official administrative and legal channels had proved inadequate. But for laws that were crafted on the other side of the Atlantic, especially after 1763, groups of colonists often acted to resist their implementation, rather than guarantee it. Maier argued, "Two other imperial efforts similarly provoked local uprisings in the colonies long before 1765 and continued to do so in long established ways during the revolutionary period: impressment and customs enforcement."[91]

Groups of colonists acted out publicly to expedite immediate, local needs and goals. Often it was to release men who were pressed or to charge men accused of theft. These mobs, Maier argued, did not display evidence of revolutionary goals or ideology. In the case of the *Gaspee*, it was the same John Brown who attempted to redress grievances through proper channels against the *Gaspee* during the spring of 1772 who led the mob that destroyed it when authorities in Boston and Newport failed to rein in the zealous Lieutenant Dud-ingston.[92]

Numerous eighteenth-century British and American writers and politicians believed that rioting was a natural and necessary part of political life among a free people. Moderate rioting was needed as a corrective to abuses in order to keep authority from deteriorating into despotism. Suppression laws passed in the wake of excessive ri-oting were temporary, as the permanent law that existed in Britain was seen by colonials as an example of arbitrary power. Colonial leaders, for the most part, understood that rioting was a symptom of a deeper problem. Certainly they claimed that most of His Majesty's subjects would live peaceably if governed wisely and justly.[93]

Captain Antrobus of the *Maidstone* and Captain Smith of the *St. John* complained in letters home that the magistrates of Rhode Is-land, "instead of preventing the outbreaks, they were 'the planners and countenancers of these riotous measures.'"[94] While local leaders allowed or even provoked resistance, they never openly defended it.[95] Invariably, magistrates offered rewards for information and decried riotous behavior. The *Gaspee* raiding party followed the script for an eighteenth-century mob; while he may have been acting *pro forma*, Governor Wanton responded appropriately by condemning their actions and offering a reward. Perhaps the whole matter would have been dropped had the raiders not returned and burned the schooner.

While the Privy Council might have been able to drop the matter of the attack on Lieutenant Dudingston, they could not ignore the destruction of a commissioned naval vessel on station. Merely offer-ing a reward for information would not be enough. While the colonists had a "formula" for how they dealt with intransient offi-cials and imperial legal conflicts, so did Whitehall. They had a "script" that they could follow for colonial conflicts as well; they would send a Royal Commission of Inquiry.

Four

Star Chamber

J UDGING FROM COLONIAL NEWSPAPERS, CORRESPONDENCE, AND diaries, most Rhode Islanders did not believe they needed a Royal Commission of Inquiry. Commissions, they recognized, could be appropriate for extreme cases of rebellion, *coups d'état*, and political assassinations, but not merely for a case of customs enforcement. Because their crucial molasses and rum trade was interrupted by overly zealous customs enforcement, many desired a return to the former laxity of *laissez-faire* salutary neglect. Only a few welcomed the commission, believing that Rhode Island politics were indeed too chaotic. Critics of Rhode Island's colonial government welcomed British reforms and perhaps saw the commission as advancing that goal. Critics pointed out the fact that some landowners waited for years for disputes to be fully settled. New justices would overturn the decisions of the previous court, as court appointments reflected the uncertainties of the shifting sands of Rhode Island politics.[1] The annual election of the governor insured that his office was highly accountable to the electorate, and it did change frequently.[2] Chief Justice Daniel

Horsmanden, one of the commissioners, indicated what he thought of Rhode Island's colonial government:

> My Lord, as to the Government (if it deserves that name), it is a downright democracy; the Governor is a mere nominal one, and therefore a cipher, without power or authority; entirely controlled by the populace, elected annually, as all other magistrates and officers whatsoever.[3]

An unknown friend of His Majesty's government wrote, "but I hope Government will make a proper use of this unheard of Event, & take this Opportunity of depriving us of what to some of us is the greatest Curse, the Charter."[4] This author doubted Whitehall would get satisfaction from Rhode Island's magistrates. At the other end of the political spectrum, Samuel Adams believed the commission was a threat to colonial liberties, describing it as a "court of inquisition . . . a star chamber . . . within this colony."[5]

An order of the King in Council was sent on August 26, 1772, from St. James's Palace, indicating that if at least three of the five commissioners, under the leadership of Rhode Island governor Joseph Wanton, convened in Newport they constituted a quorum. They were to begin "to inquire into all circumstances to the attacking, taking, plundering and burning His Majesty's schooner called the *Gaspee*."[6] But, consistent with other royal commissions of inquiry, their mission was grander than a mere criminal investigation. Their charge, which was supposed to be private but was subsequently published in several newspapers, included "taking of some fit and speedy order for securing the future peace and well-government of the said colony." It was perhaps from this statement that some Patriots saw a veiled threat to Rhode Island's charter.[7] Lieutenant-General Thomas Gage, commander-in-chief of His Majesty's forces in North America, was to stand ready to provide support to the commissioners in the event of unrest. Admiral Montagu, head of the Royal Navy's North American Squadron in Boston, was instructed to transport suspects and witnesses to England for trial. This commission passed under the Great Seal on September 2, 1772, and was signed by the king himself. On that very day, Admiral Montagu, not yet knowing about the commission or the governor's crucial role leading it, wrote to Philip Stephens at the Admiralty in London telling him that there would never be any justice for Dudingston while Governor Wanton stood in their way.[8]

Fuller instructions for the commissioners, including five separate articles, were given on September 4. Article III made it clear that the commissioners were not to circumvent the local court system but depend upon them "to arrest and commit to custody such of the persons" as the commission might recommend.[9] This was not a court of oyer and terminer.[10] The solicitor and attorney generals and American Department undersecretary John Pownall made it clear to the Privy Council in London that they could not exercise that kind of authority in a colony where courts already existed.

Consistent with previous commissions, the royal commission in Rhode Island was to examine all sides of the controversy. Newport pastor Ezra Stiles was pleasantly surprised to find that "the Commissioners were impowered to inquire into and take Information concerning any Misdemeanors and Oppressions of the *Officers of the Navy and Customs* [emphasis his]."[11] The Earl of Dartmouth assured Governor Wanton that, "His Majesty will not fail to punish with the utmost severity those who shall either wantonly or unnecessarily distress and obstruct the lawful commerce of his subjects in Rhode Island or shall otherwise injure them in their persons or properties."[12]

Admiral Montagu received the packets for the commissioners and proclamation from the King's Council on December 10, 1772, and promptly forwarded them to Governor Wanton.[13] Wanton got to work arranging the time and place for the commissioners to convene. He published the King's proclamation and reward and distributed it through his sheriffs on December 22, to be posted in the usual manner. Two days later he found out that two of the commissioners, Chief Justice Daniel Horsmanden of New York and Chief Justice Frederick Smythe of New Jersey, were already on their way to Newport in the sloop *Lydia*.[14] The other two commissioners, Robert Auchmuty, vice-admiralty judge at the Boston court and Chief Justice

Peter Oliver of Massachusetts, promptly replied to the Earl of Dartmouth that they would faithfully discharge their duty.[15] Wanton encouraged them to arrive in Newport within the week. Admiral Montagu, in Boston, indicated that he would come to Newport when the commissioners were ready for him.

On December 25, Deputy Governor Darius Sessions, Chief Justice Stephen Hopkins, John Cole, and Moses Brown wrote to Samuel Adams and sent extracts from Dartmouth's September 4 letter to Governor Wanton. They asked Adams for advice, preferably before the next meeting of the general assembly.[16] Adams replied immediately, before consulting other "gentlemen in North America," and at a later date gave a more in-depth response. The commission, he argued, was "a Matter, which in my Opinion may involve the Fate of America. . . . It has ever been my Opinion, that an Attack upon the Liberties of one Colony is an Attack upon the Liberties of all; and therefore in this Instance all should be ready to yield Assistance to Rhode Island."[17] Samuel Adams, like Richard Henry Lee and John Allen, was ready to move the *Gaspee* beyond a mere legal and investigative problem; he politicized it and viewed the ramifications in inter-colonial terms and a larger imperial context.

Governor Wanton took one other action he claimed was his duty and it infuriated the Earl of Dartmouth. The governor brought his letter and orders from Dartmouth before the Rhode Island Assembly,[18] from whence it was quickly leaked to the press and appeared "in the Boston weekly paper, and spread industriously over all New England."[19] John Adams noted on December 29, that Dartmouth's letter and the commission were "the present Topick of Conversation." After having just told Samuel Adams that he was too old for politics and public life, he got in a heated conversation with an "English Gentleman" about the *Gaspee* commission and, "I found the old Warmth, Heat, Violence, Acrimony, Bitterness, Sharpness of my Temper, And Expression, was not departed. I said there was no more Justice left in Britain than there was in Hell—That I wished for War."[20]

On December 31, 1772, commissioners Horsmanden and Smythe arrived in Newport, followed two days later by Auchmuty and

Oliver.[21] On January 2, 1773, Samuel Adams wrote his follow-up letter to Deputy Governor Sessions.[22] In this letter Adams raised the alarm that, "the Administration has a design to get your Charter vacated."[23] Adams discussed the possibility of not calling the commission or not prosecuting any of the attackers. Too much resistance, he seemed to say, could be counter-productive. He spoke in ominous terms of "a most violent political Earthquake through the whole British Empire if not its total Destruction. I have long feard that this unhappy Contest between Britain & America will end in Rivers of Blood; Should that be the Case, America I think may wash her hands in Innocence."[24]

Adams also proposed a grand jury investigation in Rhode Island as an alternative to the royal commission of inquiry.[25] He finished the letter by proposing some intercolonial communication from Rhode Island's Assembly to the assemblies of other colonies and even their agents in London. Adams wanted Deputy Governor Sessions to dissuade Governor Wanton from serving on the commission, because his service would endorse its legality. He feared more commissions would follow.[26]

Also on Saturday, January 2, Admiral Montagu reversed himself and wrote to Governor Wanton that he would not personally attend to the commission, but would instead delegate his duties to Captain Robert Keeler of the *Mercury*.[27] Because Montagu's flagship was laid up for the winter he would have had to make the more difficult overland journey. This reasoning seems hollow, as this was not a difficult trip and southern New England was experiencing an unusually mild January. Perhaps Montagu wanted to avoid the potential for harassment by disgruntled colonials along the way. Newport reverend Ezra Stiles thought that Montagu was embarrassed by his own inability to round up suspects, and was perturbed that this commission appeared to trump his authority.[28] Montagu indicated that a trip to Newport would take him away from important duties in Boston.[29] While Stiles was likely correct, it is also possible that Montagu (rightly) predicted the futility of their investigation and wanted to distance himself from the commission's inevitable failures. Montagu firmly believed that the Crown could make no progress on this matter so long as Governor Wanton was in charge. Montagu's absence, though, merely distracted the commissioners with petty squabbling over procedure and kept them from the more important matter at hand—getting *Gaspee* mariners face-to-face with suspects.

The following Tuesday, January 5, the five commissioners marched in a procession following about a dozen sea officers to the courthouse in Newport. Here Captain Robert Keeler of His Majesty's ship *Mercury* read their commission before a large crowd. This was the commissioners' only public act. Quickly it became apparent that the Privy Council had chosen the wrong location. Most of the people they wanted to question were in Providence, not Newport. Many of the witnesses used the difficulties of winter travel as an excuse for their absence or tardiness, just as Montagu had done.[30] Regardless, that same day the commissioners cited the specifics of their charge to turn suspects and witnesses over to Admiral Montagu, and insisted that he personally appear before them at the Colony House in Newport.[31] They expressed surprise and disappointment that he was not there to deliver the Royal Commission and instructions. Not wanting any of the failures of the commission laid at his feet, or to give the appearance that he was obstructing justice in some way, Montagu ultimately complied on January 14.

Horsmanden swore in Wanton who then gave the usual state oaths to the other commissioners. The commissioners then appointed James Brenton and James Clarke secretaries, sworn to the faithful exercise of their duties.[32] Darius Sessions and Chief Justice Stephen Hopkins came the first day and met with the commissioners, assuring them that no magistrates in the colonial government had any advanced knowledge of the attack and that they had been zealous in trying to gather information since June 10 of the previous year. When Judge Horsmanden asked them the true cause of such a violent outburst, the two Rhode Island officials[33] laid the blame at the feet of Lieutenant Dudingston and his insolence. They read written statements about the events surrounding the *Gaspee* and their follow-up investigation. When they expressed some concerns over the presence of the commissioners, they were assured that no one would be arrested but by the Rhode Island superior court and the civil magistrates of Rhode Island.[34] The next day, January 6, the secretaries posted an announcement in the *Newport Mercury* stating that the commissioners were meeting in the Colony House Mondays through Thursdays and that persons with any information should come forward.

Lieutenant General Thomas Gage predicted correctly that Newport would be quiet during the commission's proceedings because Rhode Island would adopt a model of passive resistance to the inquiry:

> I think the Commissioners will not be obstructed, unless they find Evidence sufficient to apprehend any Persons concerned in that atrocious Action, and in that Case, I firmly believe they will find no Magistrate who will regard or obey their Orders. I hope there will be no Riots or Insurrections, and I think there will not, but that more Subtle measures will be fallen upon to defeat the Enquiry. The Assembly it's said has met privately and their proceedings are secret. If the Commissioners should be obliged to apply for the Aid of the Troops I must no doubt send a Force to protect them, tho' I am confident, when the Troops arrive, that no Magistrate will ask the Assistance; nor do I believe they will give them Quarters.[35]

Gage noted the correctness of this prediction in another letter to Barrington one month later, after the first round of interviews produced no results. [36] While Gage never used the modern term "passive resistance," it seems to describe the "Subtle measures" he mentioned.

On January 7, Massachusetts governor Thomas Hutchinson wrote to Lord Dartmouth[37] informing him that he had received a post from Chief Justice Oliver assuring him that they had begun their business on the 5th and "had so far met with great civilities." The bad news, of course, was that Dartmouth's private letter to Governor Wanton had just appeared in the newspaper. Hutchinson enclosed the clipping.[38] But the Massachusetts governor was dealing with many more serious problems of his own. The same day Hutchinson wrote a private letter to Undersecretary John Pownall indicating that a circular letter denying the authority of Parliament was spreading through the many towns of Massachusetts. Hutchinson had just given a speech the day before as "the official 'answer' to the Boston pamphlet."[39] He carefully explained to the general court, using Massachusetts's history, their subordination to Parliament. Additionally, Hutchinson privately expressed concern to Pownall that the Massachusetts Assembly intended to send the circular letter to other assemblies on the continent.[40]

The governor's optimism grew throughout February and March. Reflecting with satisfaction upon the success of his January 6 speech, Hutchinson believed that he may have staved off the attempts of the House to distribute its circular letter. But the Massachusetts governor's orthodox views of imperial government were out of step with most of Massachusetts's towns. His speech before the general court had not been as pivotal or persuasive as he had hoped and the Boston pamphlet's radical influence continued to grow.[41]

Not only had Hutchinson's January 6 emergency session before the House failed to have the desired outcome in Massachusetts, officials in London were not pleased with his ultimatum either. Hutchinson's logical, rational approach explained to Massachusetts freemen that they must either fully submit to Parliament's authority or opt for total independence. The other options available to the commonwealth—become part of the Spanish, Dutch, or French empires, or total independence—seemed so ludicrous to Hutchinson that the logic of his case appeared irrefutable to the friends of the administration. Unfortunately for the governor, Lord Dartmouth did not see it this way. He secretly wrote to Speaker of the House Thomas Cushing looking for a way to undo some of the political "damage" done by Hutchinson's address. Lacking widespread support in the commonwealth and in Whitehall, Thomas Hutchinson's days as governor were drawing to an end.[42]

Back in Rhode Island, on January 7, Governor Wanton presented to the commissioners his pre-June 10 correspondence with Admiral Montagu, which was read and filed. Bartlett recorded that the commissioners read and filed at least twenty letters and depositions that day.[43] On January 8, the commissioners heard from one of their own secretaries, James Brenton, about the failure of the governor and a justice of the assize, Metcalfe Bowler,[44] to secure the person of Aaron Biggs. On July 17, they learned, Brenton was with the party that tried to serve a warrant for Biggs to appear before Bowler for questioning. When the arrest party approached the *Beaver*, the sentinel informed them that Captain Linzee was not on board and the crew could do nothing without orders from him. When they later found Captain Linzee at a farm house on Brenton's Point, he would not come out for fear of being arrested himself due to seizures he had made.[45] Linzee would not recognize the warrant and informed Brenton's party that he only took orders from Admiral Montagu.[46] The commissioners agreed to postpone questioning of other witnesses until Admiral Montagu was personally present.

At this point a letter arrived from Montagu indicating that he did not plan to leave Boston for another three days.[47] Montagu believed that Lord Dartmouth's instructions made it clear that he could delegate his duties to another officer (which he had done). Montagu explained that he was a busy man and could not get his flagship out this time of year. Yet ultimately, Montagu traveled overland to Newport by way of Taunton. Reverend Stiles speculated that he avoided traveling through Providence due to a fear that his unpopularity there could create a disturbance. Finally, when he sailed into Newport on January 14 with his flag attached to a lesser vessel, the fort did not fire the customary salute due an admiral in His Majesty's service. Montagu could only interpret this as a deliberate slight.[48]

On January 11, the Rhode Island General Assembly met in Providence. While members engaged in some heated debate, the assembly agreed that the best action was to take a "wait and see" attitude.[49] Rhode Island resident Nathanael Greene, famous later for his military leadership under General Washington, was quick to condemn the *laissez-faire* attitude of this body. The assembly "seems to have lost all that spirit of independence and public virtue that has ever distinguished them since they have first been incorporated, and sunk down into a tame submission and entire acquiescence to ministerial mandates."[50] When the general assembly reconvened in East Greenwich, Chief Justice Stephen Hopkins made it clear before both houses that his court would not send anyone outside of this jurisdiction for trial.[51] Rhode Island, and only Rhode Island freemen, would bring Rhode Island criminals to trial.[52]

The next day in Newport the commissioners questioned Stephen Gulley, a forty-one-year-old husbandman from Smithfield, Rhode Island. [53] For Gulley's own safety he had stayed aboard the naval vessel *Lizard* the previous week. Just prior to boarding the *Lizard*, Gulley heard about the generous reward for information and was on his way to Newport to testify before the commissioners. Other than Biggs, Gulley was the only informer to come forward. While Gulley was not an eyewitness to the destruction of the *Gaspee*, he provided a lot of hearsay evidence and names. According to Gulley, Joseph Borden, a public house landlord at the ferry in Portsmouth, assisted him by redirecting his travel around an armed mob of twenty persons who were blocking the road to keep potential informers from making the trip to Newport. Fearing that his public house might be torn down by the mob if he accommodated Gulley for the night, the innkeeper took him out at about 8:00 P.M. and showed him an alternate road to Newport. Once before the commissioners, Gulley named three men who might know something about the burning of the *Gaspee,* and the commissioners summoned them. Gulley also mentioned the Browns of Providence, but did not provide any first names.[54]

The first of the men identified by Gulley, Joseph Borden, appeared the next day, January 13. Borden testified that Stephen Gulley and another man, Thomas Aylesbury, both came to his inn. Aylesbury said that Gulley, after hearing the king's proclamation read and the size of the reward, was going to Newport to report to the commissioners. Borden believed that the two men were drunk and he did not believe the report that there were twenty men (or possibly Indians)[55] with pistols on the road. Nevertheless, he directed Gulley to a lower road that would lead him around the spot where the mob was reported. Borden did not believe there was any real danger; he did not take a weapon out that night and the rest of the night was quiet.[56] It seems that Borden saw Gulley as an opportunist, not a star witness.

Admiral Montagu finally arrived in Newport on January 14, after Borden had given his testimony.[57] He ordered Aaron Biggs, also kept on one of the Royal Navy's ships for his own safety, brought ashore to Colony House for questioning. Royal officials viewed Biggs as the most promising witness, since he had provided the only eyewitness deposition given by a colonist. This was the first time that Governor Wanton, who had worked so diligently the previous July to discredit Biggs, had a chance to question him. Biggs's testimony in January before the commissioners reflected less favorably on Linzee than had the July report. The first part of Biggs's testimony was consistent with what he had stated in July. The latter half of his testimony gave evidence of his being locked in irons, threatened with flogging and hanging, and other details that made his testimony look coerced. Apparently, when Biggs boarded the *Beaver* he did not tell anyone about the *Gaspee*; at least not until it would directly serve his self-interest. But if he was not actually coerced, Biggs certainly had an ulterior motive for appearing to be one of the *Gaspee* raiders. This was the only way he could avoid being flogged and returned to his master. His testimony raised the question before the commissioners of another scenario, one in which Biggs was merely running away from his master and found that telling *Gaspee* tales was a convenient way to avoid punishment.[58]

Having largely discredited Biggs's testimony, Governor Wanton moved on to discredit the seaman who claimed to have seen, rowed next to, and shared his tobacco with Aaron Biggs that night. Admiral Montagu provided the commissioners with Patrick Earle's written testimony from July 16. Hearing that he was aboard the *Lizard*, the commissioners summoned him to appear personally. But Earle would not retreat from what he had said exactly six months earlier, though the commissioners found out more about the conditions under which Biggs gave his testimony. Almost a month after the attack, onboard the *Beaver*, Biggs was stripped and was about to receive two or three dozen lashes when Earle claimed to have recognized him. At the time of the raid the moon had set and it was very dark during the attack, so this seems unlikely. On the other hand, Earle and Biggs could have been rowing next to each other as the dawn was breaking. Earle based his credibility upon his ability to describe what Biggs was wearing on the night of the raid.[59]

Governor Wanton also entered into evidence the treatment of the shipmaster of the *Fortune*, Rufus Greene, when his cargo was seized by Lieutenant Dudingston's master, Mr. Dundas, the previous February. While Rufus Greene did not personally appear before the commissioners, his deposition told a story of the abuse of power by British sea officers and the unnecessarily rough treatment of mariners going about their lawful business. When Greene had questioned Dudingston about his customs deputation the previous February, he got no satisfaction.[60]

After only two days in Newport, Montagu informed the commissioners that he would be leaving in four days (a total stay of less than a week). He declared that the naval department in Boston could not now be without him, though he would be happy to return to Newport at a more seasonable time of year. He wanted to know if the commissioners would need to summon Lieutenant Dudingston. The Lord Commissioners of the Admiralty in London would have to send Dudingston back to Newport. Montagu also gave the commissioners six names of men that he thought they should summon. Admiral Montagu thought it so unlikely that anyone would be prosecuted for the raid on the *Gaspee* that he grew impatient and was unwilling to give any more of his time to it. Governor Wanton kept the hearings going without him, carefully discrediting each witness as each day passed.[61]

On January 15, two people who were summoned by the commissioners asked Deputy Governor Sessions to take their depositions in Providence. One of these witnesses, Captain William Thayer, now near 70 years old, was struggling with ill health so Sessions obliged him. The captain had already traveled one day in difficult weather just to get to Providence, further aggravating his illness. Saul Ramsdale, on the other hand, was a young, healthy man and Sessions told him to continue on his way to Newport.[62] Although admitting no personal knowledge of the attack, Thayer mentioned the names Potter and Brown (or Browns) as part of "public" rumors.[63] Although having no "official" connection to the commission, some prominent Providence merchants asked Sessions to do one more thing. Barzillai Richmond, Joseph Brown, and John Brown appealed to Sessions in writing to summon Daniel Vaughan. Since Vaughan was from Newport, it seemed odd that he gave a deposition in Providence. But this testimony was elicited to further discredit Biggs. Additionally, Sessions probably did not want the commissioners in Newport to examine Vaughan in person, since he was the very gunner who fired upon the *St. John* nine years earlier. These long-time residents of Rhode Island perhaps did not want to take the chance of resurrecting prior disturbances with the commissioners.

On January 18, Darius Sessions wrote two letters to Governor Wanton. In the first, he explained that he was asked to take a deposition from Daniel Vaughan and he included the deposition from two days earlier. In the second letter he recalled the oral testimony from the seamen he interviewed on the morning of June 10 in Pawtuxet. That testimony, and midshipman Dickinson's deposition before Admiral Montagu and Governor Hutchinson, made it clear that it was too dark that night to identify anyone with confidence. Sessions added that the identification was done a month after the attack. The moon had set and the only artificial light was in the cabin where the doctor was tending to Dudingston's wounds.[64] Due to the efforts of the deputy governor, the governor, and the silence from the people of Providence, no one in Rhode Island was in any danger of arrest for involvement in the *Gaspee* raid.[65]

The next day, January 19, the commissioners heard from a former *Gaspee* mariner, Peter May. He did not offer any new information other than the last name, "Greene." He testified that it was the same man he saw on the *Gaspee* after the seizure of the sloop *Fortune*'s rum back in February. May was able to offer a description: "a tall, slender man; wearing his own hair, of brown color."[66] But the commissioners never summoned any men of the Greene family to appear before the month of May. It could have been Peter May's claim that he could identify Greene that caused so many who were summoned to fail to appear. Shortly after May's testimony potential witnesses flooded the commissioners with letters saying they could or would not appear (see table 4.1).

Also on January 19, Admiral Montagu informed the commissioners that he intended to depart from Newport and wanted to know when the court would adjourn. The commissioners replied they could not properly execute their duties without him. Desirous of questioning Dudingston in person, and given the reported difficulties of winter travel for the witnesses, the commissioners elected to adjourn until May.[67] On February 16, the Lords of Admiralty informed the Earl of Dartmouth that Lieutenant Dudingston's health precluded him from attending any kind of inquiry in Boston[68] regarding the burning of the *Gaspee*. In his stead they offered *Gaspee* midshipman William Dickinson and deck sentinel Bartholomew Cheevers.[69] Next to Dudingston, Dickinson probably had the best chance to identify the ringleaders he saw in the commander's cabin. Indeed, Lord Dartmouth hurriedly sent back a letter to the Lords of the Admiralty indicating that if Dickinson and Cheevers thought that they could identify anyone, to send them to Boston right away.[70] But the commissioners never called witnesses on both sides who might recognize each other on the same day. During this break, the commissioners and Admiral Montagu used the time to defend their actions and, in some cases, criticize the proceedings.

Montagu wrote to Philip Stephens at the Admiralty Office in London to explain the diligence with which he had carried out Lord Dartmouth's orders and how he quickly complied with the directives of the commissioners. He could not resist mentioning the fact that the fort in Newport failed to salute his vessel when the admiral's flag was clearly visible. Montagu took it as a deliberate insult and asked that Governor Wanton be instructed to demonstrate "the same respect shown it [an Admiral's flag] as in every other of His Majesty's colonies in North America." Moreover, he reported the king's proclamation was torn down just two hours after posting and "trodden under foot in the most contemptuous manner." The civil magistrate, Montagu maintained, would not do his duty, so there was no reason for him, as admiral, to stand by to receive prisoners. Montagu concluded he must return to Boston to look after his normal duties until the commissioners reconvened on May 26.[71]

From January 20 to 22, the commissioners wrapped up their first session with a letter to Lord Dartmouth that included a separate deposition from Governor Wanton. The first third of this letter described

Table 4.1 Pattern of Resistance to the Commissioners' Summons

Name	Occupation	Reason for Not Appearing
Capt. William Thayer	Innholder	Old and rheumatic
John Andrews, Esq.	Judge	Swollen hand
Daniel Vaughan	Mariner	Providence River frozen
Arthur Fenner	Law clerk	Ill health
John Cole	Attorney	Too busy with caseload
George Brown	Attorney	Too busy with caseload
Daniel Hitchcock	Attorney	Too busy with caseload
James Sabin	Vintner	Declining health and debt

Note: Hitchcock, Sabin, and Cole indicated that they would give sworn testimony before a civil authority if necessary. Andrews and Brown seemed willing to go before the commissioners if necessary. Ultimately Andrews, Brown, and Cole did appear before the commissioners in June.

the struggle the commissioners had getting Admiral Montagu to come to Newport. The middle third of the letter described Lieutenant Dudingston's insolence. The final third of the letter described the difficulty the governor had getting an audience with Aaron Biggs before now, laying the blame squarely at the feet of Captain Linzee. Rather than submitting a "progress report" of accomplishments, Wanton's commission reported complaints against three officers in the Royal Navy.[72] In case Lord Dartmouth missed the main points of the commissioners' previous letter of the 21st,[73] Wanton sent another letter on the 30th stating that "I am convinced that [the] intemperate zeal and indiscreet conduct of Captain Linzee and Lieutenant Dudingston caused the disorder."[74] If Lord Dartmouth was expecting to see ringleaders in London promptly, the response of the commissioners made clear he would not.

Rhode Island attorney general Henry Marchant believed, even after the first sitting of the commission, that more clarification about their authority was needed. He wrote to former Rhode Island governor Samuel Ward on January 28 that, "The Commissioners have adjourned themselves to the 26th of next May in order I presume to report Home [England] how Things appear to them [page torn] have more explicit Instructions—And if possible to get some better Information as to their Power and the True Nature and Design of Their Commission—-Setting aside the President [precedent] of such a commission."[75] Whether the recess was intended to allow passions to cool or to clarify the charge of the commission, some friends of government already despaired of finding any ringleaders.

During this recess two commissioners individually wrote to Lord Dartmouth reflecting upon Rhode Island politics and the progress made by the inquiry thus far. Commissioner and Chief Justice Frederick Smythe expressed surprise that instead of keeping Dartmouth's September 4, 1772, correspondence confidential, "the utmost industry seems to have been used to publish it."[76] Smythe reported, "in less than a week it was printed in Boston; and the Sunday following a seditious preacher harangued his congregation on the subject of it."[77] Smythe could not have known just how widely that "seditious" sermon would circulate and how it would alarm colonial Patriots.

After remarking on the dangers of popular government in general and delegating too much power to the people, Smythe went on to comment on the growth of illicit trade in Rhode Island. He asserted that British authority should be brought to bear. Left to discipline themselves, he believed, Rhode Islanders would do nothing. Dudingston had aroused the people's indignation precisely because he so capably fulfilled his customs duties. Smythe expressed his frustration believing the ringleaders must be known by hundreds of inhabitants, although official silence prevailed over the colony.

Smythe also expressed disappointment over Aaron Biggs's discredited testimony. He complained that few *Gaspee* mariners remained in the area and that they could provide little new information. Smythe questioned the motives of local magistrates who offered their assistance to the commissioners; he suspected that they would merely help suspects escape arrest. Rhode Island officials could not and, he believed, would not turn over any suspects to Admiral Montagu because of their popular politics.

Soon after Smythe sent his letter to Dartmouth, Commissioner and Chief Justice Daniel Horsmanden wrote Lord Dartmouth reflecting on his impressions of Rhode Island, its government, and the evidence presented so far to the commission. Horsmanden took the opportunity to say what he could not have said in the general report from the commissioners. Like Smythe, he expressed shock and disbelief that Wanton had copied Dartmouth's letter to the Rhode Island General Assembly: "the main object of our errand was become public, which, in prudence, was to be kept secret."[78] When challenged, Wanton claimed that he was obligated to disclose important colonial business by law and was sworn in his office to do so.[79] But like Admiral Montagu, Horsmanden took a low view of the colony's government: "As to the Government (if it deserves that name), it is a downright democracy; the Governor a mere nominal one."[80] To demonstrate how little power or authority the governor had, Horsmanden remarked that the commission's daily expenses came out of the commissioners' own pockets.[81]

Horsmanden's letter demonstrated just how much the presentation and interpretation of evidence was under Wanton's control. No one defended Dudingston and neither Montagu, Linzee, nor Dudley challenged the governor's interpretation of events.[82] Although he was highly critical of Wanton's government, Horsmanden accepted the governor's interpretation of Aaron Biggs's testimony and reiterated it to Dartmouth. The chief justice described Rhode Island's and Connecticut's governments as in a state of anarchy: "Justice has long since fled that country."[83] Horsmanden ended his letter by advising that only a "gentleman of very extraordinary qualifications and abilities" could unite the two chaotic colonies into one very decent royal colony. The "better sort of people," he claimed, would embrace such a change.

Dartmouth was not the only British official with whom Horsmanden and Smythe communicated during the recess. Upon their return to New York they met with Lieutenant General Thomas Gage. Gage concluded that Governor Wanton was not zealous enough in following up on the names given during the inquiry: "The whole Province protects and screens the Robbers, and I can't find that the Governor is more willing to bring them to Justice than any of his People."[84]

On April 10, the Earl of Dartmouth responded to what he considered Governor Wanton's poor judgment in making public the September 4 letter. Conceding it might have been useful to "communicate the substance of that dispatch to the other parts of your corporation," Dartmouth reprimanded Wanton for distributing copies that appeared "in the common newspapers."[85] Dartmouth seemed convinced that some in Rhode Island "failed in obedience due to the laws and authority of this kingdom."[86] Dartmouth's only encouragement for Wanton was his statement that the king was pleased by Newport's quiet[87] and respectful demeanor toward the commissioners.[88]

The commissioners were not the only ones to reflect upon the inquiry thus far. Colonial Patriots had read about the inquiry in newspapers as far away as Virginia. On February 4, 1773, Virginia Patriot Richard Henry Lee and Samuel Adams began an important correspondence. Lee started with an apology for writing to a stranger but indicated that they had a common acquaintance through his brother in London, Dr. Arthur Lee.[89] He commented that they had a union and an ease of communication through their shared cause of liberty. Lee feared that they were not getting reliable information about the *Gaspee* in Virginia. Newspapers frequently reprinted secondary and tertiary accounts, and Lee sought a letter in return from Adams.[90]

Two months later Lee wrote to Philadelphia Patriot John Dickinson[91] that "much alarm has been create[d] by a new court of criminal jurisdiction, it is said, having been lately opened in Rhode Island." While admitting that they did not have complete information, he correctly made the association[92] with the 1769 discussions in Parliament about transporting "obnoxious Americans" to Britain for trial.[93] The Treason Act under Henry VIII had indeed been discussed three years prior to the burning of the *Gaspee* in the context of removing some residents of Boston to London for their trial.[94] Lee continued, "I sincerely hope that every Colony on the Continent will adopt these Committees of correspondence and enquiry."[95]

Samuel Adams replied to Richard Henry Lee on April 10 indicating that "I have often thought it a Misfortune, or rather a Fault on the Friends of American Independence and Freedom, their not taking Care to open every Channel of Communication." He did not mention the *Gaspee* commission right away. First he remarked how information about "Bloodshed & even civil War in our Sister Colony

North Carolina"[96] came not from another colony but from England. Adams then returned to the topic of committees of correspondence:

> The Friends of Liberty in this Town have lately made a successful Attempt to obtain the explicit political Sentiments of a great Number of the Towns in this Province; and the Number is daily increasing. The very Attempt was alarming to the Adversaries; and the happy Effects of it are mortifying to them. I would propose it for your Consideration, Whether the Establishment of Committees of Correspondence among the several Towns in every Colony, would not tend to promote that General Union, upon which the Security of the whole depends.[97]

Adams assured Lee that the copies he might have seen in the newspapers of Dartmouth's letter to Wanton were genuine. Adams said that "I received it from a Gentleman of the Council in the Colony, who took it from the Original."[98] Adams went on to express regret that the Rhode Island General Assembly had not acted with more firmness toward the commission.

Two days before the commission was scheduled to reconvene, on May 24, Montagu sent Dickinson and Cheevers to Newport.[99] Montagu believed they could identify the men referred to as the "head sheriff" and the "captain." Not yet knowing that the Earl of Dartmouth and the Lords of the Admiralty agreed with him that he did not have to be personally present for the commissioners to meet, he informed the commissioners that he would not travel to Newport for another ten days. He was waiting for his flagship, the *Captain*, to return from Halifax.[100] In the meantime, the orders of the Admiralty arrived, clearly allowing Montagu to delegate his duties, which he promptly did.[101] Captain Keeler, unfortunately, in Newport, was unable to deliver Montagu's message to the commissioners because there was a writ issued against him preventing him from going ashore.[102] Finally the commission reconvened on May 31, as they chose to wait for Horsmanden and Smythe, who were tardy.[103]

Montagu believed that suspects would be brought before the *Gaspee* mariners, Dickinson and Cheevers, for identification. Instead the commissioners took statements from *Gaspee* personnel, examined them, and then returned them to the *Lizard*. The witnesses provided physical descriptions of people engaged in the assault, but they did not get to identify suspects face to face.[104] Men who may have been among the raiders either failed to appear or testified on a date when those who might be able to identify them were long gone. Witnesses were summoned and arrived according to a schedule whereby anyone who might recognize another was not called to the Colony House on the same day (see table 4.2).

Table 4.2 Timetable of Examinations of *Gaspee* Mariners and Possible Raiders[105]

Name	Occupation	Date
Aaron Biggs	Indentured servant	January 14
Might be able to identify raiders; named John Brown, Browns, and Potter		
Patrick Earle	*Gaspee* mariner	January 16
Might be able to identify raiders; named Potter		
Peter May	*Gaspee* mariner	January 19
Might be able to identify raiders; named Greene		
William Dickinson	*Gaspee* midshipman	June 1
Might be able to identify raiders; actually later saw the surgeon on the streets of Providence		
Bartholomew Cheevers	*Gaspee* mariner	June 1
Might be able to identify raiders; actually later saw two raiders in Pawtuxet		
John Cole	Attorney	June 3
Failed to appear in January; admitted hearing drum in Sabin's tavern		
John Andrews	Judge	June 5
Probably not among the raiders; dared to show his face to *Gaspee* officers and men when accompanying Sessions to Pawtuxet immediately following the raid		
George Brown	Attorney	June 5
Failed to appear in January; admitted hearing drum in Sabin's tavern		

Although named as possible ringleaders, John Brown, Joseph Brown, Simeon Potter, and Rufus Greene, Jr. were never summoned to appear before the commissioners. In the sixteen days that they met in January, the commissioners only managed to examine ten people, which was still more than they saw when the weather was milder in June. The "severe weather" complaints seem hollow. Additionally, Reverend Stiles recorded that January 1773 was unusually mild. Chief Justice Horsmanden wrote to the Earl of Dartmouth, "My Lord, the commissioners did not enter upon counter evidence, though I, myself, was inclined to do it, as we proceeded; and bring the witnesses face to face. . . ."[106]

By June, John Cole was a member of Rhode Island's committee of correspondence. *Providence Gazette* editor John Carter condemned Cole's submission to the commissioners.

"J__n C__e , Esq;" (a member of the committee of correspondence appointed by the general assembly) had, "in a very flagrant Manner, shamefully violated and betrayed the Faith and Confidence reposed in him by his Country, in yielding Obedience to a Mandate from the Commissioners of Enquiry, and answering Interrogatories before them on Oath, thereby fully acknowledging their Jurisdiction, and endeavoring to counteract the Laudable Design of the House in appointing the said Committee."[107]

Carter used such strong language that Cole filed a libel suit against him, but a grand jury refused to indict.[108] Carter was shocked by this "very extraordinary Attempt to destroy the Liberty of the Press."[109]

One week after convening, the commissioners called the justices of the superior court of Rhode Island to Colony House to present their findings. Chief Justice Stephen Hopkins and three assistant justices weighed the evidence and reported back to the commissioners several days later. They found that Aaron Biggs's testimony was not reliable and that it was made "in consequence of illegal threats from Capt. Linzee."[110] *Gaspee* mariner Peter May mentioned someone named Greene, but the justices noted that there were a great many people with that name in Rhode Island. Without a first name or a description, his testimony was of little assistance. The justices concluded that "upon the whole, we are all of [the] opinion that the several matters and things contained in said depositions do not induce a probable suspicion, that persons mentioned therein, or either or any of them, are guilty of the crime aforesaid."[111]

The Rhode Island justices ended their statement with: "And if the honorable commissioners are of a different sentiment we should be glad to receive their opinion for our better information." The following day the commissioners indicated that their sentiment regarding the evidence did not matter; the Rhode Island justices were to "act thereupon in such a manner as you conceive most likely to answer the ends of public justice."[112] A Royal Commission of Inquiry was to research both sides of an issue and present a report. They were not to override the local courts of assize. Rhode Island chief justice Stephen Hopkins had already informed both houses of the assembly the previous January that he would send no one to trial in England.

On June 10, exactly one year after the burning of the *Gaspee*, Peter Oliver, one of the commissioners, had tea with Newport's reverend Ezra Stiles. He explained to Stiles how the public perception of the commission was dangerously skewed. The commissioners were to examine both sides of the *Gaspee* affair. Finding the "ringleaders" was only part of their charge; they were also to inquire into the behavior of the sea officers, customs officials, and navy officers. Oliver explained that "the King might know what to do with his own Officers &c, so as to keep them in good Regulation and prevent their carrying their Irritation of America too far."[113] The reverend conceded that Oliver was a fair-minded person; but what if an inquiry were put into the hands of Montagu and a band of sea officers? Stiles finished his diary entry for that day by predicting the growth and expansion of committees of correspondence, a general [continental] congress, and a "Union and Confederacy of the Colonies."[114]

Chief Justice Oliver found that the public was so alarmed by the royal inquiry that while back on the circuit in Massachusetts, he had to set aside some time during each session to explain to those in the courtroom that the *Gaspee* commissioners had no power to try anyone. One can imagine the surprise of Boston Patriot Josiah Quincy, Jr. when, a year and a half later, he met with Prime Minister Frederick Lord North at St. James:

His lordship [North] spoke also upon the destruction of the "Gaspee," and in direct terms twice said that the Commissioners were appointed to try that matter, and had transmitted accounts that they could obtain no evidence. This declaration being in flat contradiction to what I had several times heard Chief Justice Oliver declare to be the case from the bench, when giving his charges to the grand jury, was particularly noticed by me. His Honor [Oliver] ever most solemnly declared in public and private that the Commission was to inquire whether any such offence had happened, in order to send word to England, that so a trial might or might not be ordered, as the evidence might be; and in the most express terms declared the Commissioners had no power to try.[115]

Lord North may not have remembered clearly exactly the charge made to the commissioners, but for colonists this was a very important distinction. Eighteen months after the commission, Lord North clearly did not recall the commissioners' role as merely gathering evidence for the Rhode Island courts to prosecute.

Back in Newport, before the commissioners adjourned, Chief Justice Smythe inquired whether the *St. John* incident "might be considered as a leading cause to the destruction of the *Gaspee*."[116] From June 21–23 the commissioners debated and deliberated, even examining some evidence, before concluding that the *St. John* was not a matter for this particular board to pursue.[117] With Oliver already gone, Smythe could not rally the remaining commissioners to expand the scope of their investigation.[118]

The commissioners submitted their final report to Lord Dartmouth and the King's Most Excellent Majesty on June 22, 1773.[119] Given the culture of silence that pervaded Rhode Island, the commissioners did not have much to report in terms of apprehending suspects and transporting them with their witnesses. So the report inevitably emphasized another duty of a royal commission; discovering the root or cause of a social problem or disturbance.[120] Echoing the sentiments of Governor Wanton's letters to Lord Dartmouth from January 21 and 30, 60 percent of this final report discussed the vindication of the commissioners and the civil magistrates of Rhode Island and the debunking of Biggs's testimony (see table 4.3). Again Dudingston's insolence was blamed for the trouble in the colony and the fact that Linzee took advantage of Biggs when he "tended too strongly to extort from a weak or wicked mind declarations not strictly true."[121]

Table 4.3 Breakdown of the Final Report of the Commissioners

Topic or Section	Words	Percentage
Introduction	248	10%
Assurance of the diligence of the commissioners	177	7%
Narrative of events	647	24%
Problem(s) caused by Dudingston's zeal	556	20%
Rhode Island Justices agree with commissioners	537	19%
Discredit Biggs's testimony	558	20%
Total Report	2,723	100%

Exactly one month after the commissioners adjourned in June 1773, former commissioner and Chief Justice Daniel Horsmanden wrote to the Earl of Dartmouth that Aaron Biggs confessed to an officer of a man-of-war at Newport that his story was fabricated. When Horsmanden was delayed getting out of Newport he found out that "at length he [Aaron Biggs] confessed 'twas all a fiction."[122] Apparently, Biggs paddled a canoe out to the *Beaver* a few days after the *Gaspee* was destroyed in an attempt to run away from his master. When Linzee prepared to flog Biggs for fleeing his master, *Gaspee* mariner Patrick Earle claimed to recognize him as one of the raiders.[123] Captain Linzee then threatened to hang Biggs from a yardarm if he did not speak about the *Gaspee*. Horsmanden believed that Biggs heard pieces of the story from the *Gaspee* mariners and then added the names of a few prominent citizens of Providence and Bristol. Reflecting on the incident, Horsmanden believed the attack was carried out "by a number of bold, daring, rash, enterprising sailors collected suddenly from the neighborhood."[124] He did not comment on what Whitehall truly wanted to know about, the leadership of the raiders.[125]

Horsmanden wrote to Dartmouth on more than one occasion to complain about the impotence of their inquiry and the need to change Rhode Island's government. He believed that property rights would be better protected and the court system would operate less chaotically if Connecticut and Rhode Island were merged into one royal colony. The governments of Rhode Island and Connecticut were about to change, but not as Horsmanden hoped.

The Reverend William Gordon wrote from Boston to Lord Dartmouth in June 1773 to congratulate him on having escaped the consequences of a successful inquiry.[126] He believed that the *Gaspee* raiders were to be tried under the Dockyard Act and he feared that sending suspects to England for trial would have "set the continent into a fresh flame." Gordon told Dartmouth that the Burgesses in Virginia were encouraging other colonies to set up committees of correspondence. He also informed Dartmouth that Admiral Montagu inflamed the situation by stating that "British Acts of Parliament will never go down in America, unless forced by the point of the sword."[127] Gordon predicted that any resistance to colonial actions from the London government would only hasten the creation of a colonial congress.

While committees of correspondence had existed previously in the colonies, the "court of inquiry" in Rhode Island prompted the desire for inter-colonial, standing committees of correspondence to report on the acts of the British Parliament and to maintain correspondence with other colonies.[128] The Virginia House of Burgesses on March 12, 1773:

Resolved that it be an instruction to the said committee that they do without delay inform themselves particularly of the principles and authority on which was constituted a court of enquiry said to have been lately held in Rhode Island with powers to transport persons accused of offences committed in America to places beyond the seas to be tried.[129]

The House then went on to encourage others colonies to do the same:[130]

> Resolved that the Speaker of this House do transmit to the Speaker of the different Assemblies of the British colonies on this continent copies of the said resolutions and desire that they will lay them before their respective Assemblies and request them to appoint some person or persons of their respective bodies to communicate from time to time with the said committee.[131]

Thus, the inquiry not only failed to produce any satisfactory results for the friends of government, it had the unintended effect of re-igniting the Patriot cause among their political opponents with a fervor not seen since the Stamp Act crisis of the 1760s.

While it seems clear now that no Rhode Islanders were going to be found guilty under Governor Wanton's leadership, historian Lawrence Henry Gipson found it surprising that Wanton did not mention some of Dudingston's pre-June 1772 behavior in the commission report. If true, such behavior reflected badly on the professional conduct of the crew and its officers.[132]

Five

An Oration

THE *Gaspee* AFFAIR LEFT AT LEAST TWO LEGACIES TO THE PRE-independence period. Many authors and historians have commented on the assembly-appointed inter-colonial committees of correspondence, but those committees did not interpret the incident for colonials. Instead, it was a little-known Baptist minister, along with Samuel Adams, who primarily interpreted the historical significance of the *Gaspee* episode for British colonial America.

With the exception of Pennsylvania,[1] every British colony in North America that would declare independence in 1776 created an inter-colonial committee of correspondence by 1774 (see table 5.1).[2]

Because these were official, standing committees of the various assemblies, these committees of correspondence were cautious; they hesitated to "speak" for the whole body. But this does not mean that they were completely devoid of political power. In the spring and summer months of 1774 the New Hampshire and North Carolina assemblies were dissolved by their governors, and their respective committees of correspondence called them back into session. This represented a shift in the balance of power. In the colonial balance

Table 5.1 The Revival of Committees of Correspondence

Date	Colony
March 12, 1773	Virginia
May 15, 1773	Rhode Island
May 21, 1773	Connecticut
May 27, 1773	New Hampshire
May 28, 1773*	Massachusetts
July 8, 1773	South Carolina
September 10, 1773	Georgia
October 15, 1773	Maryland
October 23, 1773	Delaware
December 18, 1773	North Carolina
January 20, 1774	New York
February 8, 1774	New Jersey

*Boston already had a committee to communicate with Massachusetts towns. This was the founding of a new and distinct committee.[3]

of power, the governor represented the interests of the Crown and the elected assemblies represented the interests of the freeholders. Governor Thomas Hutchinson immediately seized upon the way these committees were disrupting the traditional balance:

> The assemblies of Virginia, this province, Rhode Island, and Connecticut have appointed their respective committees of correspondence, who act in the recess of the courts; and the like committees are expected from the other assemblies when they shall be convened. This in some measure defeats and counteracts the powers reserved to the governors, in what are called the loyal governments, of proroguing or dissolving the assembly at pleasure.[4]

While these committees continued to exist in a few states, even to the end of the war, they were largely dissolved by January 1778.[5]

Prior to the 1970s, most historians ascribed great importance to these assembly-appointed inter-colonial committees of correspondence. Subsequent scholarship has shown that they did little of consequence. The historian Merrill Jensen disagreed with previous scholars, and argued that there was not a straight line of momentum toward war and independence created by these assemblies:

> The legislative committees of correspondence never had a chance to play a role in the events that led to independence, for within months power was seized by revolutionary committees, congresses, conventions, and mobs, and the legal legislatures soon disappeared forever. The legislative committees were important only as a symbol and the newspapers spelled out what the symbol meant.[6]

Those serving in colonial government chose to remain cautious about using overtly seditious language; much of the truly heated rhetoric was left to colonial newspaper editors and their often anonymous contributors.[7]

Historian Edward D. Collins came to the same conclusion as Jensen:

> We find, therefore, in the early part of the year 1774 twelve committees of correspondence existing, appointed by the legislative bodies of their respective colonies. The idea was apparently embodied in a more perfect organization than ever before. But the new type did not possess activity to match its seeming importance. These assembly committees were inactive from the first. The cause of this inactivity is not far to seek. In the first place, there was little or nothing for them to do. Since last June, wrote the Connecticut committee in November, 1773, nothing had happened worth transmitting. . . . The long intervals between their meetings denotes the lack of important business.[8]

Collins also pointed out that many of the members of the assembly-appointed committees did not live near each other. When the legislative session ended, they returned to their homes and were not able to function as an active, ongoing committee.[9]

Historian Richard D. Brown agreed that these provincial committees were hardly revolutionary cells: "The provincial committees, for example, were largely perfunctory bodies which wrote and received correspondence on behalf of provincial legislatures. They never displayed independence or initiative, and their records (where they survive) show little of significance."[10] While the founding of these assembly-appointed committees of correspondence was tied to the idea of improving communication among the colonies about the *Gaspee* Royal Commission of Inquiry, they were not a new development for Anglo-American political or religious life. Nor were these committees particularly active in moving the Patriot cause forward. It was the colonial legislatures themselves and the Second Continental Congress that moved the Patriot agenda forward.[11]

Forming committees of correspondence put the assemblies into a more adversarial and confrontational mode. Judging from the response of colonial governors, their actions might have been extra-legal. But the assembly-appointed inter-colonial committees of correspondence were a manifestation of opposition, not the driving engines of the subsequent independence movement. Their lasting legacy may be limited to the communication network that hastened the meeting of the First Continental Congress.[12] So, if the inter-continental committees of correspondence were not the chief consequence of the *Gaspee* Affair, what was its lasting legacy?

The *Gaspee*'s greatest revolutionary impact comes from an unexpected source: a Thanksgiving Day sermon given late in the year 1772. Unlike those who served on committees of correspondence, the Reverend John Allen was not well connected with colonial Patriots, and he died prematurely in 1774 at the age of 33 years.[13] But on December 3, 1772, Allen delivered the annual Thanksgiving Day sermon, *An Oration, Upon the Beauties of Liberty, Or the Essential Rights of the Americans*[14] at the Second Baptist Church in Boston.

Reverend Allen came to Boston with experience in publishing in England, but he also arrived with a checkered past. In 1764, at age 23, John Allen had been ordained and installed as the pastor of the Particular Baptist Church in Petticoat Lane, near Spitalfields, London.[15] Like most Baptist ministers, Allen had to earn his livelihood through secular work. He opened a linen-drapers shop in Shoreditch. When this business failed, Allen's debt grew, and he spent some time incarcerated at the King's Bench Prison. When the Petticoat Lane congregation dismissed him he briefly found a new pastorate at Broadstairs, near Newcastle. But in 1767 he was dismissed by the Broadstairs congregation, and in 1768 he returned to London as a schoolteacher.[16] By January 1769 he was again in financial trouble, and he was tried at the Old Bailey[17] for forging a £50 note.[18] Although he was acquitted, this trial destroyed his reputation, and its stigma followed him to Boston.[19]

In 1770, Allen published *The Spirit of Liberty*.[20] Already showing his radical political views and his sympathies for the developing American cause, this pamphlet argued for the return of John Wilkes to Parliament and defended the rights of the individual.[21] Most chroniclers believe that Allen left London for New York in 1771 though he does not re-appear in the historical record until 1772. At that time John Davis, the pastor of the Second Baptist Church in Boston, had left his post due to failing health, so the congregation was searching for a new teaching elder.[22] Davis knew of Allen and made it clear before he died that he wanted Allen to preach at Second Baptist.[23] The church committee knew something of Allen's reputation in England and so was reluctant to invite him to speak.[24] After some debate, they asked him to give the annual Thanksgiving Day Address.[25] Elder Allen served as a "visiting pastor" for just nine months, from November 1772 until July 1773;[26] Second Baptist never extended a permanent call to him.[27]

There may have been some whispering among the members at Second Baptist in Boston when the newly appointed and somewhat controversial Reverend John Allen ascended to the pulpit. Although Baptists were usually more interested in piety than politics, this was the Thanksgiving Day message. Reformed and Calvinistic preachers would typically use this opportunity to address a scriptural view of civil government. Since the Sons of Liberty had influenced his invitation, some no doubt attended to hear this address.

Allen read Micah 7:3: "That they may do evil with both hands earnestly, the prince asketh, and the judge asketh for a reward; and the great man, he uttereth his mischievous desire: so they wrap it up." This was the 1611 translation of the Authorized Version (King

James) of the Bible. In *The New England Soul*, historian Harry S. Stout quoted a more recent translation of Micah that puts the passage into stronger relief for modern ears: "'the ruler demands gifts, the judge accepts bribes, the powerful dictate what they desire—they all conspire together.'[28] That text was perfectly suited to contemporary applications and, with unprecedented fury and directness, Allen used it to broaden the attack on Parliament to include the king himself."[29]

In the sermon, Allen made five observations.[30] First, "It is then plain that a craving, absolute prince, is a great distress to a people."[31] Here Allen invoked the widely disliked White Pines Act that guaranteed the Royal Navy the choicest trees in New England for the masts of its ships.[32] He exhorted his listeners to let the king have their trees as a gift. Let the king pave the streets of England with gold, Allen said, not through taxation, but through trade.[33]

Allen then turned to the *Gaspee* commission. Unlike press reports that failed to mention the fact that no one could be removed to England for a trial without the consent of Rhode Island's governor, Allen stressed the point: "But the granting of this [removing suspects to England], in some measure, depends upon the consent of the governor."[34] On December 3, Allen could not have known this so he must have added it later for the published version of his sermon after the publication of Dartmouth's letter to Wanton. Allen exhorted the civil magistrates in Rhode Island to enforce their own laws, and he predicted (accurately) that the king would ask in vain for the perpetrators. Allen could not have known exactly what sort of resistance the Crown would meet in Rhode Island, but as long as Governor Wanton's authority remained intact, there was no danger of any Rhode Islanders traveling to London.

Allen's final example of what "the prince asketh" was that the wives and mothers of Rhode Island let their husbands, and the fathers of their children, be taken from them.[35] They were to return to the land of tyranny, from which their forefathers fled, "confin'd in the horrid kingdom of a Man-of-War's crew." Allen spoke sarcastically that this was a small favor to ask—and encouraged active resistance to such an outrageous request.

After addressing the first part of Micah 7:3, "the prince asketh," Allen proceeded to "the judge asketh for a reward [bribe]." Allen argued that judges were systematically taking away the rights of juries. He questioned the verdict of the "King-Street murderers,"[36] calling the Boston Massacre willful murder, not manslaughter. Allen claimed that they would receive justice at the judgment seat of Christ.

Allen invoked the Civil List[37] and the appointment and payment of Massachusetts's judges directly by the ministry. Patriot leaders believed that by paying officials directly from London via the Civil List, it made them less accountable to the people. It was from this point that Allen crafted the title for this sermon: "For thereby you submit the key of all your essential rights as Americans."[38] Allen argued that the judges, in order to be faithful servants of the Crown, would have to rule the way that the ministry directed them. He assured his listeners that these judges would not be interested in protecting the rights, lives, or property of Americans. He then reminded his Baptist audience that they knew what it was to struggle with unsympathetic judges; they had paid taxes to support ministers who were not their own for more than a century.[39]

Allen concluded his first observation with a very brief synopsis of the distress brought upon the ancient people of Israel by wicked rulers. Seamlessly, he moved into English history, demonstrating a similar pattern of distress caused by despotic rulers. But in the case of England, he showed Britons' unwillingness to tolerate oppression for long, and the ability of a freedom-loving people to dispose of such rulers.

Allen's second observation was that the branches of the London government were uniting in a conspiracy to subvert the liberties of Americans.[40] When rulers acted to destroy liberty, they forfeited their right to rule. He cited the biblical example of 1 Kings 12, when Israel rebelled against the extra burdens put upon them by King Rehoboam.[41] Allen also said, "Was not this the case in Zedekiah's reign?" This example is harder to understand and he did not explain it.[42] Zedekiah was a vassal appointed by Nebuchadnezzar, king of Babylon. He conspired with the Egyptian pharaoh in an ill-fated plot to rebel against Babylon. Nebuchadnezzar laid siege to Jerusalem, it fell, and Zedekiah witnessed the killing of his own children, had his eyes gouged out, and died as a prisoner. Perhaps, Allen was suggesting that by participating in a conspiracy, Zedekiah had forfeited his right to rule.

Allen moved easily from Old Testament history to current events. He mentioned the despotic will of the king of Sweden and the destruction of the rights of the people there. Doubtless he referred to the August 1772 *coup d'état* of Gustav III wherein he imposed a new constitution, restored many royal prerogatives, and imposed rigid financial reforms on Sweden.[43] What he could not have known then was that the remainder of Gustav's life would match Allen's formula for the distress caused by a tyrannical king. Subsequently, Gustav faced rebellions and mutinies before he was assassinated by a coalition of nobles in 1792.

Allen's third observation addressed another politically charged topic in Boston in the fall of 1772. He denied the legislative power of Parliament over Americans:[44] "The Parliament of England cannot justly make any laws to oppress, or defend the Americans,[45] for they are not the representatives of America, and therefore they have no legislative power either for them, or against them."[46] Here Allen was working up to the climax of his address. The tenor and pitch of his oration increased. He summarized much of what he had already said, adding as many new grievances as possible. He accused the Massachusetts Governor Thomas Hutchinson of wrongful motives when he said, "your G_____'s heart [is] not right." He concluded this section by returning to the *Gaspee*'s Royal Commission of Inquiry, warning that the violence and horror that would take place in Rhode Island was all the consequence of Aaron Biggs's testimony.[47]

After further incendiary rhetoric about blood in the streets, Allen's fourth observation[48] was: "That it is not rebellion."[49] He cited the biblical story of Naboth refusing to swap or sell his vineyard to King Ahab:[50] "Shall *Naboth*'s disputing with King *Ahab*, respecting his vineyard, be deem'd rebellion? . . . It is no more rebellion, than it is to breathe." Allen drew a simple parallel with his own day; Naboth had to protect his property from "a craving, absolute prince." Naboth, of course, was killed through trickery and conspiracy at the highest level of government. Americans could and should protect themselves; this was not rebellion but self-defense, for his audience an important distinction.

Allen also cited an example from Massachusetts history. He asked if, "the people sending home their governor in irons some years ago, [should] be deemed rebellion?" Allen was probably referring to Governor Sir Edmund Andros's failed Dominion of New England. Andros's opponents claimed that he "made law destructive of the liberty of the people, imposed and levied taxes, threatened and imprisoned them who would not be assisting to the illegal levies, denied that they had any property in their land without patents from him."[51] The removal of Andros from office was a powerful historical example for Allen's Boston listeners of justifiable, successful resistance to arbitrary civil government.[52]

Allen's fifth and final point was that there was a conspiracy, high in the government, to give the king the idea that he had a divine right to rule. He speculated about who could be behind it, Lord Bute or Lord Hillsborough. The personalities of government would come and go; what mattered was that the "mischievous design" to ruin their essential rights and liberties remained. George III, Allen argued, was no less susceptible to such designs than England's Charles I or ancient Israel's king Rehoboam. The passive submission from his subjects was all the king required to abuse his authority. Allen ended his sermon with a warning about the tyranny of taxing an increasing number of items, including, Allen added sarcastically, the light of the morning sun. The ministerial conspiracy was trying to implement a number of reforms inimical to colonial liberties. Allen quoted his Micah 7:3 text, "So they wrap it up." He exhorted his listeners to "unwrap it again."[53]

Allen began the published *Oration* with a ten-page dedication to Lord Dartmouth from a "British Bostonian." The actual sermon took up the remaining seventeen pages of the address.[54] Allen moved from topic to topic quickly, even changing references within the same paragraph. But Lord Dartmouth and colonial readers were familiar with these arguments. He mentioned the *Gaspee* and the Royal Commission of Inquiry[55] seven times, as well as the salaries of Massachusetts officials being paid by the ministry. These were among the politically charged issues in New England in the fall of 1772. Judging from what we know now about the chronology of the events, Allen must have written the sermon in November based upon incomplete and inaccurate reports in the newspapers. The dedication to Lord Dartmouth must have been written at least a month later, after Governor Wanton released his instructions to the Rhode Island Assembly and the press.[56] By the time he wrote the dedication, Allen knew that the *Gaspee* raiders were not going to be charged with piracy, but rather treason.[57]

The purpose of the dedication was to put a "human face" on the *Gaspee* crisis. The problem as Allen saw it was not the assault on the *Gaspee*, but rather the subsequent court of inquiry. This problem, Allen argued, was created by the ministry and could be resolved by them. Allen gave human agency to this crisis by personally addressing Lord Dartmouth, calling upon his Christian conscience to identify and rectify the problem. Allen's dedication, ultimately then, was a thinly veiled attack on Dartmouth and the ministry.

In the first sentence of the dedication Allen invoked the century-old charter of Rhode Island and quoted it at length.[58] He noted that freemen had to be tried locally, "without being, for it, brought to answer, by a due course of Law of this Colony."[59] After appealing to the law, Allen quickly moved to nature. He noted that the smallest creatures have liberty and freedom within their limited sphere, and the only differences between himself and Lord Dartmouth were political. Lastly, he invoked the "beauties of Christianity." Christianity, for Allen, was a "this-worldly" and "other-worldly" religion. If Lord Dartmouth oppressed his fellow creatures in this life, he left only the beauty of the next for them.

Allen appealed to Dartmouth's Christian faith. He claimed that he had dined with Dartmouth in Staffordshire and knew that His Lordship understood the "Divine Oracles" of the Christian faith. They had some common acquaintances in England, and he could testify to Dartmouth's good character. Allen combined Christianity's "Golden Rule"[60] with a series of rhetorical questions about how Dartmouth would react to having his liberties taken away by a despotic power. He concluded this section with another rhetorical question, noting that Dartmouth would, of course, "alarm the Nation" if his own birthright of liberty and freedom was about to be destroyed.

Allen began the next section of the dedication with one of his main points: those living in the British colonies in America valued their liberties as much as those subjects living in England. Primary among those rights and liberties was the right of a local trial by jury. Allen asked Dartmouth if he would prefer being tried by a jury of his peers or whether he preferred being dragged three thousand miles in irons in "a Hell upon water, through a Man of War's crew"[61] to face his trial? Dartmouth had given directions to destroy the rights and laws of the Americans and was therefore not "fit for Heaven, nor Earth," but perhaps "the Dunghill."[62]

Allen then turned specifically to the case of the *Gaspee*. He asked, "Why then must there be New Courts of admiralty erected to appoint and order the inhabitant to be confin'd, and drag'd away three thousand miles, from their families, laws, rights and liberties, to be tried by their enemies?"[63] In an essay introducing a republication of *Oration*, Reta A. Gilbert claimed that much of Allen's criticism of the judiciary was specious. She assumed that throughout *Oration* Allen was referring to the vice-admiralty courts.[64] But there had been eleven courts of vice-admiralty in North America since the end of the seventeenth century, so it would seem unlikely that Allen referred to them as "new" in 1772.[65] Additionally, the placement of Admiralty courts eliminated the need to remove suspects to England for trial. Although Allen was careless with his use of language here, in this instance he was evidently referring to the *Gaspee* Royal Commission of Inquiry, not the vice-admiralty courts.

In the next section of the dedication Allen addressed the person of George III and the limits of the power of an earthly king. He did not believe that it was "his Majesty's will and pleasure" to destroy the lives and liberties of the people.[66] At this point Allen was still content to blame the creation of the Rhode Island commission on a corrupt ministry's influence on the king. Even so, the king was not without responsibility, because Allen provocatively invoked the memory of the beheading of Charles Stuart[67] during the Puritan Revolution. English liberties were more important than any king, and any monarch who challenged them was no servant of God but a tyrant. Here Allen came dangerously close to republicanism; while indicating that he loved and revered the current English monarch, he insinuated that kings can expect beheadings if they do not protect English liberties.[68]

Allen's next main point was that the king had two different sets of laws, one designed to protect the rights of Englishmen at home and another aimed at destroying the rights of those in the colonies abroad. Allen asked Dartmouth how a colonist could resist oppression without being labeled a rebel. Certainly the *Gaspee* raiders had broken the law, and Allen assured Lord Dartmouth that when colonials broke colonial laws, they were willing to be tried by those laws in their local courts.[69]

Now Allen posed the central question: "What is rebellion?" Allen did not develop a theory of governmental legitimacy; he evoked a set of relatively current events that would have been familiar to his readers. Here he sided with North Carolina's regulators against the military actions of General Fanning and Governor Tryon.[70] Allen argued, with logic that was difficult to follow, that Fanning and Tryon crushed the liberties of the regulators in the same way that the king's ministry and Parliament were currently trying to crush Rhode Island's government. In the latter case, the king was a rebel before God for trying to overthrow Rhode Island's government. Allen defined rebellion as "persons rising up with an assumed authority and power to act, dictate and rule in direct violation to the laws of the Land."[71] Since the king was presumably violating the laws of Rhode Island, Allen argued, he was the true rebel.

With this preparation, Allen developed his main thesis: the legal and jurisdictional sphere of the Americans was different from the sphere of the English, and the two could not be reconciled.[72] He began this argument by proposing that the *Gaspee* raiders could have been "Indians out of the woods." A contemporary ballad reported that the raiders were "some Narragansett Indian men,"[73] and Allen indicated that the belief that they were Indians was "the current report."[74] Native Americans could not have broken any English law, he argued; they were never under such law. Allen then quipped at the dreadful manner in which the Native Americans had experienced English law at the end of a sword and bayonet; apparently English

Americans were about to receive the same sort of "justice." He then quoted a passage in Romans, wrongly attributing it to St. James: "Where there is no law, there is no transgression." [75] In his "separate spheres" argument, Allen concluded that an Indian could not break an English law, but neither could any American, nor could the English write laws for Americans.

Continuing with the "separate spheres," he argued that the king and the ministry broke the law. They sent an armed schooner to patrol a sphere that was not theirs, any more than Brest, France, was theirs to police. The English Crown could not claim land in America any more than it could claim it in France.[76] Doing so made George III an enemy to the laws of nature. The forefathers of these American colonists fled tyranny in England and fought for this land with their blood; therefore, they would not give it up easily to current-day English ministerial tyranny.[77]

Allen then quoted the book of St. Matthew 17:25b-26, "What thinkest thou, Simon? of whom do the kings of the earth take custom or tribute? of their own children, or of strangers? Peter saith unto him, Of strangers. Jesus saith unto him, Then are the children free."[78] Skillfully, Allen turned this biblical exchange into a commentary on the commission given to the *Gaspee* as a revenue schooner. The *Gaspee*, he argued, should have been collecting taxes from strangers, not the children of the British Empire. The children are to live free (in every sense of the word) in their own native country. Because the "children" did not recognize these "strangers" who came to collect taxes and stole their property, they had no choice but to treat them as pirates. Allen did not explain precisely who the "strangers" were— from whom the London government could and should collect revenue. But he used this passage to set up a possible justification for the burning of the *Gaspee*.

The Reverend Ezra Stiles wrote, "No one justifies the burning of the *Gaspee*," and no one had publicly excused the behavior of the raiders. So Allen's rationalization for the attack in the *Oration* was unprecedented and stunning.[79] Allen argued that the *Gaspee* officers and crew had, in fact, been prisoners. He portrayed the burning of the *Gaspee* as a kind of liberation for the officers and crew. The

schooner was a prison, and when they were brought ashore to Pawtuxet, they were freed from that prison. By burning the schooner, the
raiders had insured that the men would remain free.[80] He asks Lord
Dartmouth how he could, "hang these poor men" for freeing others?[81]

   Allen speculated that there was a "good prospect" that the Americans were going to unite "as a band of brethren" to stand up for
their liberties. He asked if the king could kill his own subjects any
more easily than a mother could murder her own children. The king's
military was prepared to fight the French, not the Americans. He
called the English soldier, "who art in general the refuse of the earth,"
no match for the free men and volunteers that America would produce to protect itself from slavery. Allen warned Dartmouth that
America could "raise a more potent army of men in three weeks,
than England can in three years." After this bellicose, even threatening language, Allen moderated his tone by declaring that Americans
were loyal subjects who loved their king and "Mother-Country."
Allen concluded his disingenuous dedication to Lord Dartmouth by
asking him to lay the Americans' grievances before the king and:

> Let the Americans enjoy their birthright, blessings, and Britain her
> prosperity, let there be a mutual union between the mother and
> her children, in all the blessings of life, trade and happiness; then,
> my Lord, both Britons, and Americans, will call you blessed.
> Wishing, from my heart, the inviolable preservation of the Rights
> and Liberties of the AMERICANS, and the growing happiness of
> ENGLAND:
> I am, my LORD,
> his MAJESTY'S Loyal Subject,
> and your LORDSHIP'S Dutiful Servant,
> A British Bostonian.[82]

Oration became one of the most popular pre-independence pamphlets in British colonial America (see table 5.2).[83] *Oration* was also
the most widely read sermon[84] and the most popular public address
in the years before independence.[85] Although the pamphlet was ad-

Table 5.2 Pamphlets sorted in order of popularity, 1765-1776[86]

Rank	Author	Title[a]	Year	N1[b]	N2[c]	Prdct[d]
1	Thomas Paine	Common Sense	1776	25	13	325
2	Jonathan Shipley	Speech	1774	12	8	96
3	Charles Lee	Strictures	1774	7	6	42
4	John Dickinson	Letters	1768	7	5	35
5	Matthew Robinson Morris Rokeby	Considerations	1774	7	5	35
6	John Allen	Oration	1773	7	4	28
7	Benjamin Franklin	Examination	1766	5	5	25
8	Jonathan Shipley	Sermon	1773	5	5	25
9	Daniel Dulany	Considerations	1765	5	4	20
10	John Hancock	Oration	1774	5	4	20
11	Richard Price	Observations	1776	5	4	20
12	Thomas Hutchinson	*Letters*	1773	5	2	10

a. Abbreviated
b. Number of editions in British America
c. Number of cities and towns in British America in which editions appeared
d. Ranking these pamphlets can be done by multiplying or adding the two numbers together, either method produces the same ranking.

vertised for sale in many newspapers, it is not evident that the text of the sermon was ever printed in a newspaper.[87]

Chronologically, the only pamphlet prior to *Oration* that enjoyed such widespread printing and distribution was John Dickinson's immensely popular *Letters from a Farmer in Pennsylvania to the Inhabitants of the British Colonies*. These twelve letters were first published anonymously in the *Pennsylvania Chronicle and Universal Advertiser* starting in November 1767. While *Letters* experienced stunning success in British North America, it was also published in London, Paris, and Dublin. More moderate and conciliatory in tone than Allen, Dickinson abhorred violence and acknowledged the need for some central coordinating agency to regulate commerce within the Empire. Dickinson, an attorney, crafted arguments that were carefully reasoned, historical, and legal. Nevertheless, *Letters* awakened the colonists to the crisis of taxation without representation in the wake of the much-despised Townshend duties.[88] Likewise, Allen's sermon alerted colonists to the purported operation of a deep ministerial conspiracy against colonial liberty.

There were more than four hundred pamphlets addressing the conflict between Britain and the North American colonies published prior to the Declaration of Independence;[89] *Oration*'s popularity placed it in the top one percent. Thanksgiving Day sermons frequently had political content. Following the repeal of the Stamp Act, eleven Thanksgiving Day sermons were "crowded with political theory."[90] While Allen had published pamphlets back in London, *Oration* started out as a sermon, and he used the months following to keep revising editions of it for the pamphlet wars.

While other forms of communication were important to the coming crisis, historian Bernard Bailyn argued, "It was in this form—as pamphlets—that much of the most important and characteristic writing of the American Revolution appeared."[91] He argued that it was their flexibility, ease of production, and low price that made the pamphlets the perfect tool for an ideological revolution like America's. By the middle of the eighteenth century, colonial British America was rife with printing presses. Bailyn considered Allen among the most imaginative pamphleteers in colonial British America, "But mere vigor and lurid splash are not in themselves expressions of imaginative intensity. Among all those who wrote pamphlets, in fact, there appear to have been only three—James Otis, Thomas Paine, and that strange itinerant Baptist John Allen—who had anything like the concentrated fury that propelled Swift's thought and imagination through the intensifying indirections of literary forms."[92]

He continued and explained that these three writers broke with colonial custom; they mirrored a more British writing style. In contrast, "The American writers were profoundly reasonable people. The pamphlets convey scorn, anger, and indignation; but rarely blind hate, rarely panic [or] fear. . . . The reader is led through arguments, not images. The [other] pamphlets aim to persuade."[93]

But six of the most popular pre-independence pamphleteers were either British (Shipley, Rokeby, and Price); or had only been in the colonies for a short time when they published (Lee, Allen, and Paine).[94]

In the most thorough scholarly treatment of Allen to date, historians John M. Bumsted and Charles E. Clark argue that Allen was
"becoming increasingly disillusioned over the English political scene"
between 1770 and 1773.[95] His three pamphlets of the period, *The
Spirit of Liberty*, *The American Alarm*, and *Oration*, showed his
growing impatience with the English monarchy and its ministries to
solve the problems facing the Empire. In the first pamphlet, written
in England, he called upon George III to end governmental tyranny;
in the second he blamed corrupt ministers for influencing the king;
and finally in *Oration* he attacked the king himself. Historian Harry
Stout argued that previously Parliament had been the target of criticism and until *Oration*, "the monarchy was virtually untouched by
colonial protests."[96] But Allen was unique not only for his attack on
the monarchy; he also took the unusual position of incorporating an
attack on chattel slavery.

Oration went through seven printings, five editions, in four different cities (see table 5.3). By the fourth edition, Allen incorporated
some of his anti-slavery views. His isolation from other Patriot leaders may have been related to his anti-slavery position.[97] Allen could
not get Boston printers Kneeland and Davis to publish his remarks
on slavery; he had to switch publishers and attach his critique to the
already-popular *Oration*.[98] Ebenezer Watson in Hartford was the
only other printer to join Ezekiel Russell, willing to include the anti-
slavery addendum.

Throughout *Oration*, ironically, as Allen attacked the king and
Lord Dartmouth, he praised their character and intentions. Of Dartmouth, he spoke of "the good and pious Character your Lordship
bears." How then could he explain the difficulties that these men
seemed to be imposing upon New Englanders? Allen did not, as seventeenth-century preachers did, attribute New England's current trials and tribulations to their own sin and God's fatherly discipline.
The only way that he could explain the disjuncture between the good
motives of the king and the trials and tribulations of those in his
North American colonies was in terms of a secret conspiracy of government officials.

Table 5.3. Publication History of *Oration*[99]

First printing: First edition; published by Daniel Kneeland & Nathaniel Davis, Queen-Street, Boston; advertised in the Massachusetts Gazette and Boston Weekly News-Letter, January 7, 1773

Second printing: Second edition, corrected; published by Daniel Kneeland & Nathaniel Davis, Queen-Street, Boston; advertised in the Massachusetts Gazette and Boston Weekly News-Letter, January 21, 1773

Third printing: Third edition, corrected; published by Daniel Kneeland & Nathaniel Davis, Queen-Street, Boston; advertised in the Boston Evening Post, May 17, 1773

Fourth printing: Fourth edition, expanded to include the rights and liberties of Africans; published by Ezekiel Russell, Union-Street, Boston, 1773

Fifth printing: Same as third edition; published by T. Green, New-London, 1773

Sixth printing: Fifth edition (with addendum); published by Ebenezer Watson, Hartford, 1774

Seventh printing: Same as second edition; published by James Adams, High-Street, Wilmington, 1775

At first glance it would seem unusual that among the almost nine thousand words of his *Dedication and Oration*, a Calvinistic Baptist like Allen used the term "Providence" only once, but mentioned "mischievous design" eight times. This would not surprise historian Gordon Wood, who wrote:

> Sermons of the period were filled with references to the "hidden intent," the "pernicious scheme," and the "intrigues and dark plots"—references that owed more to the apocalyptic beliefs of the clergy than to the Whig tradition of political jealousy and suspicion. . . . Yet ultimately it was neither the atmosphere of whiggish suspicion and mistrust nor the Christian tradition of a deceitful Satan that was fundamental to the age's susceptibility to conspiratorial interpretations; for people who were neither radical

Whigs nor devout Protestants nonetheless believed naturally in conspiracies. What was fundamental is that American secular thought—in fact, all enlightened thought of the eighteenth century—was structured in such a way that conspiratorial explanations of complex events became normal, necessary, and rational.[100]

Allen accounted for the fact that benevolent intentions by certain individuals in government could be thwarted by the "mischievous designs" of a few. Historical cause and effect, in the enlightened eighteenth century, was a very personal and moral matter; therefore, people could and should be held personally and morally responsible for their actions.

Historian Nathan Hatch demonstrated how ministers utilized the "language of civic humanism" when he said, "The fact that clergymen in Revolutionary New England came to understand the Anglo-American conflict in terms similar to those of less religious pamphleteers and orators should come as no surprise to students of colonial politics. . . . It certainly makes it unlikely that ministers were somehow deaf to this dominant language of civic humanism."[101]

In the strictest sense, Allen was not a New England clergyman. He had arrived only recently from England and had not fully imbibed the covenantal and remnant view of New England that his congregational and local Baptist colleagues shared. Although capable of making adroit references to Old Testament characters[102] and tying them into the politics of his own time, Allen never portrayed New England, as so many of his contemporaries did, in millennial terms as the New Israel. He understood Whig opposition politics; his background was Wilkesite, having pastored a church in a Wilkesite neighborhood in London and written a pamphlet advocating for John Wilkes. And, of course, as a pamphleteer, he was skilled in using imagery, exaggeration, and metaphors to alarm his readers.

The *Gaspee* Affair, in and of itself, was not a suitable topic for a Christian sermon. The task of a clergyman like Allen was to explain the larger moral and spiritual significance of an event for his parishioners. Allen placed the *Gaspee* Affair in the larger context of threats to American liberties and colonial right (as English subjects and

Christians) to resist tyranny.[103] The *Gaspee* (and the Civil List) was merely the most recent instance of tyranny in an emerging pattern. A single Royal Commission of Inquiry could have been the result of a misunderstanding, a mistake of some kind. But what Allen and other Patriot leaders saw in the *Gaspee* Affair was further evidence of a ministerial pattern of threats to subvert their liberties and enslave them. So, even as prime ministers rose and fell and new department heads in Whitehall came and went, the pattern of tyranny remained. Some confusing event or effect might be passed off as an accident—the result of somebody's mistaken intention—but a series of events that seemed to form a pattern could be no accident. Having only the alternative of "providence" as an impersonal abstraction to describe systematic linkages of human actions, the most enlightened of the age could only conclude that regular patterns of behavior were the consequences of concerted human intentions—that is, the result of a number of people coming together to promote a collective design or conspiracy.[104]

Thomas Jefferson could write in July 1774, "Single acts of tyranny may be ascribed to the accidental opinion of a day; but a series of oppressions, begun at a distinguished period, and pursued unalterably thro' every change of ministers, too plainly prove a deliberate, systematical plan of reducing us to slavery."[105] This explained how a secular and political event like the *Gaspee* Affair was appropriate material for a Sunday morning sermon. As Christians, Allen's listeners were morally obligated to resist this pattern of tyranny.

But the colonists were on their own to try to discover these secret plots. On the surface those conniving against them would seem polite and well-mannered. No one was going to tell them outright that there was a plot, because the scheme was the work of hypocrites. Therefore, plots and schemes had to be discerned by their undesirable outcomes. When Commissioner Daniel Horsmanden expressed shock and disbelief that Governor Wanton had copied Lord Dartmouth's letter to the Rhode Island General Assembly, he said "the main object of our errand was become public, which, in prudence, was to be kept secret."[106] The fact that it was to be kept secret, of course, made it all the more suspicious in the mind of the eighteenth-century radical Whig.

But the colonists were not alone in suspecting a conspiracy. In Whitehall ministry officials feared a conspiracy by colonial elites to discredit His Majesty's government and undermine royal officials serving in the colonies.[107] Charles Dudley and Admiral Montagu wrote letters to their superiors in London speculating that the attack on the *Gaspee* had been carefully planned with advanced knowledge (if not culpability) on the part of Rhode Island's civil magistrates.[108] Parliament's reactions to events in the colonies were also colored by the perception that there was a pattern of behavior among colonial elites systematically attempting to undermine royal authority.[109] Not only did letters from loyal colonists and royal officials feed this perception; a London newspaper erroneously reported that a vessel in Boston harbor had been set on fire and that a large number of persons had been arrested and confined to the local jail.[110] There had indeed been a ship fire in Boston, in daylight, in plain view of the crew, but the fire was an accident; newspaper editors on both sides of the Atlantic printed false and misleading stories.[111]

Intelligent, well-educated, and mentally sound people in the colonies and in London interpreted pre-independence events through the lens of conspiracy. Subsequent research has not found evidence of any plots or schemes by colonial governments or Whitehall. Having lost many of the traditional theistic explanations for crisis, contemporaries resorted to the conspiracy interpretive model to explain the "bad things" that were happening to their political systems.

The primary legacy of the *Gaspee*, then, was not the founding of inter-colonial committees of correspondence. It was not that it could have started the war three years earlier, as Commissioner Oliver stated.[112] It was not that Lieutenant Dudingston was the first British official shot (and nearly killed) by colonials. The legacy of the *Gaspee* was a growing belief that, as Reverend Allen so vigorously argued to New Englanders, some "mischievous design" to subvert their liberties had continued through Lord North's and Lord Dartmouth's administrations. The *Gaspee* Royal Commission of Inquiry, with its secret orders to the commissioners, fit perfectly into a pattern to prove that there was a plot of treachery against them. The quiet "lull" after the Boston Massacre (or King's Street riot) was officially over and Patriots were reminded that plots against their liberties continued. Just as John Dickinson skillfully alerted colonists to the dangers of "taxation without representation" in his *Letters* in 1767–68; John Allen re-awakened Patriot fears of a conspiracy in *Oration* in 1773. But colonists did not know that even before the commissioners could conclude their business in June, the next crisis was on its way, this time in chests of tea.

CONCLUSION

GOVERNOR WANTON TOOK SO LONG TO FORWARD THE MATERIALS from the commission to Lord Dartmouth that subsequent events in Boston overshadowed the *Gaspee* episode.[1] One historian made a connection between Wanton's passive resistance to imperial authority and the destruction of Boston's tea. John C. Miller stated, "Certainly, the failure of the British government to punish the scuttlers of the *Gaspee* was a direct encouragement to Bostonians to stage the Tea Party." Miller saw a direct relationship between the weakness of royal authority in Rhode Island and the emboldening of Patriots in Boston. He continued, "After the Rhode Island Commission had revealed the weakness of the British government, Admiral Montagu concluded that the Bostonians were 'almost ripe for independence, and nothing but the ships [in Boston harbor] prevents their going [to] greater lengths, as they see no notice taken from home of the behaviour.'"[2] Montagu believed that Dartmouth's "hands off" approach did not quell the fears of colonials, but encouraged radical Patriots to more dramatic resistance. On the other hand, historian Franklin Wickwire wrote, "the *Gaspee* commission would serve notice of the British government's hardening determination to curb violence and punish persons who destroyed Crown property. . . . It would thus foreshadow ominously the more effective punishment Britain meted out later to the port of Boston."[3] Admiral Montagu feared that the failures of the Royal Commission emboldened Patriots in Boston to take "great pains to influence the entire continent." He expected a strike at the governor, himself, or one of the customs officers any day.[4]

While the Privy Council may have given up on the efficacy of Royal Commissions of Inquiry, they were still looking for a way to remove key colonial radicals to London for a treason trial.[5] In the context of the Coercive Acts following Boston's destruction of East India Company tea, Thomas Hutchinson wrote on July 5, 1774:

> Mr. Pownall said his [own] plan was, to pass the Port bill, and to send over Adams, Molineux, and other principal Incendiaries; try them, and if found guilty, put them to death. This, he said, seemed to be at one time the determination of the Cabinet; and the Lords of the Privy Council actually had their pens in their hands, in order to sign the Warrant to apprehend them. He repeated it: —I say literally, they had their pens in their hands, prepared to sign the Warrant, when Lord Mansfield diverted it by urging the other measures.[6]

Lord North, while addressing Parliament during the debates surrounding the bill for regulating the government of Massachusetts Bay, complained that the London government had long been too patient with its North American colonies:

> I have heard so many different opinions in regard to our conduct in America, I hardly know how to answer them. . . . The Americans have . . . burnt your ships,[7] denied all obedience to your laws and authority; yet so clement, and so long forbearing has our conduct been, that it is incumbent on us now to take a different course.[8]

The Coercive Acts took a different tack: rather than trying to convict a few of the ringleaders, they punished the innocent alongside the guilty.[9] When Massachusetts governor Thomas Gage received secret orders from Lord Dartmouth in April 1775, "to arrest the principal actors and abettors in the Provincial Congress," the London government was again ready to transport colonials to England for trial.[10]

HISTORIANS do not believe that the raid on the *Gaspee* was an orchestrated first wave of a larger attack on imperial authority. In hindsight, the *Gaspee* raiders had been somewhat "surgical," or even "restrained" in their strike on Lieutenant Dudingston. He alone was shot, the raiders detained the crew only briefly, and there was not a simultaneous attack on the *Beaver* or any other vessels. Newport remained calm during the commissioners' hearings and there was no need to call for General Gage's troops or suppress any uprisings. It is possible to take the colonists at their word; they might have tried to follow the "formula" for a colonial mob. They may have just been going out to arrest Dudingston when events escalated beyond their control.[11]

In contrast, following the rhetoric of the Real Whigs, most historians have characterized the Privy Council's response as an "over-reaction." Patriots never gave the "benefit of the doubt" to those who upheld the laws of the Crown. The Crown response was not characterized as "restrained" or "surgical." While waiting for a reply from the solicitor and attorney generals, Hillsborough hastily sent letters to the colonies and misinformation circulated around them. Dartmouth recalled Hillsborough's packets upon his appointment, but the damage was already done. Perhaps because of Hillsborough's haste, some colonists even thought that Parliament and the ministry aimed the Dockyard Act directly at the *Gaspee* raiders. They told themselves and others that they were going to be tried under an act that did not even exist at the time of the offense.[12]

Ironically, Crown legal officials spent more than a month examining case precedent and rejecting unconstitutional and illegal alternatives.[13] The Privy Council could have taken more draconian measures, like closing Narragansett Bay to maritime traffic or moving Rhode Island's customs houses elsewhere.[14] They could have sent commissioners from England, who were not familiar with the colonies. In 1772, they were still utilizing their time-tested (if not always successful) formula: pardon the many and round up the few ringleaders. After the Boston Tea Party the following year, the Privy Council chose the alternative of punishing the many because, they recognized, they could not seize the leaders and bring them to England for prosecution successfully.

The Privy Council's formula did not work as well in Rhode Island as it had elsewhere. Ideally, after a disturbance involving powerful and well-connected residents, a new royal governor would be sent out to head up a commission of inquiry. This option was not available to the council; they had to accomplish their inquiry through a popularly elected governor. More than one British official and loyal colonist informed the ministry in London that no one would be arrested as long as Governor Wanton remained in office, but there was little that the London government could do about it.[15] This one factor, perhaps more than any other, doomed the commission to ineffectiveness and revealed the weakness of royal authority in this small charter colony.

Governor Wanton's options were limited as well. Samuel Adams would have had Rhode Island's governor refuse to seat the commissioners. Adams feared the precedent the Royal Commission would set for the future of colonial judicial systems. He believed that, once Wanton capitulated on the commission, there was nothing to stop Whitehall from sending an endless stream of inquiries into the colonies. But Wanton, of course, allowed the commission to have its hearings. By calling witnesses in a particular way, failing to call others, and taking an extended recess, Wanton sabotaged the commission, making the ministry lose its appetite for future Royal Commissions.

Loyal colonist Robert Carter Nicholas wrote *Considerations on the present state of Virginia Examined* in 1774:

> that, no Discovery having been made, the Court [the *Gaspee*'s Royal Commission of Inquiry] could proceed no farther; and, though *insulted* in all public Newspapers on the *Continent*, the Ministry were unwilling to proceed to Extremities, but sat down

silently under the Affront, laughed at by the Rhode Islanders and held in Derision by Foreigners.[16]

While the ministry in London exercised restraint by not proceeding to more extreme measures in the *Gaspee* investigation, Nicholas was still alarmed at the possibility of a trial in England for *Gaspee* suspects.

TYPICALLY, when political and legal historians came to analyze the *Gaspee* affair, they were most concerned with the right to a trial in the vicinage. This was also the concern of contemporaries. John Allen, in *Oration*, mentioned overseas trials twice. Samuel Adams, in *The Rights of the Colonists, A List of Violations of Rights and a Letter of Correspondence*, wrote that [in reference to the Dockyard Act], "Thus we are not only deprived of our grand right to *tryal by our Peers in the Vicinity*. . . ."[17] Two grievances cited in the Declaration of Independence have been frequently attributed to colonial "lessons learned" from the *Gaspee*: "For depriving us, in many cases, of the benefits of trial by jury"; and "For transporting us beyond seas, to be tried for pretended offenses." Historian Thomas Barrow believed that these grievances were referring more broadly to the customs service and specifically the Admiralty court system.[18] Certainly, the Administration of Justice Act, passed in May 1774, further angered colonial Patriots. It allowed for British officials serving in Massachusetts to be tried in England for capital crimes committed while putting down colonial uprisings.

When Helen Hill Miller examined nine colonial court cases for their merit in shaping subsequent revolutionary documents, she utilized the *Gaspee* case to illustrate the issue of a right to a trial in the vicinage.[19] Miller noted that the *Declaration and Resolves of the First Continental Congress*[20] cited three grievances tied to the *Gaspee*: the treason act under Henry VIII, ". . .the great and inestimable privilege of being tried by their peers of the vicinage. . .," and the Dockyard Act.[21] When the Second Continental Congress convened they adopted the *Declaration of the Causes and Necessity of Taking up Arms*. One of the many grievances outlined was:

statutes have been passed for extending the jurisdiction of the courts of admiralty and vice-admiralty beyond their ancient limits; for depriving us of the accustomed and inestimable privilege of trial by jury. . . that colonists charged with committing certain offences, shall be transported to England to be tried.[22]

Miller also tied the *Gaspee* case into the United States Bill of Rights: "In all criminal prosecutions, the accused shall enjoy the right to a speedy and public trial, by an impartial jury of the state and district wherein the crime shall have been committed"[23] Parliament, in 1769, updated the treason laws and made it clear that colonials could be transported to England for a treason trial. Again in 1772, when Governor Wanton leaked Dartmouth's letter to the press, colonials were reminded that they could be tried before the King's Bench for treason. When Parliament passed the Administration of Justice Act in 1774 for British officials serving in Massachusetts, they were enlarging the circle of persons who could be tried outside the vicinage.

While the *Gaspee* Affair was well known to the authors of these documents, they were pointing to a larger pattern of behavior that had developed after 1763. Royal Commissions of Inquiry, despite Samuel Adams's fears, did not become a recurring problem and they were not specifically mentioned in these revolutionary documents. On the other hand, overseas trials and royally appointed judges were elements that the *Gaspee* episode shared with several other pre-independence Anglo-American clashes, controversies, and institutions. The *Gaspee* case did not enjoy exclusive claim to these grievances. Nevertheless, it did fit nicely into a pattern for the eighteenth-century paranoid style that had a propensity to look for a conspiracy.[24]

Going beyond the issue of trials in the vicinage, or the *Gaspee*'s influence on the country's founding documents, the historian William Leslie argued that the constitutional significance of the *Gaspee* was that it instructed the founding generation in federalism:

Their discussions produced constitutional formulae which were a very long step toward the creation of a federal system because there was evolved through argument the first prerequisite to such a system, namely, the theory of two mutually exclusive legal and jurisdictional spheres encompassing the same area.[25]

Certainly the *Gaspee* episode was not the only experience that informed the founders' discussions about the role of federalism. Indeed, much of the discussion surrounding the *Gaspee* affair was not this sophisticated; it merely reflected simmering resentment about recent encroachments by a distant government that had previously remained aloof. On the other hand, Parliament's assertions of its superiority over other legislative bodies were a major factor fomenting the coming revolution.[26] Rhode Island's subsequent political culture did embrace the type of union outlined in the Articles of Confederation in 1778;[27] but they were more circumspect about the structure described by the Federal Constitution in 1787.[28] It was the last state to ratify that more centralized form of government, and Rhode Island's representatives only agreed to it when other states threatened to charge their merchants with steep tariffs, essentially treating them like a foreign government.[29]

OVER and over again, the *Gaspee* Affair demonstrated the limits of imperial authority in Rhode Island. These weaknesses appeared a decade before the *Gaspee* was set aflame. The deputizing of sea officers in 1763 revealed that the customs service was unable to perform its duties adequately. By expanding the "Hovering Act," Parliament declared a modified form of martial law in the bays and inlets of British North America. Martial law, typically, was declared when there was a breakdown of civilian authority or an occupying force ruled over a defeated foe. Rather than being rewarded for their faithful service during the Seven Years' War, many colonists felt as if they were being treated like a vanquished enemy. Burke explained this fact to Parliament in his *Speech on American Taxation* on April 19, 1774. He said, "The bonds of the act of navigation were straitened so much, that America was on the point of having no trade, either contraband or legitimate. They found, under the construction and execution then used, that act no longer tying but actually strangling them." Burke argued that the recent alterations and implementations of the Navigation Acts were counter-productive to the Empire, actually tearing it apart. In order to make it work, the London government tightened its enforcement policies, he continued, "with new enumerations of commodities; with regulation which in a manner put a stop to the mutual coasting intercourse of the Colonies; with the appointment of courts of admiralty under various improper circumstances." Colonial Americans perceived a pattern in the actions of the last several ministries, Burke argued, and this was the message they carried with them, "the people of America thought themselves proceeded against as delinquents, or at best as people under suspicion of delinquency; and in such a manner, as they imagined, their recent services in the war did not at all merit. Any of these innumerable regulations, perhaps, would not have alarmed alone; some might be thought reasonable; the multitude struck them with terror."[30] Rather than receiving some accolades for their faithful service against the French and their Native American allies in the last war, colonial Americans felt like they were being punished. This pattern, in the eighteenth-century radical Whig mind, suggested a malevolent conspiracy high in the government.

The difficulties associated with the customs service also suggested that Britain was unable to perform adequately one of the basic duties of any civil government: to collect revenue. Many Rhode Island residents believed that the Treasury Department still owed them money from the last war, so sending sea officers to collect more revenue from them seemed to have the situation reversed. [31]

The establishment of the "supercourt" of vice-admiralty under Judge Spry in 1764 was also an admission of failure, a public recognition that the eleven existing vice-admiralty courts were incapable of performing their duties. Supplementing the customs officers with sea officers and the establishment of the Halifax court were not criticisms of the ineffectiveness of colonial governments; these were British institutions, supposedly under London's control, that failed to perform in the colonies. Bolstering these institutions with new reforms merely revealed the long-standing weaknesses of royal authority in North America. Indeed, when Temple[32] and Robinson[33] each tried to set an example and utilize the new court, they were both frustrated in their attempts by concerted colonial resistance.

The effectiveness of colonial courts in arresting British sea officers, like Captain Brown of the *Hawke*, demonstrated the weakness of Royal Navy authority in the colonies. The *Hawke* was tied up at a pier for the entire summer of 1764, and when Brown's superior officer ordered him to sea, New York officials arrested and incarcerated him. Even during the Royal Commission hearings in Newport, British sea officers Keeler, Linzee, and perhaps even Montagu feared arrest if they went ashore. The *Gaspee* raiders had to approach Dudingston grounded at Namquid Point because he very carefully avoided setting foot on shore. He would not even go ashore when Governor Wanton "guaranteed" his safety. This displayed the incapacity of the imperial government in Rhode Island.

When Parliament added a new cadre of collections officers to the service in 1764, they created fresh tension between existing customs officers and newly deputized sea officers. Both had a financial stake in taking seizures, and disputes inevitably erupted between them. Rather than working together, officials often worked at odds with each other. Deputized sea officers carried two commissions, with the possibility of conflicting orders from superiors. In the events following the seizure of the *Fortune*, Dudingston found himself in the awkward position of not having the support of the board of customs commissioners, but retaining the unwavering support of his admiral.[34] In addition, colonial assemblies and governors had, by this point, more than seventy years of experience at "working the system" to frustrate the tasks of the customs collectors.

While some authors have treated Dudingston as a rogue officer or a "bad policeman," Dudingston's problems in Rhode Island in the spring of 1772 were not unique. Dudingston's predecessor Thomas Allen had similar difficulties in customs enforcement when he commanded the *Gaspee*. Additionally, the *Gaspee*'s sister schooners, such as the *St. John*, reported shocking encounters with colonial authorities. But colonial Patriots interpreted failure to act on these affronts to royal authority as evidence of the weakness of that authority and, as Hutchinson and Montagu suggested, may have even emboldened them toward future resistance.

As further evidence of the weakness of His Majesty's government on shore, the two informers who came forward to the commissioners, Gulley and Biggs, both had to be retained aboard naval vessels and could not return to their previous livelihoods in Rhode Island because there was no place on land where British officials could guarantee their safety. Even when Wanton promised to return Biggs to the *Beaver* (and not to the local jail), Linzee would not let him go ashore for questioning. Biggs did not appear before Wanton until Montagu could personally escort him to the commissioners in Colony House.

The number of people who effectively boycotted the proceedings at Colony House also demonstrated the weakness of royal authority in Rhode Island. While colonial newspaper editors aroused fears that Rhode Islanders would be dragged from their beds and sailed to England for treason trials, the commissioners could not convince many of those who were summoned even to appear. But Patriot newspaper editors did not portray the *Gaspee* Commission of Inquiry as "weak" or "limited." They emphasized the strong presence of naval vessels in Newport harbor, Gage's orders to provide troops if required, and permission to transport suspects to England for trial. The Newport pastor, Ezra Stiles, on the other hand, seemed to be one of the few colonists who understood the limits of the commission. He understood that the commissioners were to investigate the behavior of British officials (as well as find the ringleaders), and that they merely turned their findings over to Rhode Island's superior court for a verdict.

I_F the weakness of London's authority was everywhere present, why were Patriots so alarmed? The answer is that they were not so much afraid of what was seen, but of what was unseen. Conspiracies, by definition, did not show themselves. John Allen repeatedly warned about a "mischievous design." Allen, not Lord Dartmouth's American Department, played a key role in interpreting what the *Gaspee* commission meant for British America in his oft-reprinted *Oration*. While the commission itself turned out to be relatively harmless, and might have gone largely unnoticed, Allen infused it with dramatic and portentous meaning. Allen made it fit into a consistent pattern of tyranny over the colonies emerging from the highest ranks in the government.[35]

When the Province of Massachusetts Bay considered the March 12, 1773, resolves from Virginia's House of Burgesses, Speaker Thomas Cushing summed it up well when he said:

> That there has been long a settled Plan to subvert the Political Constitutions of these Colonies and to introduce arbitrary Power, cannot in the opinion of the House admit of Doubt.
>
> Those who have aimed to enslave us, like a Band of brothers, have ever been united in their Councils and their Conduct. . . .
>
> The Object which the Conspirators against our Rights seem of late to have had much in View, has been either to lull the Colonies into a State of Profound Sleep and Security, which is forever the Forerunner of Slavery; or to foment Divisions among them. How necessary then, how important is it to counteract and defeat them in this fatal Design?[36]

Even quiet in the colonies, or silence from London, could be viewed with suspicion by colonial Patriots who suspected a conspiratorial design in government.

While historians recognize that no scheme to enslave the colonists existed, Samuel Adams was not entirely misguided when he feared for Rhode Island's charter.

While Parliament had not debated the idea of uniting Connecticut and Rhode Island into a royal colony, loyal colonists had suggested the idea to Dartmouth's American Department on more than one occasion.[37] Since royal commissions were empowered to make suggestions, even legislative ones, based upon their investigations, a royal commission could have suggested a royal government as a solution to Rhode Island's customs, trade, and judicial "shortcomings." But given the fact that Rhode Island's popularly elected governor headed this particular commission, it was unlikely that the *Gaspee* commission would propose such a reform. Adams, though, feared the arrival of future commissions, which could recommend a royal government for Rhode Island. Indeed, political leaders in Britain took the recommendations of royal commissions seriously and frequently debated them in Parliament.

Someone writing under the pseudonym "HAMPDEN"[38] believed that both a conspiracy existed and that they might be revisited with a Royal Commission of Inquiry. "In one word there appears to be a plan concerted and established for enslaving us, and all our posterity: . . . A court of inquisition may be again appointed."[39] Some contemporaries, even within opposition circles, doubted that there was a deliberate scheme to enslave American colonists.[40] But few stopped to ask the question, "Why would Whitehall want to enslave us?" Certainly, the London government intended to get more revenue out of the colonists—but why would the ministry have to take away their traditional English rights and liberties to do it? How could the colonists explain their political woes without a "mischievous design"? Seventeenth-century British colonial Americans explained events in terms of "Providence" in a way that eighteenth-century Americans seldom did. While the former used the term in a religious sense, the latter used it in a more Whiggish sense, meaning "progress."[41] Colonists would not have invoked unseen "social forces" or the "unintended consequences of legislation" the way that twenty-first-century analysts would.

In the heated political rhetoric of the 1760s and 1770s, opinions of a leader's personality and character were paramount. Allen, in *Oration*, commented extensively on Dartmouth's good and Christian character. Vigilant eighteenth-century English subjects continually agonized over the virtue or lack of virtue in their leaders. Gordon Wood noted that "the very abilities that made patricians and gentry likely leaders also made them potential tyrants."[42] Such leaders were highly capable—so that if ambition were to get the better of them, they were also capable of great evils. Wicked and ambitious men in Whitehall could increase their power by appointing more placeholders and courtiers in a new royal colony of Rhode Island and Connecticut.

Colonial Patriots could impute motive for a pattern of oppression they believed was enveloping the colonies. Men high in government would crave more power when their personal virtue waned and their ambition got the better of them. If they could treat the English colonists as those living in "conquered lands," then they could send over more commissioners, governors, sea officers, customs officers, and naval officers to enforce more Acts of Parliament and further subvert the degree of home rule colonists had enjoyed for so many decades.

ULTIMATELY, Stiles's question remains: was the assault on the *Gaspee* treason? While we might think of the phrase "domestic terrorism," the English language did not yet have the word "terrorism."[43] A 1995 attack on a U.S. Government building did not result in the charge of treason, but rather "terrorism."[44] There have been cases where Taliban soldiers (who claimed to be American citizens) were captured by U.S. forces. Here the charge of treason could be used, but the U.S. Constitution requires two eyewitnesses to prosecute, something difficult to find in enemy terrain.[45] It is difficult to analyze the *Gaspee* affair now without invoking the word "terrorism" anachronistically. Rhode Islanders did not consider their actions treason, demonstrating how much they had distanced themselves from the political authority of the Crown.[46] Seeing their own actions as self-defense, or defending the colony's interests, displayed how unresponsive and distant they found London's government. While declaring their loyalty to the British monarch, they treated English authority as virtually a foreign government. That the perpetrators remained in Providence and did not flee to a more remote location[47] demonstrated how weak they perceived royal authority and to be the scant likelihood of being prosecuted. Given the *Liberty* and the *St. John* incidents, they had good historical precedent to assure them that they were safe in their homes. The *Gaspee* raiders felt quite safe in this small, independent, juridical enclave of the British Empire.

The legal officials of the Crown could not see the intentional destruction of a Royal Navy vessel as anything other than piracy or treason. If destroyed by a foreign government, then such action was a declaration of war; by non-affiliated seafarers, piracy; but if destroyed by British subjects (especially within the body of the colony), then it had to be treason. Given the traditional formula for a colonial sheriff and mob to approach a sea officer who they believed had made an illegal seizure, the *Gaspee* raiders could not see the destruction of a single vessel as "levying war against the King." Since 1769, Parliament had been looking for a way to utilize treason law on some colonials. They were convinced that "bringing some over" would restore calm to the troubled colonies.[48] Apparently both of these tasks were easier said than done.

The two Rhode Island politicians who played the largest roles in frustrating the Crown's *Gaspee* investigation, Joseph Wanton and Darius Sessions, broke with the assembly when it actually came to the point of raising arms against the king. Both were re-elected to their sixth year in office on April 19, 1775. That evening, they heard the alarming news about Concord Bridge, and the assembly met three days later in an emergency session in Providence. Sessions stepped down as deputy governor when he heard of plans to raise 1500 men to defend the province and join forces (if necessary) with other colonies. Wanton stayed in office, hoping to influence others against taking such action against their king, until November when the assembly finally forced him from office. Following the general election in 1776, elected officials removed their customary oath of allegiance to the king when sworn into office. On May 4, 1776, Rhode Island had, as a practical matter, declared its independence from the king of England. Wanton and Sessions, who had worked so diligently to protect their fellow Rhode Islanders from prosecution in 1773, could not take up arms against the English Crown. They believed that Rhode Island's charter was best protected from within the Empire by the English constitution.[49]

Perhaps it was the failure of the *Gaspee* commission to transport any ringleaders to England that caused it to lose some of its value as a Patriot issue in the push toward independence. Allen's pamphlet, judging from the advertisements, seems to have enjoyed its most robust sales in the first six months of 1773 (when the commission was still meeting and during its recess). When Samuel Adams's dire predictions about dragging people from their homes and an onslaught of subsequent commissions failed to materialize, the *Gaspee* episode, rather than showing an abuse of power by an overbearing tyrant, demonstrated the weakness of imperial authority. If American Patriots wanted to alarm colonists about threats to their liberties, they would have to look elsewhere for material. The *Gaspee* did reawaken Patriots from the "lull," but it could not sustain their cause. It certainly did not have the staying power necessary to make an argument for complete independence from Britain. Subsequent events in and around Boston and Philadelphia propelled the course of independence the remainder of the way.

Soon after the news of the destruction of H. M. schooner *Gaspee* reached the Admiralty, they commissioned H. M. brig *Gaspee* and put her on station patrolling the fishing grounds around Chaleur Bay and the Gaspee Peninsula. On June 10, 1774, George Washington attended fireworks in Williamsburg, Virginia, to commemorate the second anniversary of the burning of the *Gaspee*.[50] Rhode Islanders, too, swiftly memorialized the event, renaming Namquid Point "*Gaspee* Point," as it appears on a nautical chart produced in 1777.[51] Four *Gaspee* raiders participated in Fourth of July celebrations in Providence in 1826, marking the fiftieth anniversary of the Declaration of Independence.[52] Numerous businesses (from car washes to insurance companies) have utilized the *Gaspee* in their naming and promotions. The Daughters of the American Revolution had a *Gaspee* chapter that gave annual awards to students at Brown University. In 1965 Pawtuxet Village hosted the *Gaspee* Days parade and other festivities that continue to the present.[53]

Former commissioner Justice Oliver also looked back on the *Gaspee* commission, but from 1781. He drew similar conclusions: that the government was so Republican that the courts and magistrates could never find justice. He also observed that the *Gaspee* Affair almost started the war, "Indeed, the whole Continent was alarmed; & upon such an Attempt, they would have rushed into Rebellion 3 Years before they did. Perhaps it would have been better they had done so; they might have been less prepared for it, & a decent Firmness might have more easily, & at less Cost, have subdued it."[54] Later, with the perspective of hindsight at the close of the American War, Oliver did not see the *Gaspee* episode as merely a few merchants acting out against a "bad policeman." He tied the assault on the *Gaspee* into the larger chronology of events leading up to the war and independence.

NOTES

INTRODUCTION

1. Maritime historian Daniel Vickers defined "maritime culture" as those people who lived within three miles (a one hour walk) from the ocean. With the vastness and navigability of Narragansett Bay, many Rhode Islanders were living in a maritime world.

2. Howard Willis Preston, *Rhode Island and the Sea*, 33.

3. Neil R. Stout, *The Royal Navy in America, 1760-1775*, 70.

CHAPTER ONE: TRADING WITH THE ENEMY

1. James B. Hedges, *The Browns of Providence Plantations: Colonial Years*, 47.

2. See the section titled "Flags of Truce" in Preston, *Rhode Island and the Sea*, 47-58.

3. Thomas C. Barrow, *Trade and Empire: The British Customs Service in Colonial America, 1660–1775*, 161.

4. George Louis Beer, *British Colonial Policy, 1754–1765*, 92–93.

5. John. W. Tyler, *Smugglers & Patriots: Boston Merchants and the Advent of the American Revolution*, 15.

6. Stout, *Royal Navy*, 18-19. Later in 1773, Chief Justice Horsmanden proposed uniting the two small colonies under one royal governor.

7. Barrow, *Trade and Empire*, 177. Britain did not have a progressive tax scale. Many scholars have argued that the propertied classes could have contributed more to ease the national debt.

8. *The Parliamentary History of England* Vol. XVII, 1302.

9. Many British officials believed that the colonial courts were too responsive to local politics. They believed that justices would be more impartial in their rulings if the received a set income from England.

10. The Act of 3 George III, chapter 22.

11. During Dudingston's civil trial in Rhode Island, it was his customs deputation that was in question, not his naval commission.

12. The Act of 12 Charles II, chapter 18.

13. Oliver M. Dickerson, *The Navigation Acts and the American Revolution*, 7.

14. Stout, *Royal Navy*, 3.

15. The Navigation Act of 25 Charles II, chapter 7.

16. Imperial Acts of Frauds 7 & 8 William III, chapter 22.

17. Stout, *Royal Navy*, 5.

18. William III did this partly to outmaneuver an attempt by Parliament to set up its own colonial office.

19. Lovejoy, *Rhode Island Politics*, 33.

20. So important were the rum and molasses trades that John Adams, later in life, could write, "I know not why we should blush to confess that molasses was an essential ingredient in American independence. Many great events have proceeded from much smaller causes." John Adams to William Tutor, August 11, 1818, Quincy, Massachusetts. Charles Francis Adams, *The Works of John Adams, Second President of the United States* Vol. X, 345.

21. Stout, *The Royal Navy*, 70.

22. Governor Stephen Hopkins to Richard Partridge, January 15, 1759, Rhode Island. Richard Partridge was Rhode Island's London agent at the time. No register or Marshall or any other officer of the court had been appointed to assist Andrews. J. Franklin Jameson, ed., *Privateering and Piracy in the Colonial Period*, 575. See footnote 2.

23. For an excellent treatment of Boston's customs service and smuggling, see John W. Tyler, *Smugglers and Patriots: Boston Merchants and the Advent of the American Revolution*.

24. Carl Ubbelohde, *The Vice-Admiralty Courts and the American Revolution*, 5, 130.

25. Marblehead (Essex County) was one of two areas in British North America known for the construction of fast sailing vessels.

26. Lovejoy, *Rhode Island*, 32.

27. Some of the vessels were named after the (formerly French) fisheries they were to patrol (Gaspee Bay fishery, Bay of Chaleur fishery, the Gulf of St. Lawrence, and Magdalen Islands). New England fishermen at Magdalen Islands continued to cause friction. National Archives (PRO) UK. CO 5 154 fo. 59, 59d. CO 246, pp. 53-54. "That from Bay Vert to Chaleur Bay and across the last bay to Gaspey in the province of Quebec is a tract well-known to the French the most productive of fish of any part in America." Memorial of Settlers in Quebec and Nova Scotia to Earl of Dartmouth. March 20, 1773. London. CO 217/49 fo. 19.

28. Earl of Dartmouth to Lords of Admiralty March 20, 1773. "You are to order Rear-Admiral Montagu to send a small vessel to Gulf of St. Lawrence at proper season, if one can be spared, to protect fisheries in Chaleur and Gaspee Bays from interference by New England vessels." National Archives (PRO), CO 5 119 fos. 402-403d. Apparently Montagu's agenda differed from the Lords of the Admiralty. Even in 1773 they were still emphasizing the mission of keeping the French, English, Irish, and New England's fishermen apart and at peace with

one another. Montagu, obviously, had put a greater priority on Connecticut and Rhode Island smuggling. Nine years after the vessels were purchased settlers were still petitioning Dartmouth for at least one of the vessels to return to the fisheries. "To remedy which and to enforce laws and to preserve the property of the subject, it is humbly proposed that some one of His Majesty's cruisers be stationed in the Bay of Chaleur during the fishing season. . ." Memorial of Settlers in Quebec and Nova Scotia to Earl of Dartmouth. March 20, 1773. London. National Archives (PRO) UK, CO 217/49 fo. 19.

29. Stout, *The Royal Navy*, 127.

30. Looking for more cost-effective ways to collect revenue in the colonies was a government priority after 1764. Referring to the period prior to 1764 Hibbert stated the ministry believed that, "Smuggling must be stopped and an end put to the present disgraceful mismanagement, whereby it cost 8000 to collect £2000 worth of customs duties in American ports." Christopher Hibbert, *Redcoats and Rebels: The American Revolution Through British Eyes*, xviii.

31. Stout, *Royal Navy*, 128.

32. Stout, *Royal Navy*, 67.

33. Whether this was Robinson's motive or not, customs collectors were frequently jealous of sharing their percentage with sea officers who had only recently been brought into the service. "Property seized by customs officers was sold and the net proceeds divided: one-third to the governor, one-third to the informer, and one-third to the treasury. . . . Seizures by the navy were divided: one-half to the crews making the capture and one-half to the treasury." Indeed, the colonial governors were also removed from the equation under the new customs deputations for sea officers. Dickerson, *The Navigation Acts*, 202.

34. This was a small gun mounted on a vessel's gunwale or rail. Firing black powder without shot would give a loud bang for a warning. When loaded with shot, it was used primarily as a close-in antipersonnel weapon.

35. Two members of the General Assembly signed the orders to sink the *St. John* if it tried to leave the harbor.

36. Extract of a letter from Rear Admiral Lord Colville to Mr. Stepens [*sic*], dated at Halifax, the 26th of July, 1764. John Russell Bartlett, *Records of the Colony of Rhode Island and Providence Plantations, in New England* Vol. VI (Providence: Knowles, Anthony & Co., State Printers, 1861), 428-429.

37. The sources call this official a "peace officer." I am assuming it was the county sheriff.

38. Pauline Maier, *From Resistance to Revolution: Colonial Radicals and the Development of American Opposition to Britain, 1765-1776*, 11.

39. Stout, *Royal Navy*, 140.

40. The commissioners' final report claimed that two of *Liberty*'s boats were dragged through the streets and set of fire. Staples, *Documentary History*, 104.

41. James Munro, *Acts of the Privy Council of England, Colonial Series* Vol. V *1766–1783*, 227. Helen Hill Miller stated that Lord Hillsborough inquired in

reaction to the *Liberty* riot, "If any person had committed any acts which, under the statute of Henry VIII against treason committed abroad, might justify their being brought to England for trial." Helen Hill Miller, *The Case for Liberty*, 165.

42. This was not a Royal Dockyard. There were no "true" dockyards in North America; therefore the Dockyard Act of 1772 could not apply in the colonies. Halifax was merely a "careening yard." Until the introduction of metal veneers to protect wooden hulls, vessels were periodically turned hard over to one side to scrape the bottom for barnacles, to caulk, and perform other repairs. This process was referred to as "careening." By the end of the American War for Independence, 313 vessels had been coppered, greatly reducing the demand of careening on the shipyards. This technological development had psychological and sociological effects on the officers and men as they spent less time in port. One of the unintended effects of coppering was that the electrolytic action rapidly increased the corrosion of iron fastenings, creating a different maintenance problem. N. A. M. Rodger, *The Command of the Ocean: A Naval History of Britain, 1649-1815*, 374–375 and see also 402.

43. Neil R. Stout, "The *Gaspee* Affair," *Mankind* 11 (1967): 89.

44. Admiralty copies of Allen's log books are cataloged under Lieutenant Thomas Allen, *Logg [sic] and Journal of the Proceedings of His Majesty's Arm'd Sloop* Gaspee, National Archives (PRO) UK, ADM 51 3856 book 3, 3853 book 5 & 6, and ADM 52 1248 books 2, 3, & 4. The vessel's master kept a log as well as the commander. Some of these books are "duplicate" copies, one recording events day by day, another hour by hour.

45. Stout, *Royal Navy*, 86.

46. Stout, *Royal Navy*, 63.

47. Stout, *Royal Navy*, 92-93.

48. Thomas Allen, *Proceedings of His Majesty's Armed Schooner Gaspee*, National Archives (PRO) UK, ADM 51 3853 book 5.

49. The *Gaspee* went into His Majesty's Careening Yard in Halifax with some damage to her gripe and false keel on September 19, 1767. This damage was the result of running aground in Rhode Island. It may have been on this visit that the *Gaspee* was refitted as a schooner. The Oxford English Dictionary defines gripe, "*Naut. pl.* Lashings formed by an assemblage of ropes, etc., to secure a boat in its place on the deck; also, two broad bands passed respectively round the stem and stern of a boat hung in davits, to prevent swinging." In 1762 Falconer *Shipwr.* II. 102, "The boats are with fastening gripes secured." Romney in Halifax Harbor September 19, 1767 National Archives (PRO), UK, ADM 106 1153 281.

50. Hood to Admiralty December 20, 1767 National Archives (PRO), UK, ADM 1 483. Log of *Gaspee* ADM 51/3853.

51. William Dudingston, *A Journal of the Proceedings of His Majesty's Armed Schooner Gaspee*, National Archives (PRO) UK, ADM 51 4197 books 1–3. The Admiralty records catalog Dudingston's log up until April 1772, as well as the

vessel's muster, when presumably the May and early June papers were stolen, destroyed, or both by the *Gaspee* raiders.

52. Very little biographical or genealogical information is available about William Dudingston. I am indebted to Dr. John Concannon and Holly MacKenzie for the essay posted in the *Gaspee* "Virtual Archives" on the internet for what sparse material is available on Dudingston.

53. When Scharf mentioned "in Graydon and other journal-keepers of the day" he probably referred to the "supercilious behavior" of Royal officials toward the colonials before the war. Graydon's memoirs mentioned the behavior of British army and sea Officers, but did not seem to specifically mention the *Gaspee*. Graydon only mentioned one sea officer before the war, a man named "Wallace, a commander of a ship on the American station" who was noted for his brutality and insolence. Alexander Graydon, *Memoirs of a Life* (Harrisburg: Printed by John Wyeth, 1811), 65. Graydon is most likely referring to Captain James Wallace of the sloop-of-war *Tryal*. Davis Bevan of Chester County sued Dudingston in civil court.

54. James Dundas, Master & Pilot, *Logg Book of the Proceedings of His Majesty's Schooner Gaspee Lieu: William Dudingston Commander*. April 17, 1770, to April 16, 1771, ADM 52 1248 book 11 and book 12 larger copy of same.

55. *Newport Mercury*, July 17, 1769.

56. James B. Hedges, *The Browns of Providence Plantations Colonial Years*, 43-46.

57. Lovejoy, *Rhode Island Politics*, 158.

58. Walter A. Edwards, Papers Relating to the *Gaspee*, Rhode Island Historical Society, MSS 434.

59. Rufus Greene, Jr. was commander of the *Fortune*. He could not recall the exact date in February before the commissioners. Staples, *Documentary History*, 67.

60. Nathaniel Greene Jr. was a deputy from Coventry starting in May of 1772 and continuing for several years after. He is not to be confused with Nathanael Greene Jr. who was a Quaker preacher. He had eight sons and Nathanael (the third in the family with that name) was later the second in command under General Washington during the Revolution. Ephraim Bowen assured George Washington Greene, despite rumors to the contrary, that this the more famous Nathanael Greene was not present among the *Gaspee* raiders. George Washington Greene, *The Life of Nathanael Greene: Major-General in the Army of the Revolution*, 42 footnote 1. Bartlett recorded twenty-four men named Greene just in the volume that covered 1770-1776. Bartlett, *Records of the Colony of Rhode Island*, 44. The large number of people named Greene was cited by the commissioners as a reason why they could not summon anyone without knowing the first name. See also footnote 25 of Clifford P. Monahon and Clarkson A. Collins, 3rd, eds., "Nathanael Greene's Letters to 'Friend Sammy' Ward," *Rhode Island History* XVI 3 (July 1957): 85. Greene had plenty of alibis for that

night. He condemned the attitude of the Rhode Island General Assembly for not fervently resisting the Commission of Inquiry.

61. Samuel W. Bryant, "Rhode Island Justice—1772 Vintage," *Rhode Island History* 26 3 (July 1967): 66.

62. One cannot tell from the source whether the musket contained a ball or was being used merely as an audible warning device.

63. Lieutenant Dudingston to His Majesty's Customs at Boston, February 22, 1772, National Archives (PRO), UK, T 491 125.

64. This was not the same *Beaver* that was later involved in the Tea Party. Captain Hezekiah Coffin was the commander of the civilian brig, *Beaver*, carrying 112 chests of tea, that arrived on December 7, 1773, in Boston. L.F.S. Upton, "Proceedings of Ye Body Respecting the Tea," *William and Mary Quarterly* 22 2 (April 1965): 494 footnote 14.

65. Edwards, Papers Relating to the *Gaspee*, MSS 434. Of course, the *Beaver* and the *Gaspee* visited Rhode Island before it was assigned as their main station and primary cruising grounds. Montagu sent Hillsborough a clipping from the *Newport Mercury* called "Americans, take care of your property" which criticized the schooners in Narragansett Bay that were seizing their property. This clipping was from February 24, 1772. Unfortunately, February and March 1772 issues of the *Newport Mercury* have been lost and are not available to researchers. It was unusual that the Commodore of the North American fleet would write directly to the Secretary of State for the American Department. Rear Admiral John Montagu to Earl of Hillsborough. September 1, 1772, Boston. National Archives (PRO) UK, CO 5 761 fos. 189-197d.

66. The famous *Fortune* seizure was referred to commonly as "Jacob Greene's rum." But the suit was filed by Jacob Greene of Warwick, Nathaniel Greene of Coventry, William Greene, Elihu Greene, Christopher Greene, and Perry Greene of Warwick. They were all merchants in the company. Bryant, "Rhode Island Justice," 65.

67. Province of the Massachusetts Bay Court of Vice-Admiralty at Boston; Before the Honorable Robert Auchmuty Esq Judge Deputy Surrogate of Commissary of said court. National Archives (PRO), T 1 491 127–128.

68. Earlier in his career Sessions sailed the Caribbean for the Brown family business.

69. Governor Wanton had been the customs collector in Newport himself earlier in his career and had been attacked by a mob. Neil L. York, "The Uses of Law in the *Gaspee* Affair," *Rhode Island History*, 4. Charles Dudley reported that Wanton collected a mere 500 in the twenty-six years he held the post while he himself collected 16,000 in only five years in Newport's Custom House. Charles Dudley to Frederick Smyth, Rhode Island June 12, 1773, found in its entirety in Larry R. Gerlach, "Charles Dudley and the Customs Quandary in Pre-Revolutionary Rhode Island," *Rhode Island History*, 59.

70. Sixteen months later Sessions tried to recall from memory the names of the people who signed the complaint in a deposition before Governor Joseph Wan-

ton. Not having the document in front of him, he remembered John Brown, Nathan Angell, Joseph Nightingale, Job Smith, Ambrose Page, Darius Sessions, James Lovett, Nicholas Brown, and Thomas Greene. Bartlett, *The Destruction of the* Gaspee, 123. Influential men like these would have easy access to the governor and deputy governor in this small, face-to-face world. Gordon Wood, *The Radicalism of the American Revolution*, 61.

71. Wanton later admitted that only a customs house officer had to swear an oath, but anyone who used the force of arms in the colony needed to show a commission to the governor. Otherwise it was trespassing or even piracy. Staples, *Documentary History*, 94.

72. The *Liberty* was a confiscated vessel used by the Customs Service. It was burned by a mob in Newport in July 1769.

73. Staples, *Documentary History*, 5. See also Governor Joseph Wanton to Commanding Officer of Schooner near Brenton's Point. Newport, March 22, 1772. National Archives (PRO) UK, CO 5 1284 fo. 170.

74. The Chief Justice [Stephen Hopkins] gave the opinion to Darius Sessions that "any authority by force of arms or otherwise, without showing his commission to the Governor, and (if a custom house officer) without being sworn into his office, was guilty of a trespass, if not piracy." Staples, *Documentary History*, 94.

75. Commander William Dudingston to Rear Admiral John Montagu, *Gaspee*, Rhode Island. March 24, 1772, National Archives (PRO), UK, T 1 494 152-153. See also CO 5 119 fo. 218.

76. Rear Admiral John Montagu to Governor Joseph Wanton April 8, 1772, Boston. National Archives (PRO), T 1 491 141. See also T 1 494 148-149 and CO 5 1284 fo. 170.

77. Dickerson, *The Navigation Acts*, 179-80.

78. Rear Admiral John Montagu to Governor Joseph Wanton April 8, 1772, Boston. National Archives (PRO), T 1 491 142. See also CO 5 1284 fo. 173.

79. Letter from Admiral Montagu to Philip Stephens. Boston, April 18, 1772. National Archives (PRO) UK, ADM 1 484. See also CO 5 119 fo. 216. Montagu did not have the entire story correct here but was aware of the *St. John* incident.

80. Governor Joseph Wanton to Rear Admiral John Montagu May 8, 1772, Rhode Island. National Archives (PRO), T 1 494 150-151. See also CO 5 1284 fo. 175.

81. Adams, *The Works of John Adams* Vol. II, 306.

82. Admiral John Montagu was the cousin of the better known John Montagu, Fourth Earl of Sandwich. N.A.M. Rodger, *The Insatiable Earl: A Life of John Montagu, Fourth Earl of Sandwich 1718-1792*, 419. Writing from the perspective of a very accomplished British Naval historian, Rodger is able to offer American historians a very European perspective on the American War, its politics, and John Wilkes in chapters XIII and XIV.

83. Edwards, Papers Relating to the *Gaspee*, MSS 434.

84. Peter May testified before the commissioners against someone named Greene, but the commissioners found that there were too many people by that name in the colony to proceed without a first name. Staples, *Documentary History*, 95. Dudingston admitted to Montagu that he was aware of the statute indicating that the rum should be tried in Rhode Island. Apparently he heard back from the Customs Board of Commissioners in Boston (from his February 22 query) and could not count on their support. But local customs officials assured him that they could not safeguard the rum. May 22, 1772, Schooner *Gaspee*, Rhode Island. Lieutenant Dudingston to Admiral Montagu. Bartlett, *Records*, Vol. VII, 64-65. Therefore, if Providence merchants knew that Dudingston did not have the legal or political support for his actions; this might have emboldened them to seek a warrant and confront him. But alas, he had Montagu's unwavering support.

85. Staples, *Documentary History*, 10.

CHAPTER TWO: THE *GASPEE* INCIDENT

1. Apparently the raiders thought that they did. Local pilots were disliked by merchants as much, if not more, than the commanders of customs vessels. Dickinson told Montagu during his questions that "*Answer*—Yes; one of the people took me by the collar, and said, 'Damn you, where is your Pilot Doget.'[sic] I answered he was discharged six weeks ago. He answered, 'Damn your blood, you lie;' and said they would find him, and [illegible] him alive." Mr. Dagget, who had been on the *Beaver* the previous six months, unwisely went ashore to a sheep shearing a few days after the burning of the *Gaspee* and was sheared himself by a mob. *Providence Gazette*, June 13, 1772.

2. Commander John Linzee, *A Journal of the Proceedings of His Majesty's Sloop Beaver Commencing the 29 day of June 1771 & Ending the 28 day of October 1772*, National Archives (PRO) UK, ADM 52 1166.

3. Staples claimed that Bowen confused two packet masters named Lindsey. Benjamin, not Thomas, was on the *Hannah*.

4. Staples, *Documentary History*, 13.

5. Broad Street Pay Office Book for the *Gaspee*, National Archives (PRO) UK, ADM 33 645. Two hundred and thirty officers and crew served on board the *Gaspee* during its eight years of service. There were twenty-seven men for whom nothing was written in the paybooks about their discharge or desertion. It can be assumed that those men were aboard (or should have been aboard) on June 9, 1772. Indeed, this assumption bears true for those known to be on board at the time. The paybook for the *Gaspee* was closed on October 14, 1772, the date of Lieutenant Dudingston's court martial.

6. Lieut. General Thomas Gage heard that the *Gaspee* struck a rock while pursuing a smuggling vessel. Lieut. General Thomas Gage to Lord Barrington (Secretary at War) Cavendish Square 1 July 1772. Carter, *Correspondence of Thomas Gage* Vol. II, 611.

7. Court Martial of Lieutenant Dudingston. October 14, 1772. National Archives (PRO), ADM 1 5305.

8. Not to be confused with the Moses Brown (born January 23, 1742, Salisbury, MA) who went on to become a captain in the U.S. Navy. Edgar Stanton Maclay, *Moses Brown Captain U.S.N.*

9. Moses Brown's papers, *Diary Journal of voyage to Philadelphia, 1760*, Rhode Island Historical Society MSS, Series II: Subject Files, Box 3, folder 62.

10. In a letter to his brother, pre-medical student Solomon Drowne reported that, "I was on the wharf when the boats were manned and armed, and know the principal actors." Solomon Drowne to William Drowne June 23, 1772 Providence. Seebert J. Goldowsky, M.D., "Solomon Drowne and The *Gaspee* Affair: A Premedical Student Views Historic Event." *Rhode Island Medical Journal 55* 9, 287.

11. Whipple was commander of the privateer *Game Cock* during the Seven Years' War. Whipple later was listed among John Adams's roster of persons suitable for naval commands and achieved the rank of commodore.

12. Deputy Governor Darius Sessions testified under oath before the commission that he heard about a dozen 10-14 year old boys playing with a drum in the street opposite his house. He heard no other disturbance that night. Staples, *Documentary History*, 57. Daniel Hitchcock, John Cole, and George Brown testified (in writing) likewise, p. 71-72. Cole indicated that he could not believe that they were designed for mischief because they were so public.

13. Unsigned Letter from Newport, RI, June 16, 1772, National Archives (PRO), UK CO 5145 fo 131. Also Darius Session recalled in January of 1773 that some of the crew of the *Gaspee* reported to him back in June that some of the raiders were ". . . blackened or negroes, but it was so dark we could not tell which." Staples, *Documentary History*, 80. Sessions used this information to indicate that it would be difficult, if not impossible, to positively identify Biggs, a black indentured servant who testified against several prominent Rhode Island merchants. A ballad about the *Gaspee* raid indicated that the men dressed up like Narragansett Indians, 109. Staples himself believed that they "assumed no disguise of any kind," 108. See also William R. Staples, *Rhode Island in the Continental Congress*, 7. John Allen, in his dedication to Lord Dartmouth stated, "the *Gaspee* Schooner is destroyed . . . by Indians out of the woods, or by Rhode-Islanders, I cannot say who . . ." *Oration*, x.

14. Dr. John Concannon calculated the tides, sun, and moon for Providence on June 9-10, 1772. See the *Gaspee* "Virtual Archives" on the internet. He concluded that Bowen's report of 3:00 PM for the time of the *Gaspee*'s grounding is not consistent with the tide ebbing for two hours. Darius Sessions recalled in January of 1773 interviews he had with *Gaspee* crew members back in June; they confirmed that the moon had set. Staples, *Documentary History*, 80.

15. Reports indicated one, three, or six deck sentinels on duty that night. Cheevers claimed that he was alone on deck in his examination before the commissioners. Staples, *Documentary History*, 88.

16. Helen Hill Miller incorrectly identified Whipple as the sheriff of Kent County. Helen Hill Miller, *The Case for Liberty*, 169. The sheriff was Mr. Henry

124 Notes to Pages 17–18

Rice. John Russell Bartlett, *Records of the Colony of Rhode Island and Providence Plantations in New England* Vol. VII 1770-1776, 45.

17. John Brown was the sheriff of Bristol County. Although in Kent County, the *Gaspee* was aground very close to the Bristol/Kent County line. If Brown had a warrant, he could have made a legal argument for his actions but instead opted for silence. Brown and/or Greene might have known that Dudingston lacked support from the Boston Customs Commissioners and was himself aware that he was violating a statute in the *Fortune* case. This may have been the correspondence that they were looking for in his cabin before the *Gaspee* burned.

18. Lieutenant Dudingston to Admiral Montagu June 12, 1772. Pawtuxet, RI. T 1 494 136–137. Dudingston told his version of the events. See also ADM 1 484 115-116 and CO 5761 fo. 152.

19. Dickinson told this to Massachusetts governor Thomas Hutchinson and Admiral Montagu in Boston. An unsigned and unaddressed letter from Newport June 16, 1772, suggested that Dudingston fired first. National Archives (PRO) CO 5 145 fo 131.

20. Biggs claimed that John Brown shot Dudingston. Staples, *Documentary History*, 65. The colonists lived in a personal, face-to-face world where individuals were held personally and morally responsible. Even though Dudingston was acting on orders that were part of larger Imperial reforms, he was singled out for retaliation. Gordon Wood would not be surprised by this, it fit into the larger world of conspiracy and the paranoid style. "If a merchant's cargo was seized for violating the navigation acts, then a particular and well-known official could be singled out." Wood, *The Radicalism of the American Revolution*, 61.

21. This fits with Aaron Biggs's account that there were 17 longboats. Later historians who believed Biggs's testimony explained the higher number by arguing that some could have been held in reserve to gauge the resistance provided by the *Gaspee*'s guns and crew. Dudingston, in his petition to the King, claimed that there were seventeen armed longboats with about 200 men. Navy pension: petition of Capt William Dudingston, late commander of the *Gaspee* schooner, concerning dangerous wounds he received on the coast of Rhode Island, America and asking for relief from the King. December 17, 1772, referred to the Admiralty. National Archives (PRO), PC 1 15 93. William Checkley, the collector of customs in Providence believed that it was only six or seven boats. Letter to the collector of the Port of Rhode Island from William Checkley, June 11, 1772, Providence. T 1 491, 131-132.

22. Or Daggert or Doget. *Gaspee* sources never gave his first name but he is believed to be Sylvanus. Charles Edward Banks, *The History of Martha's Vineyard, Dukes County, Massachusetts* Vol. III, 131.

23. Deposition of William Dickinson before Governor Thomas Hutchinson and Admiral John Montagu, taken under oath June 12, 1772, National Archives (PRO), UK, ADM 1484 pages 107-110. See also T 1 494 154-156 and CO 5 761 fo. 112. The Admiralty forwarded this testimony to Hillsborough on July 15. CO 5 119 fos. 253-260d.

24. Staples, *Documentary History*, 76. Historians who believed Biggs's testimony argued that Biggs took the hanger (sword). Staples related this story "Mr. John Howland says, that on the morning after the affair, Justin Jacobs, a young man, was parading himself on 'the great bridge,' then the usual place of resort, with Lieutenant Dudingston's gold laced beaver on his head, detailing to a circle around him the particulars of the transaction, and the manner in which he obtained the hat from the cabin of the *Gaspee*. It required sharp words to induce him to retire and hold his peace. There were others, probably, equally indiscreet; and yet not an individual could be found who knew anything about the affair," 108. Dudingston submitted a receipt for the loss of his personal possessions totaling £363. A breakdown can be seen at: Account of the effects and cash cost or burnt on board HMS *Gaspee* belonging to Lieutenant William Dudingston. National Archives (PRO), T 1 496 167. £363 still would not cover Jacob Greene's losses; but perhaps Dudingston's personal items would have sold for more than their market value.

25. They did not report seeing a vessel heading to Bristol.

26. The raiders could have claimed that the fire started by accident while they were searching for documents. Or Providence's elite could have claimed that they lost control of the mob and shifted the blame to a few less well-connected members of the raiding party. But instead they opted for group cohesion and silence.

27. Lieutenant William Dudingston to Rear Admiral John Montagu June 12, Pawtuxet, National Archives (PRO) UK, CO 5 761 fo 152. Montagu forwarded this letter to Prime Minister Frederick Lord North on June 18, 1772. T 494 138-139. Also on June 18, Montagu forwarded two letters to the Earl of Hillsborough; Dudingston's letter and Checkley's June 12 letter to the commissioners of customs at Boston. See also CO 5 761fos. 150-155d.

28. Aaron Biggs testified the following January that one of the men in the boats was shot in the thigh. Staples, *Documentary History*, 65.

29. Court Martial of William Dudingston, October 14, 1772, testimony of Captain John Linzee, National Archives (PRO), UK, ADM 1 5305. Dudingston credited Linzee with rescuing him twice from his enemies. London, December 1, 1772. T 1 495 274-275.

30. Dexter, *Literary Diary*, 242. Samuel Hopkins, pastor of the First Congregational Church in Newport, early anti-slavery advocate, and founder of the hyper-Calvinistic school of "The New Divinity" failed to mention the *Gaspee* in his 236 page autobiography. Stephen West, *Sketches of the Life of the Late Rev. Samuel Hopkins, D.D., written by himself.* Hopkins (Congregational) in 1776 and John Allen (Baptist) in1773 were among the first non-Quaker voices against chattel slavery in British Colonial America.

31. John Rowe was unique among Boston's merchant elites; he supplied the British military forces, was a Patriot, and a smuggler. See Tyler, *Smugglers & Patriots*, 16.

32. Anne Rowe Cunningham, *Letters and Diary of John Rowe, Boston Merchant*, 229. Rowe entertained Montagu and Linzee on more than one occasion.

Linzee married the daughter of another Boston merchant, Ralph Inman. The newlyweds took Dudingston to England on the *Beaver* to stand his court-martial. Montagu claimed that he did not have enough vessels to convene a court-martial in Boston.

33. Rhode Island had its own Vice-Admiralty Court, where merchants had picked a sympathetic Judge Andrews to preside. This made the sending of seizures to Boston more maddening to Rhode Island's merchants. Ubbelohde, *The Vice-Admiralty Courts*, 30.

34. Staples, *Documentary History*, 90.

35. Staples, *Documentary History*, 90. Following the Boston Tea Party, Parliament did not elect to punish a few ringleaders but rather closed the entire Port and relocated the customs house.

36. The commissioners' final report indicated that they did not reach Pawtuxet until June 11.

37. Acts and Resolves of the Colony of Rhode Island, August, 1772. Rhode Island State Archives. Daniel Vaughan was not considered a great friend of the navy or the customs service. He fired upon HMS *St. John* from Fort George in 1764. To his credit, though, he merely shot through the mainsail and did not sink the vessel. He was later reprimanded for not following orders to sink the vessel.

38. William Checkley never gave his title in his *Gaspee*-related correspondence. Stiles, *Literary Diary* Vol. I, p. 58 footnote 1.

39. William Checkley to Commissioners of His Majesty's Customs June 12, 1772, Providence, National Archives (PRO), UK CO 5 761 fo 154. See also T 1 494 134 and ADM 1 484 121. On June 18, Montagu forwarded this letter to the Earl of Hillsborough. CO 5 761 fos. 150-155d.

40. Rear Admiral John Montagu to Philip Stephens June 12, 1772, National Archives (PRO), UK CO 5 119 fo 255. Montagu is referring to the fact that he sent a letter also to Wanton with Dickinson's testimony. See also Montagu's letter to Lord North. Rear Admiral Montagu to Lord North June 12, 1772, Boston in New England. T 1 494 154.156. Montagu's letter was forwarded by the Admiralty to Hillsborough on July 15. CO 5119 fos. 253-260d.

41. The Admiralty paid Dudingston five shillings a day in addition to his half-pay. The expenses of his cure were covered as if he had been wounded in combat. Dudingston recovered in a French spa and returned to duty off of the New England coast. James Munro, *Acts of the Privy Council of England* Vol. V, 358.

42. Governor Thomas Hutchinson to Earl of Hillsborough June 12, 1772, National Archives (PRO), UK, CO 5 761 fo 108.

43. Staples, *Documentary History*, 21. See also Proclamation by Governor Wanton, June12, 1772, Newport. National Archives (PRO) UK, CO 5 1284 fos. 183-186d.

44. In defending himself against Montagu's accusations, Wanton wrote to Hillsborough that back in March he could not be certain about the legitimacy of the

Gaspee or Dudingston's commissions. Governor Joseph Wanton to Earl of Hillsborough. Newport, RI, 20 May 1772. National Archives (PRO) UK, CO 5 1284 fo. 170.

45. Bartlett, *Records* VII, 81.

46. Governor Joseph Wanton to Earl of Hillsborough June 16, 1772, Newport, RI. National Archives (PRO) UK, CO 5 1284 fo 183.

47. Little Compton, RI, birth records do not have an Aaron Biggs or Briggs. Stiles believed that he was born to an Indian mother there. Contemporary newspapers usually referred to him as "Aaron the mulatto," and did not provide a last name. See *Providence Gazette*, January 30, 1773, 3. When John Carter reprinted a brief history of the *Gaspee* affair from the *Providence Gazette*, "PROVIDENTIA" referred to him as a "mulatto" and a "servant." *Newport Mercury*, January 18, 1773, 2. Because Staples and Bartlett (Bartlett was largely derivative of Staples) both spelled his name as Briggs, most secondary literature refers to him as such. Aaron's name was spelled Biggs on the warrant for his arrest. Rhode Island State Archives C# 00554 number 29. Biggs was illiterate, he signed the original deposition with an X. Regardless, that document would be considered the most reliable, since it was drafted in his presence. It repeatedly spelled his name Biggs. The Colonial Office, Admiralty, and Treasury documents (some of which are derivative of each other) copied and preserved the name as Biggs.

48. Admiral Montagu to Governor Wanton July 8, 1772, Boston. Staples, *Documentary History*, 30.

49. Simeon Potter's case was a classic example of Rhode Island justice falling prey to factional politics. A Ward court found him guilty of assaulting an Anglican priest. A newly elected Hopkins court voided his conviction, sentence, and even the records of the court. Lovejoy, *Rhode Island Politics*, 96. A colonel in the militia, Simeon Potter was later appointed major general of the colony by the general assembly in 1774. He was responsible for all of the men under arms, 173.

50. See also Charles Dudley's letter to Lord North July 11, 1772. National Archives (PRO), T 1 491 137-139.

51. Daniel Vaughan testified that Biggs knew nothing about the *Gaspee* until Captain Linzee ordered him tied to the mast to be whipped (for running away from his master). Staples, *Documentary History*, p. 79. The commissioners believed that Captain Linzee may have threatened to hang him at the yard arm. P. 94. Biggs later confessed to an officer of a man-of-war in Newport that his testimony was fabricated. It was given under duress. Daniel Horsmanden to Earl of Dartmouth July 23, 1773, New York, National Archives (PRO), UK, CO 5 1104 fo 378-379.

52. Admiral Montagu to Lord North, September 1, 1772. Boston in New England. National Archives (PRO), T 1 491 pp. 143-144. See also CO 5 761 fo. 189. "It is a measure of the crisis that, as well as reporting to the Admiralty, Montagu corresponded on the subject of the *Gaspee* directly with the Secretary of State, something the commodore of the North American station did not usu-

ally do." K. G. Davies, *Documents of the American Revolution 1770-1783* (Colonial Office Series) Vol. V, 7.

53. Montagu moved the *Swan* and the *Mercury* to Rhode Island after the attack. Linzee had moved Biggs to the *Swan* and had his shackles removed.

54. Affidavit of Aaron Biggs to Charles Bardin, National Archives (PRO), UK, CO 5 761 fo 191. See also T 1 491 143–148.

55. Biggs claimed that there were several vessels on the island. He knew of one of his master's boats that wouldn't sail, but he took a "little fishing boat of two oars." Examination of Aaron Biggs, January 14, 1773, Council Chamber, Newport, National Archives (PRO) UK, CO 5 1285 fo 242.

56. Apparently Biggs was coached by *Gaspee* seafarers. They may have made up the part about Potter and a vessel from Bristol, as the other accounts made no mention of it. Captain William Thayer did hear rumors about Potter. Deposition of Captain William Thayer, of Mendon. Bartlett, *Destruction of the Gaspee*, 95. Simeon Potter was a well-know privateer and he owned a ropewalk in Bristol, and was for some reason the target of this testimony. Admiral Montagu described Potter as "the most infamous character possible to describe and is guilty of almost every vice a pirate can be guilty of." Admiral Montagu to Lord North July 11, 1772. National Archives (PRO), T 1 494 pp. 146 -147. See also CO 5 761 fo. 164. See also Admiral Montagu to Philip Stephens July 11, 1772, ADM 1 484 124 -125. For a kinder treatment of Potter's character see William Harold Munro, *Tales of an Old Sea Port*, Part I. Chapter 1 is devoted to Potter, 37–47. Samuel Faulkner, one of Thompkin's laborers, testified before the commissioners that Aaron "was looked upon by the people where he worked as a person much addicted to lying."Staples, *Documentary History*, 93. Potter may have been known by the mariners because he was a sea captain and militia colonel. Horsmanden thought that Dr. Weeks may have been Biggs's master's family physician. Chief Justice Horsmanden to Earl of Dartmouth July 23, 1773, New York. National Archives (PRO), CO 5 1104 fo. 378.

57. Earle appears in the sources sometimes as Earns or Earls. W.E. May, "The *Gaspee* Affair," *The Mariner's Mirror* 63 2, 132, 134.

58. Deposition of Patrick Earle before Charles Bardin, Justice of the Peace, July 16, 1772, Newport, RI, National Archives (PRO), UK, ADM 1 484 141. See also T 1 491 143–148 and CO 5 761 fos. 189-197d.

59. Ultimately, Linzee was arrested under charges from Biggs's master, and Montagu posted his bail and defense at the Crown's expense. Rear-Admiral John Montagu to Philip Stephens September 2, 1772, Boston, National Archives (PRO), UK, CO 5 119 fo 356.

60. (Lat.) Within the body of the county. The common-law courts have jurisdiction *infra corpus comitatus*: the admiralty, on the contrary, has no such jurisdiction, unless, indeed, the tide-water may extend within such county. 5 How. 441, 451. William Edward Baldwin, D.C.L. *Bouviers Law Dictionary*, 547. The location of the attack was important to distinguish between piracy on the high seas and treason within the colony.

61. Governor Wanton to Admiral Montagu July 22, 1772, Newport, RI. Staples, *Documentary History*, 35.

62. Charles Dudley to Rear-Admiral John Montagu July 23, 1772. National Archives (PRO), UK, CO 5 761 fo 195. See also T 1 491 138-139.

63. Frank J. Hinkhouse, *The Preliminaries of the American Revolution as Seen in the English Press 1873-1775*, 159.

64. Hinkhouse, *Preliminaries*, 80.

65. Rear Admiral John Montagu to Philip Stephens June 12, 1772. Boston. National Archives (PRO) UK. CO 5 119 fo. 255. Montagu sent his dispatches with Captain Squire of the *Bonetta*. Governor Hutchinson's letter may have actually arrived first at the Admiralty. K. G. Davies, *Documents of the American Revolution 1770-1783* (Colonial Office Series) Vol. V, 6. Governor Thomas Hutchinson to Earl of Hillsborough June 12, 1772. Boston. National Archives (PRO) UK. CO 5 761 fo. 108.

66. David S. Lovejoy, "Henry Marchant and the Mistress of the World," *William and Mary Quarterly* 12 3, 395-397. The news appeared in London newspapers two days later. Governor Wanton had not given up on getting money from the Treasury for expenses from the late war. See Gertrude Selmyn Kimball, *The Correspondence of the Colonial Governors of Rhode Island 1723-1775*, Vol. II, 431. See also Governor Joseph Wanton to Earl of Dartmouth February 16, 1773. Newport, RI. National Archives (PRO) UK, CO 51285 fos. 164-179d.

67. Earl of Hillsborough to Attorney-and Solicitor-General, August 7, 1772, Whitehall. National Archives (PRO) UK. CO 5 159 fos. 22-25d. Their original report, Edward Thurlow and Alexander Wedderburn to the Earl of Hillsborough August 10, 1772, Lincoln's Inn, was "mislaid." *The Manuscripts of the Earl of Dartmouth* Vol. II American Papers (London: Eyre and Spottiswoode, 1895), 87. John Pownall indicated that the Attorney General considered this business "five times the magnitude of the Stamp Act." John Pownall to Lord Dartmouth August 29, 1772, *The Manuscripts of the Earl of Dartmouth* Vol. II American Papers (London: Eyre and Spottiswoode, 1895), 91. A copy of the August 10, 1772, letter has since been found. As Pownall indicated, it dismissed the Dockyard Act and allowed for high treason with a trial in Rhode Island or England. CO 5 159 fo. 26.

68. Nathanael Greene was troubled by the practice of eliciting testimony with a promise of so much reward. He feared that it preyed upon the weak to perjure themselves and corrupted the virtue of the nation. Clifford P. Monahon and Clarkson A. Collins, eds., "Nathanael Greene's Letters to 'Friend Sammy' Ward," *Rhode Island History* XVI 3, 85.

69. The Dockyards etc. Protection Act of 1772 Anno duodecimo George III Chapter 24 was passed on April 15, 1772, but the colonists had not heard of it prior to the burning of the *Gaspee*. The act allowed for capital punishment, without benefit of clergy, for arson in His Majesty's dockyards and surrounding buildings. Offenders could be tried in the realm where the act was committed or in London. Sir James Fitzjames Stephen, K.C.S.I., D.C.I., A Judge of the High

Court of Justice, Queen's Bench Division, was unable to identify what (if any) particular occasion prompted the act. *A History of the Criminal Law of England* Vol. II, 293. Thomas Hutchinson thought that it was prompted by a fire in the King's storehouses in Portsmouth. Thomas Hutchinson, *The History of the Colony and Province of Massachusetts-Bay* Vol. III, 262. The Dockyard Act was not repealed until the Criminal Damage Act of 1971, ss 11 (2), (8), 12 (6), Schedule, Pt III. Samuel Adams, Ezra Stiles, and the Rhode Island newspapers clearly thought that this Act was going to be used in the *Gaspee* case. Adams understood that the Act (and the rehabilitation of the Henry VIII treason statute) was a reaction against the 1769 Resolves. He noted that the North American colonies had not even been contemplated in the 1540s. Cushing, *The Writings of Samuel Adams* Vol II, 367.

70. The first person to be tried under the Dockyard Act was James Hill (Hinde) or James Actzen or Aitken (known by the name John the Painter) on March 6: 17 George III A.D.1777. A full trial transcript taken in shorthand by Joseph Gurney is available in the library at Lincoln's Inn. For a biography see Jessica Warner, *John the Painter: Terrorist of the American Revolution.*

71. Upon closer examination of the issues involved, Hillsborough's August 7 packet had to be recalled and cancelled. Earl of Hillsborough to Lords of Admiralty, August 7, 1772, Whitehall. National Archives (PRO) UK, CO 5 250 pp. 45-47. See Lieut. General Thomas Gage to Earl of Dartmouth January 6, 1773, New York. National Archives (PRO)CO 5 90. Also see cabinet minutes on recall from August 20, 1772, in *The Manuscripts of the Earl of Dartmouth* Vol. II American Papers, 88.

72. Hillsborough came up against powerful investors when he opposed a new western colony, Vandalia. The investors were unable to defeat Lord North; consequently, Hillsborough took the political fall. Hillsborough announced his resignation on August 1 but did not actually leave until August 14. Lord Dartmouth enthusiastically endorsed the Vandalia claims on August 14. Lord Frederick North and William Legge (the second Earl of Dartmouth) were stepbrothers. Ray Allen Billington, *Westward Expansion: A History of the American Frontier,* 151.

73. Barrow, *Trade and Empire*, 226.

74. While Dartmouth personally opposed bringing colonists to London for trial; he could not resign over this issue after so recently taking the position in his stepbrother's government. It would have publicly embarrassed Lord North. Dartmouth had to remain silent on this important issue. Dartmouth's letter to Wanton was, "worded with Caution and Ambiguity on that Head." Dexter, *Literary Diary* Vol. I, 350.

75. Orders of the King in Council, August 26, 1772, St. James's. National Archives (PRO) UK. CO 5 1278 fo. 114. The very next day Dartmouth found out about Aaron Biggs (and his naming of "principal" persons) from the Admiralty. Lords of the Admiralty to Earl of Dartmouth, August 27, 1772, Admiralty. CO 5 119 fos. 309-314d.

76. Earl of Hillsborough to Lieut. General Thomas Gage August 7, 1772, White-hall. Clarence Edwin Carter, *The Correspondence of General Thomas Gage* Vol. II, 146. See also Lieut. General Thomas Gage to Earl of Hillsborough October 7, 1772, New York. National Archives (PRO), CO 5 90 fo. 77. Gage indicated that, against the advice of Governor Hutchinson, he did not believe that they needed to increase lookouts for vessels around Castle-William above their current levels.

77. Earl of Dartmouth to Lieut. General Thomas Gage September 4, 1772, Whitehall. Carter, *Correspondence of Gage* Vol. II, p. 149. See also National Archives (PRO) UK, CO 5 90 fos. 51-52d.

78. Commission of Inquiry into Burning of *Gaspee*, September 2, 1772. Westminster. National Archives (PRO) UK. CO 5 204 p. 3.

79. Lord Dartmouth to the Governor of Rhode Island September 4, 1772, Whitehall, National Archives (PRO), UK, CO 5 1284 fo 187-194. Undersecretary John Pownall actually wrote this letter on Dartmouth's behalf. Franklin B. Wickwire, *British Subministers and Colonial America, 1763-1783*, 143. As the September 4 packet was about to be sent, Pownall expressed concern over how the *Gaspee* affair had already been misrepresented in newspapers. John Pownall to Lord Dartmouth, 9:30 PM September 6,1772, *The Manuscripts of the Earl of Dartmouth* Vol. II American Papers, 95. Edmund Burke warned the New York Committee of Correspondence about the reliability of debates printed in the newspapers. "On mentioning this Debate, I take the Liberty of cautioning you against giving Credit to the Speeches printed in the News papers. They are rarely genuine; they are for the most part extremely misrepresented, often through Ignorance, often through design; and very frequently the whole is a mere matter of invention." May 4, 1774, to the Committee of Correspondence of the General Assembly of New York. Lucy S. Sutherland, ed. *The Correspondence of Edmund Burke,* Vol II, 532.

80. Governor Hutchinson to Secretary Pownall, Boston, August 29, 1772, Bartlett, *Records*, 102.

81. The Newport pastor Ezra Stiles, commented that "No one justifies the burning of the *Gaspee*. But no one ever thought of such a Thing as being Treason." Ezra Stiles to the Reverend Elihu Spencer, at Trenton, New Jersey, Newport, February 16, 1773, Franklin Bowditch Dexter, *The Literary Diary of Ezra Stiles* Vol I, 349.

82. Rear Admiral Montagu to Philip Stephens, National Archives (PRO), UK, ADM 1 484, 135-137.

83. Earl of Dartmouth to Lords of Admiralty September 5, 1772, Whitehall, National Archives (PRO), UK, CO 5 119 fo 328-329.

84. Stout, *Royal Navy*, 131.

85. Staples, *Documentary History*, 96.

CHAPTER THREE: THREE THOUSAND MILES TO BE HANGED

1. Boston January 2, 1773, to Darius Sessions [MS., Samuel Adams Papers, Lenox Library], Cushing, *Writings of Samuel Adams* Vol. II, 400.

2. I first heard this figure from a less-bookish source; a PBS special titled "Rebels and Redcoats (How Britain Lost America)" narrated and presented by British historian Richard Holmes. This program seemed to rely heavily upon the work of Christopher Hibbert. "After all, it was their homelands which were to be protected, and their taxes were so relatively slight that it was calculated that an American paid no more than sixpence [£0.025] a year against the average English taxpayer's twenty-five shillings [£1.25]." This figure is actually fifty times greater. Christopher Hibbert, *Redcoats and Rebels: The American Revolution Through British Eyes*, xviii.

3. A "sea officer" was a commissioned officer serving on a vessel. A "naval officer" was a civilian nominated by and subordinate to the governor and was charged with keeping detailed records of every vessel that entered a given jurisdiction. He was to report this information back to England. Much of this was a duplication of the efforts of the customs officers; ideally serving as a check on each other's work. Rhode Island had been disputing with the London government since 1743 over whether this office was appointed by their popularly elected governor or by the Crown. July 19, 1771, Whitehall, Earl of Hillsborough to Attorney and Solicitor-General. National Archives (PRO) UK, CO 51284 fo. 135.

4. Hedges, *Browns*, 49.

5. "The first of the excerpts from Blackstone were gruesomely apropos for the perpetrators of the *Gaspee* incident because it described in detail the punishment inflicted on those convicted of high treason. It told how the offender was drawn to the gallows, hanged by the neck, cut down and while still alive, had his entrails removed and burnt, and finally how his head was cut off and his body divided into four parts to be thereafter at the disposal of the king." William R. Leslie, "The *Gaspee* Affair: A Study of Its Constitutional Significance," *The Mississippi Valley Historical Review* 39 2, 249.

6. *The Public Advertiser* September 11, 1773. Found in William B. Willcox, ed. *The Papers of Benjamin Franklin*, Vol. 20, 397.

7. Historian William Leslie noted that "Pownall had been directed to 'attend the Attorney & Solicitor General & to communicate to them such Papers as he apprehends may be useful for their Information upon the Occasion.' They consist of a ten-page report entitled 'State of the Business of Rhode Island proposed to be considered on Thursday the 20th of August' together with twenty-six appendixes. Some of the appendixes directly support the statement in the report. Others are such 'as tend to shew the controuling power which has been exercised by the Crown in different Instances over the Charter and proprietary Governments, & the Opinions of the Law Servants of the Crown touching the Exercise of such Power; as also a precedent of the proceeding in the Privy Council in 1702, in the Case of Bayard & Hutchins tried, convicted & condemned for High Treason in the Province of New York.'" Leslie, "The *Gaspee* Affair," 240. See "421. The Trial of Colonel Nicholas Bayard, in the Province of New-York, for High-Treason: 14 William III. A.D. 1702." T.B. Howell, *A Complete Collection of State Trials and Proceeding for High Treason and other Crimes and Misde-*

meanors from the Earliest Period to the Present Time Vol. XIV, 472-516. Colonel Bayard and Alderman Hutchins were charged with gathering signatures at a coffee house on three addresses; one to the King, one to Parliament, and one to Lord Cornbury. These addresses were found to be "scandalous libel" and therefore disturbing the peace and harmful to peoples' views of the government.

8. DeVaro, *Impact of the* Gaspee, 160.

9. Court of oyer and terminer is defined as a commission empowering a judge in Great Britain to hear and rule on a criminal case at the assizes. Pownall did cite a case of establishing a court of oyer and terminer in Labrador at a time when there was no local judicial system.

10. Since at least the 1970s historians have tried to understand the Atlantic world through a more transnational, "spheres of influence" approach. This approach downplays the "inevitability" of the American Revolution and emphasizes other cultural factors (e.g., religion) over against a monolithic nation-state. See Nicholas Canny, "Writing Atlantic History: or, Reconfiguring the History of Colonial British America," *The Journal of American History* 86 3. The Nation and Beyond: Transnational Perspectives on United States History: A Special Issue (December 1999): 1093-1114.

11. Hugh McDowall Clokie and J. William Robinson, *Royal Commissions of Inquiry: The Significance of Investigation in British Politics*, 28.

12. Harold F. Gosnell, "British Royal Commissions of Inquiry," *Political Science Quarterly* 49 1, 88. Horsmanden was still seeking reimbursement for his expenses one year later. Chief Justice Daniel Horsmanden to Earl of Dartmouth, December 10, 1773, New York. National Archives (PRO) UK, CO 5 1105 fos. 72-75d.

13. W. Harrison Moore, "Executive Commissions of Inquiry," *Columbia Law Review* 13 6, 502.

14. Clokie and Robinson, *Royal Commissions*, 50.

15. When Virginia's backcountry planters met resistance from Native Americans over their expansionist European agricultural practices; western planters called for a policy of armed expansion. Mercantile interests in the eastern part of Virginia resisted the aggressive anti-Indian policy while the planters grew impatient. Led by a wealthy western planter, Nathaniel Bacon, settlers began indiscriminately murdering Indians on the frontier. Virginia deteriorated into a civil war with the "General of Virginia," Bacon, leading one faction, and Governor Berkley trying to hold on to the loyal government from the eastern shores of the Chesapeake. By the time the Privy Council was able to respond, the situation had largely resolved itself.

16. Wilcomb E. Washburn, *The Governor and the Rebel: A History of Bacon's Rebellion in Virginia*, 95.

17. Were he alive, Bacon could have been tried in Virginia or in England.

18. Washburn, *Governor and the Rebel*, 130.

19. Warren M. Billings, "Berkeley, Sir William (1605-1677)." In *Oxford Dictionary of National Biography*, article 2225.

20. Washburn, *Governor and the Rebel*, 135. For a more sanguine view of the commissioners (and conversely, a more jaded Berkeley) see Stephen Saunders Webb, *1676: The End of American Independence*, esp. pp. 100-137.

21. Parke's grandson, Daniel Parke Custis, was Martha Washington's first husband.

22. Sir Allan Burns, *History of the British West Indies*, 424.

23. June 9, 1710, St. Jago de la Vega in Jamaica, 262. Cecil Headlam, *Calendar of State Papers, Colonial Series, America and West Indies, 1710-June, 1711*, 113.

24. Headlam, *State Papers 1710–June, 1711*, 441-457. See also *Acts of the Privy Council of England Colonial Series Vol. II AD 1680–1720* Appendix 1, 797.

25. Headlam, *State Papers July, 1711–June, 1712*, 78.

26. Morris Schonbach, *Radicals and Visionaries: A History of Dissent in New Jersey*, 17.

27. Donald L. Kemmerer, *Path to Freedom: The Struggle for Self-Government in Colonial New Jersey 1703–1776*, 200.

28. After the burning of the *Gaspee*, New York chief justice and *Gaspee* commissioner Daniel Horsmanden proposed uniting anarchic Rhode Island and Connecticut under one Royal governor. More than one Patriot feared troops being sent into Rhode Island from New York. Critics of Rhode Island's government accused it of being too responsive to the people as well. For an excellent discussion on the fears that undiscriminating "democracy" could overthrow the balance of the constitution, see Bernard Bailyn, *The Origins of American Politics*, 152-158.

29. Kemmerer, *Path to Freedom*, 223.

30. Kemmerer, *Path to Freedom*, 236.

31. An indentured servant, Aaron Biggs testified before the *Gaspee* commissioners about Captain Linzee, "the captain saying he did not want to know any thing about the poor people, but only the heads." The *Gaspee* commissioners were charged with finding the "Head Sheriff" and the "Captain" and they were empowered to pardon anyone else who offered information, excepting only the man who shot Dudingston.

32. Douglas Hay discussed the increasing number of capital and property crimes in the latter half of the eighteenth century in Britain and the simultaneous increase in pardons. See his essay in *Albion's Fatal Tree: Crime and Society in Eighteenth-Century England*, esp. 20-23. Additionally, there is the practical matter of trying to punish the many; it is easier to punish a few leaders. The Royal Navy expended enormous resources when they ended "the golden age" of piracy earlier in the eighteenth century.

33. Jeanne G. Bloom, *Sir Edmund Andros: A Study in Seventeenth-Century Colonial Administration*, 146.

34. Dudingston was treated gently by the Admiralty for the loss of His Majesty's Schooner *Gaspee*. It did not hurt his career as he soon returned to service in North America and retired as a Rear Admiral many years later.

35. Trading with the enemy was a sore point between Whitehall and Rhode Island's government. Rhode Island still had not been reimbursed (in 1772) by the Treasury for expenses it incurred during the Seven Years' War. Many in England believed that Rhode Island's merchants traded with French Islands during that war with connivance of the civil magistrates of the colony. This was the context in which the Privy Council considered the charge of treason for the *Gaspee* raiders.

36. May 15, 1712, Governor Lord A. Hamilton, Jamaica, to the Council of Trade and Plantations, 423 Headlam, *State Papers July, 1711–June, 1712*, 287.

37. The location of the attack was important. If they were "within the body of the colony" it was treason. If they were on the high seas, it was piracy.

38. For a discussion of the debates surrounding transporting colonials to England for treason trials, see Richard M. Deasy's introduction to Staples, *Documentary History,*1990 reprint, especially xlii to liv. Resolutions passed December 15, 1768 (House of Lords) and February 8, 1769 (House of Commons) allowed the Treason Statute from the reign of Henry VIII (to have the trial within this Realm) to be used in the North American colonies. Found in *Journals of the House of Lords, beginning anno undecimo Georgii Tertii*, 1769. Vol. XXXII. Vol. 32. [London], [1796?]. 33 vols. Eighteenth Century Collections Online. Gale Group. 210. Rhode Island's Assembly responded on October 25, 1769, upholding the right to a trial in the vicinage.

39. Member of Parliament Edmund Burke was the London agent for the Provincial Assembly of New York from 1771-1776. In a private letter to John Cruger, Speaker of the Assembly of New York, April 16, 1773, Burke condemned the use of 35 Henry VIII ch. 2 in the *Gaspee* case. Lucy S. Sutherland, *The Correspondence of Edmund Burke* Vol II, 430. Burke wrote to the New York Committee of Correspondence at least nineteen times while their agent.

40. Paul Langford, *The Writings and Speeches of Edmund Burke* Vol. II, 331.

41. James Willard Hurst, *The Law of Treason in the United States: Collected Essays*, 15.

42. J.G. Bellamy, *The Law of Treason in England in the Later Middle Ages*, 16. Sir Edward Coke, in the third part of his Institutes noted that 25 Edward III covered "To violate, or carnally to know the king's consort or queen, the king's eldest daughter unmarried, or prince's wife."

43. John Bellamy, *The Tudor Law of Treason: An Introduction*, 133.

44. Bradley Chapin, *The American Law of Treason: Revolutionary and Early National Origins*, 13. These two changes to the statute under Henry VIII had significant implications for the *Gaspee* raiders. Ironically, contrary to the claims of Samuel Adams and John Allen, these were upheld in Rhode Island's earliest charter; although suspects were to be found guilty by the General Assembly before being sent to the King's Bench. See Proceedings of the First General Assembly of "The Incorporation of Providence Plantations," and THE CODE OF LAWS adopted by that Assembly in 1647. Found in John D. Cushing, ed., *The Earliest Acts and Laws of the Colony of Rhode Island and Providence Plantations 1647–1719*, 16.

45. John Brown was one of the founders of the *Providence Gazette* in 1762. Helen Hill Miller, *The Case for Liberty*, 168.

46. Leslie, "*Gaspee* Affair," 246.

47. Early American Imprints, 1st series, no 11512 Virginia Resolves, May 16, 1769.

48. George Louis Beer, *The Old Colonial System*, 244.

49. *Providence Gazette*, December 19, 1772, and January 9, 1773; *Newport Mercury*, December 21, 1772, and January 18, 1773.

50. Leslie, "Gaspee *Affair*," 248.

51. Richard Henry Lee and Samuel Adams are on Pauline Maier's "short list" of seven key radicals who emerged during the Stamp Act crisis and remained strong throughout the war. Maier, *From Resistance to* Revolution, xiii.

52. James Curtis Ballagh, *The Letters of Richard Henry Lee* Vol. 1, 82.

53. Many historians have considered the time following the Boston Massacre to represent a "lull" in Patriot activity. John Miller claimed "So well did North succeed that, for over two years, the colonies were not so much as mentioned in parliamentary debates." John C. Miller, *Origins of the American Revolution*, 325. Samuel Adams wrote of the *Gaspee* commission that, "It should awaken the American Colonies, which have been too long dozing upon the Brink of Ruin." December 28, 1772, Boston, Samuel Adams to Darius Sessions. Cushing, *The Writings of Samuel Adams* Vol II, 391-392. Mercy Otis Warren skipped from 1770 to 1773 in her *History of the Rise, Progress and Termination of the American Revolution*. Prior to the Boston Tea Party, the *Gaspee* was virtually the only other event since the Townshend Act crisis of 1767–70 to receive public commentary and report in British newspapers. Benjamin Woods Labaree, *The Boston Tea Party*, 190.

54. Paul Leicester Ford, *The Works of Thomas Jefferson* Vol. 1, 9-10.

55. Barrow, *Trade and Empire*, 87.

56. Barrow, *Trade and Empire*, 87.

57. Barrow, *Trade and Empire*, 90.

58. Being a tidewaiter was dangerous work, and according to a former English tidewaiter, it did not pay an adequate wage to a family man. See Thomas Stayley, *The Statue of Truth in the Garden of Allegory. Addressed to Lord North containing such Remarks as may not be unworthy his Lordship's Notice. Useful to the Manager of his Majesty's Revenues, &c. &c. &c.* (London: Printed for the Author, 1773), 10. This one shilling, 42-page pamphlet is available through Goldsmiths' Kress library of economic literature, S1, reel 173, no. 11048. Stayley wrote it to defend himself against, he claimed, false charges of impropriety.

59. Barrows, *Trade and Empire*, 93. The *Liberty* was a customs yacht, a civilian vessel serving under the Treasury Department. The *Gaspee* was merely a schooner; a man-of-war is significantly larger and has much greater fire power than a schooner. But, significantly, they both have a military commission and serve in the Royal Navy under the Admiralty.

60. Barrow, *Trade and Empire*, 95.

61. Lovejoy, *Rhode Island Politics*, 35.

62. The Morgans devoted a sympathetic twelve-page chapter to Robinson in Edmund S. Morgan and Helen M. Morgan, *The Stamp Act Crisis: Prologue to Revolution*, 40-52.

63. Stout, *Royal Navy*, 66.

64. While geographically in northern New Jersey, Sandy Hook is the landmark spit of land that marks the entrance to New York harbor.

65. Stout, *Royal Navy*, 72.

66. Jesse Lemisch, *Jack Tar vs. John Bull: The Role of New York's Seamen in Precipitating the Revolution*, 27. "Collective amnesia" was also a problem in Rhode Island following the burning of the *Gaspee*.

67. Stout, *Royal Navy*, 48–49.

68. John Robinson was greatly disliked by Patriots. He attacked James Otis in a Boston coffee house in 1770, giving him head wounds from which he never fully recovered. O.M. Dickerson, "The Commissioners of Customs and the 'Boston Massacre,'" *The New England Quarterly* 27 3, 309.

69. On board the *Cygnet*, Newport Harbor, August 30, 1765, The Collector, &., of the Customs, in Newport, to the Governor and Company of Rhode Island. Robinson and his staff took refuge on a naval vessel and closed the port until Rhode Island officials could restore order. Bartlett, *Records* Vol. VI, 453.

70. A Vice-Admiralty Judge is supposed to represent the interests of the Admiralty and the Crown. Andrews, it seemed, more often than not represented the interests of Rhode Island's merchants. "In Rhode Island the Vice-Admiralty Court was established under the colonial government, the power of appointment resided here, and the local judge was sworn to his office by the governor." Richard M. Deasy, Introduction to Staples's *Documentary History* reprint in 1990, xiv. Because of their unique politics, Rhode Island merchants were successful in manipulating their Vice-Admiralty Court where other colonies failed. See Ubbelohde, *The Vice-Admiralty Courts*, 32-33.

71. Lovejoy, *Rhode Island Politics*, 46.

72. Even if these events had happened in Newport instead of Massachusetts, Rhode Island did not yet have its own Vice-Admiralty Court and its cases were heard in Massachusetts.

73. Fort George was on Goat Island in Newport.

74. Capt. Charles Leslie to the Governor of Rhode Island Dated on board the *Cygnet*, Rhode Island harbor, Sunday, Sep'r 1st, 1765 to Samuel Ward, Esq. Leslie cited the St. John incident from the previous year as evidence that his fears were not unfounded. Ward dismissed these rumors as "idle" and "chimerical." Wanton dismissed Dudingston's fears in a similar manner. Bartlett, *Records* VI, 456.

75. Stout, *The Royal Navy*, 69-70. See also Ubbelohde, *The Vice-Admiralty Courts*, 67-69; Barrow, *Trade and Empire*, 192.

76. The *Newport Mercury* claimed that five hundred people participated in the riot.

77. The Governor of Rhode Island to Capt. Charles Antrobus, Newport July 12, 1765. Bartlett, *Records*, 447. Again this seems consistent with the desire to prosecute "ringleaders." There was little interest in the "others."

78. Lovejoy, *Rhode Island Politics*, 38.

79. Early American Newspapers, *Newport Mercury* June 10, 1765, page 3 column 1.

80. Barrow, *Trade and Empire*, 205. This helps to explain why men who admitted to being in Sabin's Tavern on the evening of June 9, 1772, spent so much of their testimony explaining why they did not think that the audible drumming in the streets of Providence was significant. Apparently this was a means of gathering resistance. For further discussion on the "hue and cry," *posse commitatus*, and the local militia see Maier, *From Resistance to Revolution*, Ch. 1 section II.

81. R.S. Longley, "Mob Activities in Revolutionary Massachusetts," *New England Quarterly* 6 1, 120.

82. Pauline Maier, "Popular Uprisings and Civil Authority in Eighteenth-Century America," *William and Mary Quarterly* 27 1, 10.

83. Considerable debate surrounds the testimony of tidewaiter Thomas Kirk. We may never know exactly what was on board the *Liberty*. See Barrow, *Trade and Empire*, 231.

84. See the section titled, "Boston Adopts Unilateral Nonimportation August 1768–March 1769," in Tyler, *Smugglers & Patriots*, 114-115.

85. For a detailed description of the *Liberty* riot, see chapters 9 & 10 John Phillip Reid, *In a Rebellious Spirit: The Argument of Facts, The Liberty Riot, and the Coming of the American Revolution*, 86-99.

86. Ubbelohde, *Vice-Admiralty*, 126-127. Hancock was not charged based upon Kirk's testimony of what may or may not have been aboard *Liberty*. He was charged with a rarely enforced statute that required a permit before loading a vessel. See Barrow, *Trade and Empire*, 232. John Adams used the opportunity of this painfully long trial to get his Whiggish views heralded up and down the seaboard.

87. Dudley was an Englishman, he replaced John Robinson back in 1768. This attack started on board the *Polly*. Dudley complained that he received no aid from the navy. He doubted that he would survive this attack. He claimed that he was not attacked by the "lowest class of men, it came from men who are styled merchants and the masters of their vessels." April 11, 1771, Newport, RI. Charles Dudley to Commissioners of Customs at Boston. National Archives (PRO) UK, CO 5 72 fo. 283.

88. Franklin Bowditch Dexter, *The Literary Diary of Ezra Stiles* Vol. 1, 270-271. This is a fantastic claim but difficult to verify either through customs records or vessel logs.

89. It is not the intent of this study to provide an exhaustive list of colonial resistance; but merely to itemize those events that would have been known to well-informed people living in the maritime regions of Rhode Island in 1772.

90. In addition to those killed in March, eleven-year-old Christopher Snider was killed two weeks prior. From the sixteenth to the eighteenth century, a "massacre" could refer to the murder of an individual if done in a cruel or atrocious manner.

91. Maier, *From Resistance to Revolution*, 6.

92. Maier, *From Resistance to Revolution*, 12.

93. Maier, *From Resistance to Revolution*, 26.

94. Lovejoy, *Rhode Island Politics*, 39.

95. Maier, *From Resistance to Revolution*, 125.

CHAPTER FOUR: STAR CHAMBER

1. The Rhode Island General Assembly annually elected the five judges of the Superior Court of Judicature, Court of Assize and General Gaol Delivery. Court appointments were not immune to the politics of the colony. The governor also nominated the colony's naval officer, frequently a merchant, creating a potential conflict of interest. A former merchant was less likely to zealously enforce customs regulations on his neighbors and former business associates. William Wanton became naval officer upon his father's election as governor in 1769. Lovejoy, *Rhode Island*, 22, 94.

2. For an excellent treatment of the Ward/Hopkins political factions see Lovejoy, *Rhode Island Politics*, esp. the introduction.

3. Chief Justice Daniel Horsmanden to the Earl of Dartmouth, New York, February 20, 1773, Staples, *Documentary History*, 120. Horsmanden reiterated this theme again in December, complaining that judicial inquiries are ineffectual and the need for a royal colony to replace the anarchy. Chief Justice Daniel Horsmanden to Earl of Dartmouth, December 10, 1773, New York. National Archives (PRO), CO 5 1105 fos 72-75d. Sheriffs, justices of the peace, judges and clerks were elected by the Assembly. The system was driven by factional concerns and low pay invited bribery and corruption. See Lovejoy, *Rhode Island Politics*, 22, 94-95.

4. Unsigned and unaddressed letter from June 16, 1772, Newport, RI, National Archives (PRO) CO 5 145 fo. 131.

5. Samuel Adams used the phrase "court of inquisition" to invoke revulsion at Spanish and Portuguese heresy trials. He used these phrases in the *Providence Gazette* Saturday, December 26, 1772, writing under the name "Americanus." He mentioned the "star chamber" to remind his readers of the English equivalent of a court of inquisition. Star Chamber trials in the fifteenth through seventeenth centuries took place in secret because they examined issues of national security. Adams explained in a letter to Darius Sessions why the Star Chamber was inconsistent with justice and had to be removed from the British judiciary system. Darius Sessions from Samuel Adams December 28, 1772, Boston (MS., Samuel Adams Papers, Lenox Library) found in Cushing, *Writings of Samuel Adams* Vol. II, 391. The phrase "court of inquisition" also appeared in a letter to Richard Henry Lee. Cushing, *Writings* Vol. III, 27. John Adams used the same

language in his diary, "The high Commission Court, the Star Chamber Court, the Court of Inquisition. . ." December 29, 1772, L. H. Butterfield, *The Adams Papers: Diary and Autobiography of John Adams* Vol. II, 73.

6. National Archives (PRO) CO 5 1278 fo. 114.

7. "You will not be alarmed when I tell you that they have determined to vacate the charter of that colony." December 26, 1772, *Providence Gazette*. "It is surmised, that they are going to deprive you of your charter." Extract of a letter from a gentleman in Boston, to his friend, in this town, dated December 14, 1772. Bartlett, *Destruction of the* Gaspee, 62.

8. Rear-Admiral John Montagu to Philip Stephens, Boston September 2, 1772. National Archives (PRO), CO 5 119 fo. 356.

9. Bartlett, *Destruction of the* Gaspee, 61.

10. Court of oyer and terminer is defined as a commission empowering a judge in Great Britain to hear and rule on a criminal case at the assizes. The assizes were one of the periodic court sessions formerly held in each of the counties of England and Wales for the trial of civil or criminal cases.

11. Dexter, *Literary Diary of Ezra Stiles*, 346. Dexter italicized parts of Stiles's diary. How Stiles might have emphasized points in his original writing is unclear. See page 2.

12. Earl of Dartmouth the Governor Joseph Wanton September 4, 1772, Whitehall National Archives (PRO) CO 5 1284 fo. 187.

13. Montagu explained to the Admiralty the difficulty of holding the inquiry in winter weather. The *Captain*, his flagship would be laid up for the entire winter. He also inquired about purchasing a vessel to replace the *Gaspee*. Admiral Montagu to Philip Stephens December 16, 1772, Boston. National Archives (PRO), ADM 1 484 187-189. Apparently Captain Howe, of the sloop-of-war *Cruizer*, left England in early September, encountered bad weather and landed in South Carolina on November 10. He did not arrive in New York until December 10 and the documents were rushed to Boston from there. *Providence Gazette*, December 19, 1772, 3.

14. Governor William Franklin to Earl of Dartmouth January 4, 1773, Burlington. Apparently Franklin did not get Dartmouth's letter of August 4 until December 22. Smythe set out for Rhode Island almost right away. National Archives (PRO), CO 5 992 fos.3-4d.

15. December 21, 1772, Boston, Robert Auchmuty to Earl of Dartmouth endorsed January 30, 1773, National Archives (PRO) CO 5 762 fos. 22-23d. December 29, 1772, Middleborough Chief Justice Peter Oliver to Earl of Dartmouth endorsed February 23,1773, National Archives (PRO), CO 762 fos. 41-42d.

16. William V. Wells, *The Life and Public Services of Samuel Adams*, 14.

17. Cushing, *Samuel Adams* Vol. II, 389, 392.

18. At one point Wanton claimed that the letter was addressed to the "Governor and Company of Rhode Island"—but could not later find the cover. Another

time he claimed that Rhode Island law required that he share official correspondence with Assemblymen. Lastly, in a letter to Dartmouth he claimed that he showed his charge only to other commissioners. Regardless, the other commissioners and Dartmouth believed that it represented a breach of trust and demonstrated Wanton's lack of discretion.

19. Chief Justice Horsmanden to the Earl of Dartmouth February 20, 1773, New York, Bartlett, *Destruction of the* Gaspee, 130–131.

20. After that outburst, John Adams reprimanded himself for his boyish rashness and failure to govern his tongue. Butterfield, *The Adams Papers*, 76.

21. Chief Justice Horsmanden to Earl of Dartmouth January 5, 1773, Newport, RI. National Archives (PRO), CO 5 1139 5-6. See also Governor Thomas Hutchinson to Earl of Dartmouth, December 30, 1772, Boston. CO 5 762 fos. 29-36d and Governor William Tryon to Earl of Dartmouth, December 30, 1772, New York, CO 5 1104 fos. 36-37d. Governor William Franklin to Earl of Dartmouth, January 4, 1773, Burlington. CO 5 992fos. 3-4d.

22. We know that in between the two letters Samuel Adams consulted "gentlemen of North America." Samuel Adams may not have wanted to mention their names in a letter. We know that some *Gaspee* correspondence arrived already opened. But John Adams did not have to be so careful in his diary. On the evening of December 30, 1772, Samuel Adams entertained John Adams, Cushing, Hancock, Phillips, Hawley, Elbridge Gerry, Hutchinson, Sewall, Quincy, &c. &c. and they had "much Conversation about the State of Affairs." Butterfield, *The Adams Papers*, 74.

23. Cushing, *Samuel Adams* Vol. II, 396.

24. Adams's response should be read in the context of the concurrent formation of the Boston committee of correspondence and the Massachusetts controversy over the Civil List. Cushing, *Samuel Adams* Vol. II, 398.

25. Although this seems hard to believe, Rhode Island justice James Helme admitted to the commissioners that when he called the Grand Jury of the Superior Court of Judicature together the previous October, he completely forgot about the *Gaspee* and sent the jurors home. Staples, *Documentary History*, 91.

26. Wells, *Samuel Adams*, 17. Cushing shows this letter not being written until sometime in February 1773, after the commissioners had adjourned until May. His advice would have been coming a little late. Cushing, *Samuel Adams* Vol. II, 427.

27. Bartlett, *Destruction of the* Gaspee, 67.

28. Dexter, *Literary Diary* Vol. I, 346.

29. The commissioners and Montagu went back and forth (five letters between January 2 and 14) on the topic of his personal presence in Newport. See National Archives (PRO) UK, CO 5 1285 fos. 141-159d. A letter to Governor Wanton seemed to indicate that the duties could be delegated, but the instructions to the commissioners indicated that his personal presence was required. In March the Admiralty sent a letter to Montagu stating that they agreed that a "senior cap-

tain" could certainly tend to the commissioners' needs. March 26, 1773, the Lords of the Admiralty to Admiral Montagu. Bartlett, *Destruction of the* Gaspee, 112-113. In April clarification was sent to the commissioners from London that persons arrested could be delivered to the commander-in-chief of British ships in North America or to commanders of British ships in Rhode Island. April 5, 1773, St. James, CO 5 1301, 470-471.

30. March and April (Rhode Island's mud season) are actually more difficult months for overland travel. In January the ground is frozen and Providence and Boston were not considered difficult journeys from Newport.

31. Bartlett, *Destruction of the* Gaspee, 69. See also Commissioners of Inquiry to Admiral Montagu. January 5, 1773. Newport, RI. National Archives (PRO) UK, CO 5 1285 fos.141-159d.

32. James Brenton had defended Dudingston the previous July. James Clarke was Rhode Island's naval officer.

33. Session was elected deputy governor by freemen and Hopkins was appointed chief justice by the general assembly.

34. They were, of course, referring to the three gentlemen from Rhode Island sitting in the room. The governor, the deputy governor, and the chief justice would have to concur with their findings and issue the writs for any arrests. Dexter, *Literary Diary* Vol. I, 346. Stiles indicated that this was less formal conversation, some of which did not take place in Colony House. Bartlett recorded the appearance of Sessions and Hopkins before the commissioners on January 7 and indicated that the commissioners asked them to write out their testimony under oath. Sessions's written deposition was accepted on January 9.

35. Lieut. General Thomas Gage to Lord Barrington [private] January 6, 1773, New York. Carter, *Correspondence of Thomas Gage* Vol. II, 631.

36. Lieut. General Thomas Gage to Lord Barrington February 3, 1773, New York. Carter, *Correspondence of Thomas Gage* Vol. II, 635.

37. *Gaspee* correspondence uses the titles the Earl of Dartmouth and Lord Dartmouth interchangeably.

38. Governor Thomas Hutchinson to Earl of Dartmouth January 7, 1773, Boston. National Archives (PRO), CO 5 762 fo. 37.

39. Richard D. Brown, *Revolutionary Politics in Massachusetts: The Boston Committee of Correspondence and the Towns, 1772-1774*, 86.

40. Governor Hutchinson to John Pownall [private] January 7, 1773, Boston. National Archives (PRO), CO 5 246, 55.

41. Brown, *Revolutionary Politics*, 90-91.

42. For an excellent treatment of the January 6, 1773, speech and it aftermath, see Bernard Bailyn, *The Ordeal of Thomas Hutchinson*, 205–220.

43. Bartlett, *Destruction of the* Gaspee, 73.

44. Metcalfe Bowler wrote to the commissioners on January 11, 1773 indicating that he would assist them. Staples, *Documentary History*, 59.

45. Linzee was visiting Dudingston, who was moved to this farmhouse for his own safety and recovery from his wounds.

46. Bartlett, *Destruction of the* Gaspee, 75.

47. Admiral Montagu to Commissioners of Inquiry January 8, 1773, Boston. National Archives (PRO) UK, CO 5 1285 fos. 141-159d.

48. Montagu told the Admiralty of this slight. Rear-Admiral John Montagu to Philip Stephens January 19, 1773, Rhode Island Harbour. National Archives (PRO), CO 5 119 fo. 382. See also ADM 1 484 196-199. The Lords of the Admiralty told the Earl of Dartmouth of this slight on March 1, 1773, National Archives (PRO), CO 5 247, 117–121. Dartmouth told Wanton that, "the King, who is justly incensed at such an Indignity, . . ." desired that the Admiral's flag "be saluted in such manner as is usual in all other Parts of His Majesty's Dominions in America." Lord Dartmouth to the governor and company of Rhode Island, Whitehall, March 3, 1773. Gertrude Selmyn Kimball, *The Correspondence of the Colonial Governors of Rhode Island 1723-1775* Vol. II, 430.Wanton replied that the failure to salute was a cost-saving measure adopted many years earlier. He expected that the Assembly would now order the usual salute. Governor Joseph Wanton to Earl of Dartmouth July 1, 1773, Rhode Island. CO 5 1285 fos. 196–197d.

49. Lieutenant General Thomas Gage believed that the assembly had met in secret and prepared a "Spirited Answer to Lord Dartmouth's Letter, which was agreed to be suspended . . ." until they could see the outcome of the proceedings. He believed that the civil magistrates of the colony were under orders to not obey the commission. Carter, *The Correspondence of Thomas Gage* Vol. II, 634.

50. George Washington Greene, *The Life of Nathanael Greene: Major-General in the Army of the Revolution* Vol. 1, 43.

51. Apparently the Rhode Island supreme court had become highly partisan with the Sons of Liberty attaining a majority among the justices in 1770. Chief Justice Stephen Hopkins "had several years past publicly declared the King and Parliament had no more right to pass any Acts of Parliament to govern us than the Mohawks." July 22, 1771, Newport, Rhode Island. John, Thomas and Samuel Freebody to Earl of Hillsborough. National Archives (PRO) UK, CO 5 1284 fo. 150.

52. Dexter, *Literary Diary* Vol. I, 349.

53. When he turned informer, he joined the British navy.

54. Bartlett, *Destruction of the* Gaspee, 82.

55. It is unclear from his testimony if they believed that these were really Narragansett Indians or colonists dressed as Indians. "Then Aylesbury told him he would not get to Newport, as there were a number of Indians with brass pistols in the road, who would take care of him; but this deponent in fact sayeth that he did not know, neither has he any reason to believe, there were any Indians in the road leading to Newport, and the deponent supposed that Aylesbury told this story to Gulley with no other design but to frighten him. After Aylesbury left the room Gulley asked the deponent what he should do; and as he recollected

Aylesbury was in liquor, and did not know but there might be some disturbance between him and Gulley, he, the deponent, told Gulley there was a lower road that he might go in, by which he might avoid that which Aylesbury had told him the Indians were in, and if he would pay his reckoning he would go and direct him to that road; on which he asked the deponent if he would not take a weapon with him; whereupon he replied that he should not take a weapon with him, as he did not believe any body would hurt him, the deponent, or the said Gulley, and then immediately proceeded to show him the road, by going with him as far as his barn, which is about twenty rods from the deponent's house, and showed him a pond near to which was a road, and directed him to take that road and steer southward till he came into the main road, which he would soon do." Staples, *Documentary History*, 62.

56. Staples, *Documentary History*, 62-63.

57. Staples (and Bartlett, who relied heavily on Staples) disagree with the copy of the letter found in the colonial office records. It showed Montagu arriving on the 13th. National Archives (PRO), CO 5 1285 fo. 141.

58. Examination of Aaron Biggs January 14, 1773, Council Chamber, Newport. National Archives (PRO), CO 5 1285 fo. 242.

59. Staples, *Documentary History*, 68.

60. East Greenwich, Rhode Island, January 14, 1773, Rufus Greene before Justice of Peace Hopkins Cooke. Staples, *Documentary History*, 67.

61. Bartlett, *Destruction of the* Gaspee, 91.

62. Saul Ramsdale was a Providence shoemaker who had recently moved from Mendon, MA. He allegedly gave *Gaspee* information to Captain William Thayer. Gulley and Ramsdale had been friends for several years. Although he might have had first-hand information, it does not appear that Ramsdale ever made it to Newport.

63. Deposition of Captain William Thayer, of Mendon by Darius Session, January 15, 1773. Staples, *Documentary History*, 78. Although Ephraim Bowen and Dr. Mawney do not mention a boat from Bristol or Simeon Potter, Biggs, Earle, Vaughan, and Thayer do. Of course, Earle would have been Biggs's coach, but Thayer had no connection with these two. Vaughan's deposition indicates the possibility of coaching, since Biggs claimed no knowledge on their first meeting but then knew names "two or three days afterwards." Deposition of Daniel Vaughan given to Darius Sessions, Providence January 16, 1773. Bartlett, *The Destruction of the* Gaspee, 97. Stiles claimed that Potter gave an alibi to Governor Wanton, a white woman (perhaps a house servant) in the family, which trumped the testimony of this black man [Biggs]. Dexter, *Literary Diary*, 350.

64. Deputy Governor Sessions to Governor Wanton, relative to Barzillai Richmond, Joseph Brown, John Brown and Daniel Vaughan. Providence January 18, 1773. Deputy Governor Sessions to Governor Wanton, relative to the Deposition of the Negro Aaron Briggs, &c. Providence January 18, 1773. Bartlett, *Destruction of the* Gaspee, 97-98.

65. Many in the *Gaspee* raiding party (whose identity we do know) were related by blood, marriage, and business ties. The Ward/Hopkins political factions did not exploit the situation; silence was near unanimous.

66. Staples, *Documentary History*, 76.

67. The Council Chamber to Admiral Montagu January 19, 1773, Colony House, Newport, RI. National Archives (PRO), ADM 1 484 200. Library of Congress archivist John C. Fitzpatrick believed that the commission "paused" to let emotions cool and to assure colonists about the benign nature of their mission. John C. Fitzpatrick, *The Spirit of the Revolution: New Light from Some of the Original Sources of American History*, 105.

68. Apparently the Admiralty thought that the inquiry was taking place in Boston. The North American Squadron and Admiral Montagu were in Boston, so it made sense to send the men through that port anyway.

69. Lords of Admiralty to Earl of Dartmouth February 16, 1773, Admiralty, National Archives (PRO), CO 5 119 fos. 372-373d.

70. Earl of Dartmouth to Lords of Admiralty February 19, 1773, Whitehall, National Archives (PRO), CO 5 119 fos. 374-375d. On March 4 the Lords of the Admiralty wrote to the Earl of Dartmouth that Dickinson and Cheevers could identify some persons and that they would sail to Boston the very next week. CO 5 119 fos. 394-395d.

71. Rear-Admiral John Montagu to Philip Stephens January 19, 1773, Rhode Island Harbour. National Archives (PRO), CO 5 119 fo. 382. See also ADM 1 484 196-199.

72. Bartlett, *Destruction of the* Gaspee, 107-110.

73. Commissioners of Inquiry to Earl of Dartmouth. January 21, 1773. Newport, Rhode Island. National Archives (PRO) UK, CO 5 1285 fo. 141.

74. Governor Wanton to the Earl of Dartmouth January 30, 1773, Rhode Island. National Archives (PRO), CO 5 1285 fos. 162-163d. Wanton also explained that they had the wrong location. The raid took place thirty miles away.

75. Clifford Monahon, *Correspondence of Governor Samuel Ward May 1775–March 1776* (Providence, RI: Rhode Island Historical Society, 1952), 22–23.

76. Chief Justice Frederick Smythe to Earl of Dartmouth, February 8, 1773, New York, National Archives (PRO), CO 5 1278 fo. 144. Dartmouth acknowledged Smyth's "very sensible remarks." Earl of Dartmouth to Chief Justice Frederick Smyth. April 10, 1773. Whitehall. CO 5 1003, 66.

77. One can assume he is referring to John Allen here.

78. Bartlett, *Destruction of the Gaspee*, 130.

79. Wanton told a different story later claiming that he only gave copies of the September 4 letter to the other commissioners. Governor Joseph Wanton to Earl of Dartmouth, July 1, 1773, Rhode Island. National Archives (PRO) UK, CO 5 1285 fos. 198-199d.

80. Chief Justice Daniel Horsmanden to Earl of Dartmouth February 20, 1773, New York, National Archives (PRO), CO 5 1104 fos. 113-118d. Dartmouth ac-

knowledged Horsmanden's "very sensible remarks." Earl of Dartmouth to Chief Justice Daniel Horsmanden, April 10, 1773. Whitehall. CO 5 1141, 241.

81. Indeed, Horsmanden cited a particularly appropriate expense: the commissioners had to pay for their own firewood in Colony House. Since Dudingston's crew allegedly stole firewood from local farmers and created a fuel shortage by his zealous enforcement of customs, Horsmanden's choice of firewood seemed especially fitting. Admiral Montagu complained to Governor Hutchinson about his un-reimbursed expenses as well. February1, 1773, Boston Governor Thomas Hutchinson to Earl of Dartmouth, National Archives (PRO), CO 5 762 fo. 47.

82. DeVaro, *Impact of the* Gaspee *Affair*, 232.

83. Bartlett, *Destruction of the* Gaspee, 132. Horsmanden tells us here that he has served on two royal commissions previously in Rhode Island.

84. Lieut. General Thomas Gage to Lord Barrington February 8, 1773, New York. Carter, *Correspondence of Thomas Gage* Vol. II, 637.

85. Staples, *Documentary History*, 124. Wickwire explained the construction of the September 4 letter in some detail. Part of the reason that its release was so controversial was that it indicated that the suspects would be tried for high treason. Franklin B.Wickwire, *British Subministers and Colonial America, 1763-1783*, 141-143.

86. Bartlett, *Destruction of the* Gaspee, 134.

87. The *Virginia Gazette* falsely reported a clash between British regulars and Rhode Islanders with fatalities on both sides. Perhaps this was why Richard Henry Lee was reluctant to rely on the "uncertain medium of newspapers." Merrill Jensen, *The Founding of a Nation: A History of the American Revolution 1763-1776*, 430. See footnote 112.

88. Earl of Dartmouth to Governor Joseph Wanton April 10, 1773, Whitehall. National Archives (PRO), CO 5 1285, fos. 184-185d. Governor Wanton expressed surprise that the September 4 letter was in the newspapers. He claimed (to Dartmouth) that he gave copies only to the commissioners themselves. Governor Wanton to Earl of Dartmouth July 1,1773, Rhode Island. National Archives (PRO), CO 5 1285 fos. 198-199d.

89. Samuel Adams first conceived of the idea of corresponding societies in every colony in a letter to Arthur Lee almost a year and a half earlier. Samuel Adams to Arthur Lee, September 27, 1771, Boston. Cushing, *Writings of Samuel Adams* Vol. II, 234.

90. Richard Henry Lee to Samuel Adams February 4, 1773, Chantilly. Ballagh, *Letters of Richard Henry Lee*, 82-83.

91. Sometimes spelled John Dickenson. His *Letters from a Pennsylvania Farmer* were widely published in newspapers in 1767 and 1768.

92. Most colonists thought that any arrested *Gaspee* raiders would be tried under the Dockyard Act. The House of Representatives of Massachusetts described it as, "a measure repugnant to justice, highly derogatory to our rights, and shakes the very foundation of our constitution . . ." House of Representa-

tives of Massachusetts to Earl of Dartmouth, March 5, 1773. Massachusetts Bay. CO 5 762 fo. 149.

93. Richard Henry Lee to John Dickinson, April 4, 1773, Chantilly in Virginia. Ballagh, *Richard Henry Lee* Vol. I, 83.

94. Indeed Secretary of War William Barrington wrote to Governor Francis Bernard saying that Boston would never be quiet "unless some legal examples be made of persons concern'd in the late violences committed there." Lord Barrington to Governor Bernard September 6, 1768, Cavendish Square. Edward Channing and Archibald Cary Coolidge, eds, *The Barrington-Bernard Correspondence and Illustrative Matter 1760-1770*, 166.

95. Ballagh, *Richard Henry Lee* Vol. I, 84.

96. Adams must be referring to the Regulator Insurrection of 1766-1771 here.

97. Cushing, *Samuel Adams* Vol. III, 26. For an excellent discussion of the Adams/Lee communications, see Brown, *Revolutionary Politics*, 122-124.

98. Cushing, *Samuel Adams*, Vol. III, 27.

99. Dudingston still had not recovered fully enough to travel. Dickinson and Cheevers had arrived in Boston on April 29. Admiral Montagu to Philip Stephens April 29, 1773, Boston. National Archives (PRO), ADM 1 484 220.

100. Admiral Montagu to the Commissioners, &c. May 24, 1773, Boston. Bartlett, *Destruction of the* Gaspee, 113.

101. His Majesty's Commissioners at Rhode-Island from J. Montagu. June 14, 1773, Boston. Staples, *Documentary History*, 86. The Lords of Admiralty had inquired of the Earl of Dartmouth if Rear Admiral Montagu's continuing presence was absolutely necessary at the Inquiry. March 18, 1773, Admiralty. National Archives (PRO) UK, CO119 fos. 400-401d. Dartmouth replied that the duties could be entrusted to a senior captain of the Royal Navy, March 20, 1773. Whitehall. CO 5 119 fos. 404-405d.

102. Staples, *Documentary History*, 85. Keeler complained about being served with four writs in one day and asked for "every support in this disagreeable service" (referring to customs service, not naval service). Captain Robert Keeler to Admiral Montagu October 2, 1772, HMS *Mercury* at Rhode Island. National Archives (PRO) ADM 1 484 159. See also same to same on October 5, 1772. ADM 1 484 166.

103. Horsmanden was 76 years old, could not walk without assistance, and brought his wife, a carriage and two horses with him. We know this because he was still seeking a £200 reimbursement for his expenses in 1777 that he asked Dartmouth for in 1773. Chief Justice Daniel Horsmanden to Governor Tryon April 19, 1777, New York. Staples, *Documentary History*, 127.

104. Commissioner and Chief Justice Horsmanden wanted those summoned to see each other face to face.

105. Dr. John Concannon lists all of the probable/possible raiders presently known on the Internet at "*Gaspee* Virtual Archives." Concannon gives sources and comments on the strength of the evidence.

106. Chief Justice Horsmanden to the Earl of Dartmouth, New York, February 20, 1773. John Russell Bartlett, *Records of the Colony of Rhode Island and Providence Plantations in New England* Vol. VII 1770-1776, 183.

107. *Providence Gazette*, July 3, 1773, in *Early American Newspapers*, 3.

108. Actually, lawsuits to protect one's good name were not uncommon in a society based upon face-to-face contact and patronage. Wood, *The Radicalism of the American Revolution*, 60.

109. *Providence Gazette*, July 3, 1773, in *Early American Newspapers*, 3.

110. Staples, *Documentary History*, 94.

111. Staples, *Documentary History*, 95.

112. Staples, *Documentary History*, 95.

113. Dexter, *Literary Diary*, 383.

114. Dexter, *Literary Diary*, 382-385.

115. Quincy met with Lord North for about two hours on November 19, 1774. Quincy, *Memoir of the Life of Josiah Quincy*, 200. See also *Massachusetts Historical Society Proceedings October, 1916–June, 1917* Vol. L, 440. MHS published *to try* and *no power to try* in italics.

116. Personal and family ties and patronage were strong among Rhode Island's merchants and civil magistrates. Governor Joseph Wanton's son was Deputy Governor in 1764 when Daniel Vaughan fired upon the *St. John*.

117. Staples, *Documentary History*, 96.

118. Official business required Oliver to leave early. Chief Justice Peter Oliver to Earl of Dartmouth, July 20, 1773, Middleborough. National Archives (PRO) UK, CO 5 762 fos. 384-385d. Larry R. Gerlach discovered a previously unknown letter at the American Philosophical Society Library in Philadelphia from Customs Collector Charles Dudley to Frederick Smythe on June 12, 1773. This letter seemed to be the impetus for bringing up the matter of the *Liberty* and the *St. John* so late in the proceedings of the commission. Gerlach received permission to print the letter in its entirety in Larry R. Gerlach, "Charles Dudley and the Customs Quandary in Pre-Revolutionary Rhode Island," *Rhode Island History* (Spring 1971): 55-59. Lawrence DeVaro suggested that there might have been two meetings between Dudley and Smythe, where a second (more recent) meeting emphasized the *St. John*. DeVaro, *Gaspee Affair*, 280, footnote 73.

119. Whitehall received the report on August 17, 1773. Earl of Dartmouth to Commissioners of Inquiry at Rhode Island acknowledging letter of June 22 and report. National Archives (PRO), CO 5 1285 fos. 200-201d.

120. Royal Commissions were also used to recommend legislation. The commissioners did not recommend any changes to the current system of customs or collection of revenue from the colonies.

121. Staples, *Documentary History*, 107. See also Commissioners of Inquiry to Earl of Dartmouth (and to the King), June 22, 1773, Newport, Rhode Island. CO 5 1285 fos.186-195d.

122. Daniel Horsmanden to Earl of Dartmouth, July 23, 1773, New York. National Archives (PRO) CO 1104 fos. 378-379d. Biggs was detained on the *Swan*, Captain James Ayscough, commander.

123. Biggs, in his testimony before the commissioners, remembered the *Gaspee* mariner who recognized him that day by the name of Paddy Alis.

124. Chief Justice Daniel Horsmanden to Earl of Dartmouth July 23, 1773, New York. National Archives (PRO), CO 5 1104 fo 378.

125. Dartmouth was not satisfied with the final report to the King. He wanted to examine the evidence for himself and requested it in August. Lord Dartmouth to the Commissioners of Inquiry in Rhode Island, Whitehall, August 17, 1773. National Archives (PRO) 5 1285 fo 401-404. Perhaps this made Wanton nervous that Whitehall might draw its own conclusions from the evidence. He did not send it along until the following April after which it would certainly be overshadowed by events in Boston. Joseph Wanton to Lord Dartmouth, Rhode Island, April 15, 1774. National Archives (PRO), CO 5 1285 fo 433-436. Wanton sent copies, the originals remain in Rhode Island. See Deasy's introduction in Staples, *Documentary History*, xxxvi. The commissioners' papers were catalogued by Dudley. Chief Justice Daniel Horsmanden to Earl of Dartmouth, December 10, 1773, New York. CO 5 1105 fos. 72-75d.

126. Gordon was pleased that no one was going to be sent to England for trial; but a truly successful inquiry would not have re-invigorated and unified Virginia's and New England's Patriots.

127. The Reverend William Gordon to Lord Dartmouth June 16, 1773, Jamaica Plain. *The Manuscripts of the Earl of Dartmouth* Vol. II American Papers, 156.

128. The Virginia Committee consisted of Peyton Randolph, Robert Carter Nicholas, Richard Bland, Richard Henry Lee, Benjamin Harrison, Edmund Pendleton, Patrick Henry, Dudley Digges, Dafney Carr, Archibald Cary, and Thomas Jefferson.

129. The language of these resolves was carefully constructed to avoid accusations of treason by their political opponents. Richard Henry Lee to John Dickinson, April 4, 1773, Chantilly in Virginia, Ballagh, *Letters of Richard Henry Lee* Vol. I, 83. See also E. I. Miller, "The Virginia Committee of Correspondence of 1773-1775," *William and Mary College Quarterly Historical Magazine* 22 2 (October 1913): esp. 101-102, ft. 9.

130. Rhode Island responded with a committee of correspondence in May 1773. The committee consisted of Stephen Hopkins, Metcalfe Bowler, Moses Brown, John Cole, William Bradford, Henry Marchant, and Henry Ward.

131. Commissioners for Trade and Plantations to the King, July 1, 1773, Whitehall. National Archives (PRO), CO 5 1369 356-360.

132. Lawrence Henry Gipson, *The Triumphant Empire: Britain Sails into the Storm 1770–1776*, 25. Gipson is correct that the *final report* only mentioned Dudingston "disturbing and obstructing their vessels and boats, firing at and searching them . . ." Governor Wanton did testify under oath to the commissioners that Dudingston paid fifteen dollars to a Mr. Faulkner of Portsmouth

after his crew felled about thirty trees on his property on Gould Island. Staples, *Documentary History*, 74. *American Culture Series* microfilm reel 282.

CHAPTER FIVE: AN ORATION

1. Historian Merrill Jensen attributed Pennsylvania's refusal to form a committee of correspondence at this juncture largely to the work of Speaker Joseph Galloway. Merrill Jensen, *The Founding of a Nation: A History of the American Revolution 1763-1776*, 431, see footnote 121. Speaker of the Pennsylvania House Joseph Galloway replied to the Speaker of the House of Burgesses on September 25, 1773, Philadelphia, "I embraced the earliest opportunity to communicate your favor of the 19th of March, with the Resolves of the House of Burgesses of the Colony of Virginia to the Assembly of this province, and I have it in command from them to assure your honorable House that they esteem it a matter of the greatest importance to co-operate with the representatives of the other Colonies in every wise and prudent measure which may be proposed for the preservation and security of the general right and liberties, and that it is highly expedient and necessary a correspondence should be maintained between the Assemblies of their several Colonies." Galloway went on to explain that the assembly ran out of time in this session and would take it up again in the next. The speaker seemed to be procrastinating, since it took him six months to reply to the initial correspondence. Found in H.W. Flournoy, *Calendar of Virginia State Papers and Other Manuscripts* Vol. VIII, 28. Ultimately Pennsylvania did form a committee, but it came out of a Philadelphia mass meeting to consider the implications of the Boston Port Bill. See Miller, "The Virginia Committee of Correspondence," 103, and footnote 13.

2. Fitzpatrick, *The Spirit of the Revolution*, 105.

3. Miller, "The Virginia Committee of Correspondence," 103. For more nuances see the detailed study by Brown, *Revolutionary Politics*, especially 143, footnote 62.

4. Thomas Hutchinson to Lord Dartmouth, July 10, 1773, cited in Collins, *Committees of Correspondence*, 255. See also National Archives (PRO) UK, CO 5 762 fo. 380. Promoting adversarial relations with the London government was not the only function of inter-colonial committees of correspondence. Miller cited a case of colonies cooperating to strengthen their counterfeiting laws. But, clearly parties on both sides of the Atlantic understood the revolutionary potential. See Miller, "The Virginia Committee of Correspondence," 106.

5. Fitzpatrick, *Spirit of the Revolution*, 115. New Hampshire and Connecticut kept their committees of safety throughout the war.

6. Merrill Jensen, *The Founding of a Nation: A History of the American Revolution 1763–1776*, 431. Jensen argued that, "On the whole, the newspapers between 1763 and 1776 were more aggressive in promoting extreme ideas than the writers of pamphlets." Merrill Jensen, *Tracts of the American Revolution 1763-1776*, xiv.

7. See Richard Henry Lee to John Dickinson, April 4, 1773, Chantilly in Virginia. Ballagh, *Letters of Richard Henry Lee* Vol. I, 83.

8. Edward D. Collins, "Committees of Correspondence of the American Revolution," *Annual Report of the American Historical Association for the Year 1901* Vol I, 252-253.

9. Collins, *Committees of Correspondence*, 253.

10. Richard D. Brown, *Revolutionary Politics in Massachusetts: The Boston Committee of Correspondence and the Towns, 1772-1774*, viii.

11. Staples, *Documentary History*, xxxvii. Even the First Continental Congress was not an entirely new idea, with precedent in the Stamp Act Congress of 1765.

12. Euguene Wulsin, "The Political Consequences of the Burning of the *Gaspee*," *Rhode Island History* II (April 1944): 56.

13. While most sources placed his death in 1774, *The Oxford Dictionary of National Biography* dated his death between 1783-88. Bumsted and Clark argued that it could be as late as 1789. John M. Bumsted and Charles E. Clark, "New England's Tom Paine: John Allen and the Spirit of Liberty," *William and Mary Quarterly* 21 4, 569.

14. Allen must have acquired his *Gaspee* commission information from the newspaper. October 26, 1772, *Newport Mercury* (taken from a September 2 story, 2) and October 29, 1772, *Massachusetts Gazette and Boston News-Letter*. Admiral Montagu did not receive the official packet from London and Wanton did not leak the information until later in December. These early newspaper stories were inaccurate. Whether they were purposely misleading or not is a matter for debate. DeVaro, *Impact of the* Gaspee *Affair*, 170, footnote 2. Leslie, "*The* Gaspee *Affair*," 242. When Allen was writing his sermon in November he was doing so based upon inflammatory, inaccurate, and misleading information. Allen's statement, "I have seen what is said to be an authenticated copy of your Lordship's Letter to the Governor of Rhode-Island . . ." must have been added later. Captain Howe, of the sloop-of-war *Cruizer*, did not arrive in New York until December 10 and the official packet was rushed to Boston from there. *Providence Gazette*, December 19, 1772, 3.

15. Prior to this he had served as a preacher and writer. He may have preached in Salisbury and wrote *The Spiritual Magazine: or the Christian's Grand Treasure*. See Edward C. Starr, ed., *A Baptist Bibliography: Being a register of printed material by and about Baptists; including works written against the Baptists*, Section A, 63.

16. *The Oxford Dictionary of National Biography* dated his death between 1783-88. The exact nature of the behavior that accounted for his dismissal by the Broadstairs congregation remains unknown.

17. The transcript of the trial is available online at http://www.oldbaileyonline.org/Reference Number: t17690112-46.

18. Allen found the note in the street. A simple handwriting sample cleared him of the charge of forgery. But the fact that he tried to cash it in did not reflect well on his character.

19. Kneeland and Davis, the publishers of *Oration* in Boston, tried to help salvage the reputation of their very successful pamphleteer by publishing the entire

twenty-page transcript of his trial in 1773. See *Early American Imprints*. First Series, no 13047.

20. Allen was a high Calvinist with supralapsarian leanings. He was considered to be slightly unorthodox in some of his views; the Canons of Dordt (1618-19) adopted the infralapsarian order. While praising John Wesley as a gentleman, scholar, and historian, Allen questioned his Christian faith in *The Spirit of Liberty*. Allen showed little regard for the rising Arminianism of his day.

21. "John Wilkes's career was crucial to the colonists' understanding of what was happening to them; his fate, the colonists came to believe, was intimately involved with their own." Bernard Bailyn, *The Ideological Origins of the American Revolution*, 110–112. Bailyn cited Pauline Maier, "John Wilkes and American Disillusionment with Britain," *William and Mary Quarterly* 3rd Series 20 (1963): 373-395 for a detailed discussion. Rodger described Wilkes as "an established charlatan." N. A. M. Rodger, *The Insatiable Earl: A Life of John Montagu, Fourth Earl of Sandwich, 1718-1792*, 216.

22. Church historian Albert Henry Newman stated that Davis was driven out of Boston by harsh treatment in the press for his active role in the Baptist Association's resistance to ecclesiastical taxes and certificates. Albert Henry Newman, *A History of the Baptist Churches in the United States*, 352. He left for Philadelphia in August 1772 in failing health and died the following February at age 36. It appears that Allen was preaching at Second Baptist before Davis died in Philadelphia. Reta A. Gilbert cited Bumsted and Clark as her only source for the fact that Davis died at his post in Boston. Bumsted and Clark, "New England's Tom Paine," 564. Davis was among a group of Baptist leaders who were planning to appeal to the British Crown for relief from unjust taxation, not from Parliament, but from the Massachusetts authorities. Isaac Backus, *A History of New England with Particular Reference to the Baptists*, 176. Boston's Patriots did not want Baptists bringing their grievances about Massachusetts's ecclesiastical taxation before the Crown in 1773. The intervention of George III on behalf of Ashfield, Massachusetts's Baptists is in Frederick G. Howes, *History of the Town of Ashfield*, 63-86. They could not be taxed "for the maintenance of another society which they do not belong unto," 86.

23. Allen praised Davis's work on behalf of imprisoned Baptists in New England in *The American Alarm*.

24. The Sons of Liberty were more interested in Allen than the Baptists. Some suspected Allen had sympathy for the much-despised Sandemanian sect because of comments he made in *The Spirit of Liberty*. For more on the Sandemanians see Williston Walker, "The Sandemanians of New England," *Annual Report of the American Historical Association for the Year 1901* Vol. I, 133-162.

25. G. Jack Gravlee and James R. Irvine, *Pamphlets and the American Revolution: Rhetoric, Politics, Literature, and the Popular Press*, ii.

26. William G. McLoughlin, *New England Dissent, 1630-1833: The Baptists and the Separation of Church and State* Vol. I (Cambridge, MA: Harvard University Press, 1971), 584.

27. William G. McLoughlin, *Soul Liberty: The Baptists' Struggle in New England, 1630–1833* (Hanover and London: Brown University Press and University Press of New England, 1991), 147.

28. New International Version, 1973, 1978, 1984 International Bible Society. More literal than a paraphrase; some scholars refer to the NIV as a "dynamic equivalent." The NIV committee tried to capture the meaning and flavor of a verse, and, when possible—idiom that would be lost in a more "wooden" translation of the text.

29. Harry S. Stout, *The New England Soul: Preaching and Religious Culture in Colonial New England*, 277.

30. Allen claimed that he was going to make six observations, but only made five.

31. *Oration*, 19. Allen used the term "craving" the way we would use "greedy." Rigid customs enforcement and white pines were examples of resource extraction at the expense of loyal British colonists.

32. In 1763 the Crown resumed enforcement of the 1722 White Pines Act. Suspects could be tried in Vice-Admiralty Courts. See Joseph J. Malone, *Pine Trees and Politics: The Naval Stores and Forest Policy in Colonial New England, 1691-1775*. Having access to large stands of trees was important for the Royal Navy. Making a mast form a single tree was much cheaper than a "made" mast. Maine was still a part of Massachusetts and much of the controversy surrounded the clearing of Maine timber. New Englanders had to "prove" that their homes were built by locally harvested trees.

33. Many of Boston's entrepreneurs wanted to sell Maine's trees on the open market for a fair price.

34. *Oration*, 20.

35. Women rarely appeared in the *Gaspee* sources. Allen's appeal to women, not to let their husbands submit to the Commission, especially if they had children, was one of the few references to women (and that they could influence the outcome) in the whole *Gaspee* Affair.

36. The King Street riot is more commonly known among Americans as the "Boston Massacre." Five colonials were killed when British sentinels fired into a hostile crowd in front of the customs house in Boston in 1770. Captain Preston and four men were acquitted and two men were found guilty of manslaughter after being defended by John Adams.

37. In 1760 the whole cost of the Civil List (judges' and ambassadors' salaries) fell under Parliament, not the Crown's budget, which is how it remains to this day.

38. *Oration*, 22.

39. Many Baptists were viewed as mere tax evaders when they sought certificates to exempt them from paying ecclesiastical taxes in Massachusetts. *Oration*, 23.

40. Historian Bernard Bailyn discussed how Allen's pamphlets fit into a wider belief in high-level governmental conspiracy in "Chapter IV: The Logic of Rebellion" in Bailyn, *Ideological Origins*, 94-159.

41. Allen cited this as a case of tax revolt. But the term "yoke" was typically used to describe the oppression of the Israelites by foreigners. This may have been a revolt over harsh, forced labor. 1 Kings 12:18 described Adoram as "who was over the tribute" (King James Version)—"who was in charge of forced labor" (New International Version). Rehoboam, nonetheless, acted in a boastful and arrogant manner and, like the advisors of his generation, thought that his rule was absolute.

42. One commentator complained that, "To effectively catch the nuance of the oration, a reader would have to be familiar with the lives of King Ahaz, Micah, Hezekiah, Rehoboam, Naboth, Jeroboam, Zedekiah as well as the familiar Saul, David, Solomon, and Cain." G. Jack Gravlee and James R. Irvine, *Pamphlets and the American Revolution: Rhetoric, Politics, Literature, and the Popular Press* (Delmar, NY: Scholars' Facsimiles & Reprints, 1976), v. Allen did enlist many references without giving the biblical citation or even any background. Just to understand the Zedekiah reference, one has to see 2 Kings 24:17, 18:1; Chronicles 3:15; 2 Chronicles 36:10; and Jeremiah 37:1.

43. Or Gustavus III. See Robert Nisbet Bain, *Gustavus III and His Contemporaries, 1743–1792: An Overlooked Chapter of 18th Century History* Vol. I, 105-140.

44. In the repeal of the Stamp Act in 1766, Parliament asserted their right in the Declaratory Act to legislate for and bind the colonies "in all cases whatsoever."

45. The efforts to raise more revenue in the colonies were ostensibly to pay for their own defense. Indeed, Britain left a military presence in the colonies following the Seven Years' War. Some calculations indicate that their efforts were not cost-effective. Britain was actually paying more trying to collect revenue than they were getting from the colonies. For the participants in the debate upon the "Old Colonial System," see Barrow's Introduction, *Trade and Empire*, 1-3. John Adams may have started this debate with his comments on the lucrative trade that existed under George II, just in molasses. John Adams to William Tutor, Quincy, August 16, 1818. Adams, *The Works of John Adams*, 348.

46. *Oration*, 26.

47. "To be confin'd, and tried for his life, by the accusation of a negro." *Oration*, 27.

48. There was no fourth observation. Allen failed to correct this omission until his fourth edition when he switched to a number of "remarks" instead of "observations."

49. *Oration*, 28.

50. Allen also mentioned this story previously on page 24. 1 Kings 21:1-28. Canaanite kings could legally seize the land of their subjects. Naboth saw his land as his family's inheritance following the conquest (Joshua 13-21), so it was not negotiable.

51. Lawrence Shaw Mayo, ed., *The History of the Colony and Province of Massachusetts-Bay by Thomas Hutchinson* Vol. I, 334. Andros was also cited in John Pownall's research as a colonial case tried in England in chapter 2.

52. Andros was still fresh in the minds of colonial Patriots and cited as an example of tyranny. Governor Hutchinson to Earl of Hillsborough October 1, 1772. He enclosed an essay from the *Massachusetts Spy*, Vol. II, No. 82 which cited Andros as an example of an appointed governor who was "positively annihilating all our legislative bodies." National Archives (PRO) UK, CO 5 761 fo. 224.

53. *Oration*, 31.

54. For the purpose of analysis here, I am using the original publication found in *Early American Imprints*, Series I: Evans. John Allen, *An oration, upon the beauties of liberty, or The essential rights of the Americans* (Boston: D. Kneeland and N. Davis in Queen-Street, 1773).

55. Allen used the phrase "court of admiralty" seven times; five of these references clearly referred to the Royal Commission of Inquiry in Rhode Island.

56. See page vi of the dedication in *Oration*.

57. See page vii of the dedication in *Oration*.

58. See "An Act for Declaring the Rights and Privileges of His Majesties Subjects within this Colony" and "Laws made and past by the General Assembly of His Majesties Colony of *Rhode-Island* and *Providence-Plantations* in *New-England*. Begun and Held at Newport, the first day of March 1662," in Cushing, ed., *Earliest Acts and Laws*, 139.

59. Contrary to the claims of John Allen, 35 Henry VIII chapter 2 was upheld in Rhode Island's earliest charter; although suspects were to be found guilty by the General Assembly before being sent to the King's Bench. See "Proceedings of the First General Assembly of 'The Incorporation of Providence Plantations,' and THE CODE OF LAWS adopted by that Assembly in 1647," in Cushing, ed., *The Earliest Acts and Laws*, 16. Women were executed in only a slightly less gruesome manner than men. The March 1, 1662, Rhode Island treason laws were vaguer; see 140. Of course, the Rhode Island Assembly challenged and protested Parliament's extension of 35 Henry VIII ch. 2 to the colonies in 1769.

60. Matthew 7:12 "Therefore all things whatsoever ye would that men should do to you, do ye even so to them: for this is the law and the prophets." Allen used the Authorized (King James) Version of the Bible.

61. *Oration*, vi.

62. *Oration*, vii.

63. *Oration*, vii.

64. See Gravlee and Irvine, eds. *Pamphlets and the American Revolution*, iii. Later, on page xiii in *Oration* Allen stated, ". . . that General Gage, hold the troops in readiness to assist this assumed court of admiralty . . ." This was also a reference to the court of inquiry in Rhode Island, not the vice-admiralty courts. On pages 22–23, Allen referred to the "courts of judiciary of this province." He was voicing concerns about Massachusetts judicial salaries being paid by the British Ministry rather than coming from the local legislature (or general court).

65. Ubbelohde, *Vice-Admiralty Courts*, 5.

66. *Oration*, vii.

67. Allen spelled his name Charles Steward. Perhaps this was a play on words where Allen later reminded the king of his duty to be a steward to his people. ". . . which is only a power to protect them, and defend their rights civil and religious; and to sign, seal, and confirm as their steward such laws as the people of America shall content to." *Oration*, xii. ". . . give an account of thy *stewardship*, that thou mayest be no longer steward," 19.

68. See sections on republicanism and monarchy in Wood, *Radicalism of the American Revolution*. Much of the next section appears to be sections, paraphrases, and quotes taken from *Vidiciae Contra Tyrannos, a defence of liberty against tyrants, or, Of the lawful power of the Prince over the people, and of the people over the Prince*: being a treatise written in Latin and French by Junius Brutus (attributed to Philippe Duplessis-Mornay) (London: Printed by Matthew Simmons and Robert Ibbitson, 1648). Allen wrote under the pseudonym Junius junior. Decimus Junius Brutus Albinus (died 43 BC) was a Roman politician and general of the 1st century BC, one of Julius Caesar's assassins.

69. Although this seems incredible, apparently the local courts "forgot" to try the *Gaspee* case. James Helme told the Royal Commissioners, "The examination of James Helme, Esq., of South Kingstown, in the county of King's county, and colony of Rhode Island, &c., taken on oath at Newport, in said colony, this fifth day of June, A. D. 1773: Who saith, that in October following the burning the schooner *Gaspee*, the Superior Court of Judicature, &c., for said colony, sat at East Greenwich, in the county of Kent, at which Court I presided, being the eldest Justice of the same present. Before the sitting of said Court I had heard of the said schooner's being burnt, and of Lieutenant Dudingston's being wounded. I did not give any charge to the grand jury at that court, nor is it usual in this colony to give either general or special charges to grand juries; but before the meeting of said court I informed my brethren that if I presided at said court I fully intended to give the affair of burning the said schooner and wounding the Lieutenant in charge to the jury; but having been near two months on the circuit it entirely went out of my mind when the grand jury was empanelled, and there being no business laid before said jury, they were soon dismissed; immediately after, I recollected the omission of what I intended, and then mentioned to some of the other judges of the court, that I had entirely forgot to give the business of destroying the *Gaspee* and wounding Lieutenant Dudingston in charge to the grand jury, which I had designated, and further this deponent saith not." Staples, *Documentary History*, 91.

70. In 1768 and 1771 the governor called upon the general to raise a group of provincials to put down the rebellion in North Carolina.

71. *Oration*, ix.

72. This seemed like an odd tack to take since he had just accused the king of having two different sets of laws. Now Allen argued that they were two separate spheres.

73. Staples, *Documentary History*, 109.

74. *Oration*, x.

75. Allen was incorrect: it is actually Romans 4:15: "Because the law worketh wrath: for where no law is, there is no transgression." Authorized (King James) Version of the Bible, 1611. The Apostle Paul did not have the civil magistrate or civil law in mind here. He was referring to the promise (or covenant) given to Abraham four hundred years before the law given to Moses. Therefore, salvation could not be dependent upon keeping the law of God.

76. This was a de facto declaration of independence.

77. *Oration*, xi.

78. Allen misused this passage. It is referring to the Temple Tax (what the Authorized Version translated "custom or tribute") from Exodus 30:13. Christ addressed the civil tax code quite differently in Matthew 22:21. "They say unto him, Caesar's. Then saith he unto them, Render therefore unto Caesar the things which are Caesar's; and unto God the things that are God's." Regardless, so as not to offend anyone, Christ gave Simon Peter the money (in a very creative way) to pay the Temple Tax anyway.

79. The Newport pastor Ezra Stiles commented that "No one justifies the burning of the *Gaspee*. But no one ever thought of such a Thing as being Treason." Ezra Stiles to the Reverend Elihu Spencer, at Trenton, New Jersey, Newport, February 16, 1773. Dexter, *Literary Diary of Ezra Stiles*, 349.

80. Most of the *Gaspee* officers and crew were on the *Beaver* the very next day.

81. *Oration*, xii.

82. *Oration*, xiv.

83. Bernard Bailyn attributed authorship to John Allen. Bailyn, *The Ideological Origins of the American Revolution*, 18, footnote 23. John Adams attributed authorship to John Allen. Adams, *Works of John Adams*, 320. L. H. Butterfield, ed. *The Adams Papers Series I: Diary and Autobiography of John Adams*, 83. Adams indicated that "common people" were hearing and reading *Oration*. The local paper identified Allen as the author a week later. December 10, 1772, *Massachusetts Gazette and Boston Weekly News-Letter*. Historian Alice M. Baldwin attributed it to Isaac Skillman, who became pastor of the church in 1773. Alice M. Baldwin, *The New England Clergy and the American Revolution*, 117. Philip Davidson showed doubt about Skillman. Philip Davidson, *Propaganda and the American Revolution*, 214, see footnote 8. Bumsted and Clark, using Thomas Adams's scholarship, have settled the issue beyond reasonable doubt. Bumsted and Clark, "New England's Tom Paine," 561-562, see footnote 1. Thomas R. Adams, *American Independence: The Growth of an Idea*, 68-70. Isaac Skillman is still listed in *Early American Imprints* as an "additional index point" so that researchers who look for *Oration* under his authorship will find it. Skillman was born and educated in New Jersey, so the pen name "a British Bostonian" seems an unlikely choice.

84. Harry S. Stout, *The New England Soul: Preaching and Religious Culture in Colonial New England*, 277.

85. Eric Foner, *The Story of American Freedom*, 12. Foner mistakenly identified the author as Joseph Allen on page 12 but correctly as John Allen on page 33.

86. Gravlee and Irvine created this table from Adams's earlier work. Unfortunately, this does not tell us anything about the size or volume of a particular printing. See Thomas R. Adams, *American Independence: The Growth of an Idea*, 69-70. This table was taken from G. Jack Gravlee and James R. Irvine, eds. *Pamphlets and the American Revolution: Rhetoric, Politics, Literature, and the Popular Press*, viii.

87. Using the powerful mark-up and searching tools in *Early American Newspapers*, I was able to find seven different advertisements for Oration in 1773, but not the text itself. Unlike *Letters*, *Oration* was not released in a series that fit comfortably into a four-page newspaper. As of this writing, there are still some gaps in *EAN* that will be filled as more sources are scanned into the computer.

88. Forrest McDonald, *Empire and Nation: Letters from a Farmer in Pennsylvania, John Dickinson and Letters from the Federal Farmer, Richard Henry Lee*, xiii.

89. Bailyn, *Pamphlets* Vol 1, vii, 8. There were more than 1500 pamphlets published between 1750-1783.

90. Bailyn, *Pamphlets* Vol I, 5.

91. Bailyn, *Pamphlets* Vol I, 3.

92. Bailyn, *Ideological Origins*, 17-18.

93. Bailyn, *Pamphlets* Vol I, 17.

94. Gravlee and Irvine, *Pamphlets and the American Revolution*, x.

95. Bumsted and Clark, "New England's Tom Paine," 568.

96. Harry S. Stout, *The New England Soul: Preaching and Religious Culture in Colonial New England*, 277.

97. Even though Kneeland and Davis were in "economic straits," they would not publish the antislavery remarks. Patricia Bradley, *Slavery, Propaganda, and the American Revolution*, 107.

98. Ibid., 106.

99. Compiled from Thomas R. Adams, *American Independence: The Growth of an Idea*, 69-70.

100. Gordon S. Wood, "Conspiracy and the Paranoid Style: Causality and Deceit in the Eighteenth Century," *William and Mary Quarterly* 3rd Ser. 39 3, 420-21.

101. Nathan O. Hatch, *The Sacred Cause of Liberty: Republican Thought and the Millennium in Revolutionary New England*, 57.

102. Allen, though, did not utilize Haman's treachery from the story of Esther. This would seem like an obvious choice; a high-level royal conspiracy, orchestrated by the king's ministers, against a particular subset of people in the kingdom. Haman told the king that the laws of the Jews were different from his (Esther 3:8).

103. Allen was certainly in the right place at the right time. The Boston Committee of Correspondence met in Faneuil Hall from October 28 to November 2, 1772, and published (largely written by Samuel Adams) a forty-six-page pamphlet, "to state the Rights of Colonists and of this Province in particular, as Men, as Christians, and as Subjects . . . with the infringements and violations thereof." After being printed in Boston, five pages of it were printed as a broadside. It also appeared in London and Dublin. See *Early American Imprints* (Evans) no. 12332. Also Adams, *American Independence*, 66-67.

104. Wood, *Conspiracy*, 419.

105. "Draft of Instructions to the Virginia Delegates in the Continental Congress" this was the manuscript text of "A Summary View of the Rights of British America," in Julian P. Boyd, ed., *The Papers of Thomas Jefferson* Vol I 1760-1776, 125.

106. Bartlett, *Destruction of the Gaspee*, 130.

107. Bernard Bailyn brought this to the foreground of historical discussion with his classic *Ideological Origins of the American Revolution*, especially the section titled, "A Note on Conspiracy."

108. For an excellent discussion on conspiratorial beliefs on both sides of the Atlantic see Lawrence J. Devaro, "The *Gaspee* Affair as Conspiracy," *Rhode Island History* 32 4, 109-110.

109. "All other avenues seemed to be exhausted, and their duty as ministers of the Crown and as Englishmen was to uphold the most perfect of all constitutions in the face of a sinister [colonial elite] conspiracy to subvert it." Rodger, *The Insatiable Earl*, 217.

110. *Newport Mercury*, June 7 and September 27, 1773.

111. Admiral Montagu informed Lord Sandwich that the store ship burned to the water's edge. June 1, 1773, Admiral Montagu to the Earl of Sandwich, First Lord of the Admiralty. G.R. Barnes and J.H. Owen, *The Private Papers of John, Earl of Sandwich* Vol. I, 50-51. Montagu wrote, "In short, they are almost ripe for independence, and nothing but the ships prevents their going to greater lengths, as they see no notice taken from home of their behaviour."

112. Douglass Adair & John A. Schutz, *Peter Oliver's Origin & Progress of the American Rebellion*, 99.

CONCLUSION

1. In early June, the May 10, 1773, Tea Act was still at the "rumor" stages in the Boston press. Benjamin Woods Labaree, *The Boston Tea Party*, 87-88.

2. John C. Miller, *Origins of the American Revolution*, 1959), 329.

3. Wickwire, *British Subministers*, 141.

4. June 1, 1773, Admiral Montagu to the Earl of Sandwich. Barnes and Owen, *Private Papers of John, Earl of Sandwich* Vol. I, 50.

5. Earl of Dartmouth to Attorney- and Solicitor-General, February 5, 1774, Whitehall. National Archives (PRO) UK, CO 5 160 fo. 1. Dartmouth enclosed

a four-page summary of the deteriorating conditions in Boston leading up to the disposal of the tea. He ended his letter with two queries about whether the case amounted to the crime of high treason and the proper and legal method of proceeding against chargeable persons. Attorney- and Solicitor-General to Earl of Dartmouth, February 11, 1774. CO 5 160 fo. 40. The law servants of the crown believed that the case was high treason, levying of war against His Majesty. They also believed that the chargeable persons could be tried in some county in England. See also Attorney- and Solicitor-General to Earl of Dartmouth, December 13,1774. Massachusetts Bay was considered to be in open rebellion and at war. Certain persons were charged with overt acts of treason. CO 5 159 fo. 3.

6. Peter Orlando Hutchinson, *The Diaries and Letters of His Excellency Thomas Hutchinson*, Esq. Vol. I, 183. July 5, 1774. Later Hutchinson seemed to tell the story differently when he indicated that, "the Attorney and Solicitor General were in doubt whether the evidence was sufficient to convict them: but he said things never would be right until some of them were brought over." August 14, 1774, 219.

7. Since Lord North used the plural (ships), he must be referring to the *Liberty* and the *Gaspee*. No persons were apprehended or punished in either case. During the Boston tea crisis, "Legion" wrote in the *Newport Mercury*, ". . . it may be safely affirmed, that it [tea] will not be suffered to be sold here; and that if landed, which is scarce possible, it will bereshipp'd on board the LIBERTY, and sent to GASPEE, the first favourable wind and weather." December 13, 1773.

8. *The Parliamentary History of England* Vol. XVII, 1280.

9. In the debates surrounding the passage of the Coercive acts, member of Parliament Mr. Dunning speaking in the Commons, asserted that the Boston Tea Party was neither open resistance nor was it treason. It was merely a mob. But, even after the failure of the Royal Commission of Inquiry in Rhode Island, he seemed to think that inquiries were still an appropriate means to seek after traitors. "Had any thing appeared that bore the least similarity to treason or rebellion, my hon. and learned friends would have told us that it was treason, and I will give them credit for their willingness upon such an occasion; but there was treason, there were traitors, they would have been known and punished; and if not known, they would at least have been enquired after; but as no enquiry had yet been set on foot, I will be bold to say, there was neither treason nor traitors." *The Parliamentary History of England* Vol. XVII. MP Mr. Byng was leery of this "new tack"—punishing the innocent alongside the guilty. He told the House of Commons, "It has been said, Sir, that there has been treason and traitors, but that the traitors are not known. There can be no treason without traitors, therefore endeavor to find out the traitors first, that they may be punished, to save the destruction of an innocent people," 1310.

10. The Administration of Justice Act moved British officials, not colonials, to England for trials involving capital crimes. Robert Gross, *The Minutemen and their World*, 113.

11. Trial attorney Leonard Bucklin (a direct descendant of Joseph Bucklin, the man who shot Dudingston) believes that that is why Montagu was so interested

in the attorneys who gathered at Sabin Tavern. Montagu encouraged the Commissioners to summon and question them. They may have been laying the legal grounds for a warrant at the tavern just before the mob departed for the *Gaspee*.

12. The authors of the U.S. Constitution inserted two clauses to prohibit *ex post facto* laws and trials 15 years after the *Gaspee* Affair. The Dockyard Act passed in April 1772 but colonists did not hear/read about it until after the *Gaspee* burned in June. Governors in America were not officially notified about the Act (and six other Acts of Parliament relating to America) until after July 1, 1772. Circular letter to Governors in America from John Pownall, July 1, 1772, Whitehall. National Archives (PRO) UK, CO 5 241 419–421.

13. In the case of Boston's destruction of East India Company tea, the law servants originally ruled that the ringleaders could be tried in England for treason, but later they reversed themselves and left it up to Parliament to act punitively against the port of Boston. Labaree, *Boston Tea Party*, 174-176.

14. These were the actions (close the port and move the customs house) that Parliament punished Boston with one year later.

15. Charles Dudley, the Collector of Customs in [Newport] Rhode Island, wrote, "I am persuaded the choice of commissioners was not a good one: would you think of asking a man to make a discovery which would ruin himself. . .?" Apparently Dudley sent this to Montagu, who forwarded it to Sandwich. June 14, 1773, Charles Dudley to Admiral Montagu. Barnes and Owen, *The Private Papers of John, Earl of Sandwich* Vol. I, 53.

16. Robert Carter Nicholas, *Considerations on the present state of Virginia Examined*, 16. *Early American Imprints*, Series I Evans 13500. Nicholas "repeatedly sought accommodation with Britain" but reluctantly adapted to Virginia's more radical Patriots. *Oxford National Biography*, doi: 10.1093/ref:odnb/ 68720.

17. Adams's piece was adopted by the Town of Boston November 20, 1772. Adams, like most colonists, would have still believed that the Dockyard Act was going to be used in the *Gaspee* case. For his comments on vicinage, he had the 1769 resolves in Parliament and the Dockyards Act (April 1772) at his disposal. The debate over transporting ringleaders from the Boston Tea Party and principal actors and abettors from the Provincial Congress—who may have been in hiding in Lexington and Concord—was still in the future. Cushing, *Writings of Samuel Adams*, 367.

18. Barrow, *Trade and Empire*, 256.

19. Helen Hill Miller, *The Case for Liberty*, 163-184.

20. Adopted by the First Continental Congress October 14, 1774.

21. Miller, *Case for Liberty*, 182. Taken from Richard L. Perry, ed., *Sources of our Liberties: Documentary Origins of Individual Liberties in the United States Constitution and Bill of Rights*, 286-289. Perry did not tie theses documents directly to the *Gaspee*.

22. Perry, *Sources*, 295-300. Adopted July 6, 1775.

23. Article VI. Miller, *Case for Liberty*, 163.

24. James H. Hutson preferred the use of the term *jealousy* over *paranoid*. In the eighteenth century the term *jealousy* was more closely aligned with *suspicion*. Revolutionaries like Samuel Adams were on their guard against corrupt power. The term *paranoid* places too much emphasis on psychosis and other psychological categories. James H. Hutson, "The Origins of 'The Paranoid Style in American Politics': Public Jealousy from the Age of Walpole to the Age of Jackson," found in David D. Hall, John M. Murrin, and Thad W. Tate, eds., *Saints & Revolutionaries: Essays on Early American History*, 332-372.

25. Leslie, "The *Gaspee* Affair," 256.

26. Most members of Parliament understood the supremacy of the English Parliament (and the subsequent elimination of Scotland's Parliament) as the grand settlement of the Glorious Revolution of 1688. Giving colonial legislatures authority over taxation issues would revert back to the politics of the Stuart era. The Stuarts played the Parliaments against one another to serve the monarchy's political advantage. Rodger, *The Insatiable Earl*, 214-215. On April 28, 1707, the last Scottish Parliament was dissolved. It did not sit again until 1999.

27. Irwin H. Polishook, *Rhode Island and the Union 1774-1795*, 18. The general assembly voted its ratification of the Articles of Confederation unanimously.

28. Judge Staples wrote the definitive nineteenth-century works on the *Gaspee* and Rhode Island's roles in the Continental Congresses and subsequent Constitutional Convention. He did not make a link between the *Gaspee* and federalism. See Staples, *Continental Congress*, 686–87.

29. Rhode Island was the only state to wait until 1790 to approve the new government. Arnold noted that the historic precedent for federal union may have had its roots in Rhode Island after all: "The similarity between the New England Confederacy of 1643 and the National Confederation of 1783 has been often remarked; but there is yet a stronger resemblance in the relative position of the four towns of Rhode Island in 1647, and the States of the Federal Union under the constitution of 1787." Samuel Greene Arnold, *History of the State of Rhode Island and Providence Plantations* Vol. I, 211, footnote 2.

30. Paul Langford, ed., *The Writings and Speeches of Edmund Burke* Vol. II, 433.

31. Ironically, the new U.S. government would have to arm revenue cutters in 1790 to curtail smuggling and collect tariff revenue. With the "War on Drugs" (and now the "War on Terror" as well), twenty-first-century Americans expect government vessels to interdict merchant liners and pleasure craft for a host of reasons.

32. Customs Surveyor Temple tried to set an example in January 1764 with the *Rhoda*, the vessel escaped, and he was humiliated into offering a reward for recapture.

33. Customs Collector Robinson failed with at least three different vessels to get justice in Halifax.

34. Montagu later complained that his Royal Navy Sea Officers were not getting support from Customs in America. Rear Admiral Montagu to Philip Stephens, July 11, 1772, Boston. Extract of a letter found enclosed in John Robinson to John Pownall, enclosed for Lord Dartmouth's information, October 26, 1772. Treasury. National Archives (PRO) UK, CO 5 145 fos. 115-120d.

35. Bailyn, *The Ideological Origins*, "A Note on Conspiracy," 144-159. Also see Wood, "Conspiracy and the Paranoid Style," 401-441.

36. John Pendleton Kennedy, *Journals of the House of Burgesses of Virginia 1773-1776*, 50.

37. A report made by the Privy Council to the king in early 1760 recommended voiding the charters of Connecticut and Rhode Island. Thomas Hutchinson, George Roome, and Daniel Horsmanden all proposed annulling the charter in favor of a royal colony. Thomas Williams Bicknell, *The History of the State of Rhode Island and Providence Plantations* Vol. II, 735-736.

38. Hampden (if it was the same person) wrote 5 separate pieces of "An Alarm" attacking East India Tea in 1773 and published in New York. While Samuel Adams more frequently wrote under the pseudonym "Americanus," the style here is very suggestive of Adams. Publishers insisted upon knowing the identity of the authors who submitted work, but they would not reveal it to others, often taking that information to the grave. See Roger B. Berry, "John Adams: Two Further Contributions to the *Boston Gazette*, 1766-1768" *The New England Quarterly*, 31 1, 94, esp. footnotes 6,7, and 8.

39. POSTSCRIPT to the *Newport Mercury*, May 2, 1774. *Early American Newspapers*.

40. Bailyn, *The Ideological Origins*, 148-149.

41. Wood, *The Radicalism*, 360.

42. Wood, *The Radicalism*, 108.

43. The word "terrorism" made its way into the English language between 1795-1798 while reflecting upon the Reign of Terror in France. *Oxford English Dictionary*.

44. Timothy McVeigh (Oklahoma City Federal Building) was charged with murder and conspiracy, not treason. Since no one died in the *Gaspee* incident, the charge of murder was not an option (although attempted murder could have been utilized). Jamal Badawi and Fahd Mohamed al-Qasaa (USS *Cole*) were indicted in US District Court in New York on fifty charges, including terrorism. Not being U.S. citizens, the charge of treason was not applicable.

45. John Walker was the first of several Americans captured by US forces in Afghanistan and Iraq.

46. Ironically, Rhode Island is the only state to have charged someone with treason. Thomas W. Dorr was "elected governor" by his supporters and Rhode Island had two governments for a short time in 1841–42. Rhode Island governor King had Dorr tried for treason and sentenced to life in prison in 1844. The U.S. Supreme Court ruled that one could not commit treason against a state government and Dorr was pardoned.

47. Third vice-president of the United States, Aaron Burr, fled to the western parts of the United States and Mexico when it became apparent that he was going to be charged with treason.

48. Hutchinson, *Diaries and Letters*, 384. Later Hutchinson seemed to tell the story differently when he indicated that, "the Attorney and Sollicitor General were in doubt whether the evidence was sufficient to convict them: but he said things never would be right until some of them were brought over." August 14, 1774, 219.

49. Lovejoy, *Rhode Island Politics*, 181.

50. This was the understanding of Donald Jackson, ed., *The Diaries of George Washington* Vol. III, 255.

51. A Topographical Chart of the Bay of Narraganset in the Province of New England by Charles Blaskowitz. Engraved & Printed for W[illia]m Faden, Charing Cross, as the Act directs July 22nd 1777. Library of Congress, Washington, DC.

52. *Manufacturers and Farmers Journal*, July 6, 1826.

53. This is not the location of "*Gaspee* Point." Pawtuxet is just north of "*Gaspee* Point," partly in Cranston and partly in Warwick. It was where the officers and men were taken by the raiders and left on June 10, 1772. The organization of this elaborate two-hour parade to honor the *Gaspee* raiders requires the work of one hundred "*Gaspee* Days" volunteers each year.

54. Douglass Adair & John A. Schutz, *Peter Oliver's Origin & Progress of the American Rebellion*, 99.

BIBLIOGRAPHY

PRIMARY SOURCES

American Antiquarian Society.
  Early American Newspapers: *The Newport Mercury* (Newport, RI)
  Early American Newspapers: *The Providence Gazette*
Brown University. John Carter Brown Library. American Manuscripts.
  The Brown Papers, 1772-1774. Brown Family Records Collections:
  Brown Family Papers Project
  Manuscript Records. *Gaspee* commission.
Brown University. John Hay Library.
  [Anonymous] Account of Events Pertaining to Destruction of
  Schooner *Gaspee*.
  Rider Collection. Documents Respecting the Destruction of the
  Schooner *Gaspee*, June 10, 1772.
Brown University. John D. Rockefeller, Jr. Library.
  Original publications of Staples and Bartlett.
National Archives. Kew, London, UK.
  Admiralty (ADM) ADM 1 484 Contains valuable correspondence
  among Commanders and Admiralty administrators
  ADM 1 5305 Court Martial of Lieutenant Dudingston
  ADM 106 1153 Contains materials about *Gaspee* prior to 1772
  ADM 33 Broad Street Pay Office Book for the *Gaspee*
  ADM 36 7248 Muster for the *Gaspee*
  ADM 51 3853 ADM 51 4197 ADM 52 1166 ADM 52 1248
  Gaspee Logs
  Colonial Office (CO) CO 5 Contains correspondence with the Amer-
  ican Department administrators in the Colonial Office
  Privy Council (PC) PC 1/15/93 and PC 2/116-117 Privy Council
  records and correspondence pertaining to the *Gaspee*
  Treasury Department (T) T 1 491, T 1 494, T 1 495, & T 1 496
  Correspondence retained by the Treasury Department relating Cus-
  toms and Customs Deputations
Newport Historical Society.
  Henry Marchant Letterbook
Rhode Island Historical Society.
  Rhode Island Miscellaneous Manuscripts. Papers Relating to the
  Gaspee, compiled by Walter Edwards Mss, 434

Moses Brown Papers
John Waterman, Journal of Remarkable other material things. Journal of Col. John Waterman
Rhode Island State Archives.
Acts and Resolves of the Colony of Rhode Island. *Gaspee* Commission Papers
Rhode Island Colony Records
Gaspee Papers
Rhode Island Journal, House of Deputies and Journal of the Senate

SECONDARY SOURCES

Adair, Douglass and John A. Schutz. *Peter Oliver's Origin and Progress of the American Rebellion*. San Marino, CA: Huntington Library, 1781, 1961.

Adams, John. *The works of John Adams, second President of the United States. With a life of the author, notes, and illus. by his grandson, Charles Francis Adams*, 1-10. Freeport, NY: Books for Libraries Press, 1850-56, 1969.

Adams, Thomas R. *American Independence: The Growth of an Idea*. Providence, RI: Brown University Press, 1965.

Alden, John Richard. *General Gage in America*. New York: Greenwood Press, 1948.

Allen, John. *An oration, upon the beauties of liberty, or The essential rights of the Americans*. Boston: D. Kneeland and N. Davis in Queen-Street, 1773.

Andrews, Charles M. *The Colonial Period of American History*, 1-4. New Haven and London: Yale University Press, 1938, 1964.

Appleton, Marguerite. "The Agents of the New England Colonies in the Revolutionary Period." *New England Quarterly* 6 2 (Jun 1933): 371-387.

Arnold, Samuel Greene. *History of the State of Rhode Island and Providence Plantations*, 1-2. 1859–60.

Backus, Isaac. *A History of New England with Particular Reference to the Baptists*. New York: Arno Press & New York Times, 1969.

Bailyn, Bernard. *The Origins of American Politics*. New York: Vintage Books, 1967.

Bailyn, Bernard. *Pamphlets of the American Revolution 1750-1776*. Cambridge, MA: Belknap Press of Harvard University, 1965.

Bailyn, Bernard. *The Ideological Origins of the American Revolution*. Cambridge, MA: Belknap Press of Harvard University, 1992.

Bailyn, Bernard. *The Ordeal of Thomas Hutchinson*. Cambridge, MA: Belknap Press of Harvard University, 1974.

Bailyn, Bernard. *To Begin the World Anew: The Genius and Ambiguities of the American Founders.* New York: Alfred A. Knopf, 2003.

Bain, Robert Nisbet. *Gustavus III and His Contemporaries 1742-1792: An Overlooked Chapter of 18th Century History,* 1-2. New York: Bergman Publishers, 1894, 1970.

Baldwin, Alice M. *The New England Clergy and the American Revolution.* Durham, NC: Duke University Press, 1928.

Ballagh, James Curtis. *The Letters of Richard Henry Lee,* 1-2. New York: Macmillan, 1911.

Banks, Charles Edward. *The History of Martha's Vineyard, Dukes County, Massachusetts,* Vol. 1-3. Edgartown, MA: Dukes County Historical Society, 1966.

Bargar, B. D. *Lord Dartmouth and the American Revolution.* Columbia: University of South Carolina Press, 1961.

Barnes, G. R. and J. H. Owen. *The Private Papers of John, Earl of Sandwich, First Lord of the Admiralty, 1771-1782,* 1-4. [London]: Navy Records Society, 1932-1938.

Barrell, John. *Imagining the King's Death: Figurative Treason, Fantasies of Regicide 1793-1796.* Oxford: Oxford University Press, 2000.

Barrow, Thomas C. *Trade and Empire: The British Customs Service in Colonial America 1660-1775.* Cambridge, MA: Harvard University Press, 1967.

Bartlett, John Russell. *A History of the Destruction of His Britannic Majesty's Schooner Gaspee in Narragansett Bay on the 10th June, 1772.* Providence: A. Crawford Greene, Printer to the State, 1861.

Bartlett, John Russell. *Records of the Colony of Rhode Island and Providence Plantations in New England,* 1-10. Providence: Knowles, Vose and Anthony, 1856-65.

Beer, George Louis. *British Colonial Policy, 1754-1765.* New York: Peter Smith, 1933.

Beer, George Louis. *The Old Colonial System 1660-1754,* 1-2. New York: Peter Smith, 1933.

Bellamy, J. G. *The Law of Treason in England in the Later Middle Ages.* Aberdeen: Cambridge University Press, 1970.

Bellamy, John. *The Tudor Law of Treason: An Introduction.* London: Routledge & Kegan Paul, 1979.

Berry, Roger B. "John Adams: Two Further Contributions to the *Boston Gazette,* 1766-1768." *New England Quarterly,* 31 1 (March 1958): 90-99.

Bicknell, Thomas Williams. *The History of the State of Rhode Island and Providence Plantations*, 1-2. New York: American Historical Society, Inc., 1920.

Bloom, Jeanne Gould. *Sir Edmund Andros: A Study in Seventeenth-Century Colonial Adminstration*. Yale University: Unpublished Dissertation, 1962.

Boyd, Julian P. *The Papers of Thomas Jefferson*. Princeton, NJ: Princeton University Press, 1950.

Bradley, Patricia. *Slavery, Propaganda, and the American Revolution*. Jackson: University Press of Mississippi, 1998.

Bridenbaugh, Carl. *Mitre and Sceptre: Transatlantic Faiths, Ideas, Personalities, and Politics 1689-1775*. New York: Oxford University Press, 1962.

Brown, Charles W. "Hurricanes and Shore-Line Changes in Rhode Island." *Geographical Review* 29 3 (July 1939): 416-430.

Brown, Richard D. *Major Problems in the Era of the American Revolution*. Boston: Houghton Mifflin, 2000.

Brown, Richard D. *Revolutionary Politics in Massachusetts; the Boston Committee of Correspondence and the Town, 1772-1774*. Cambridge, MA: Harvard University Press, 1970.

Bryant, Samuel W. "HMS 'Gaspee'—The Court-Martial." *Rhode Island History* 25 3 (1966): 65-72.

Bryant, Samuel W. "Rhode Island Justice—1772 Vintage." *Rhode Island History* 26 3 (1967): 65-71.

Bryant, Samuel W. *The Gaspee Syndrome—a Tory View*. Unpublished Thesis, 1967.

Bumsted, John M. "New England's Tom Paine: John Allen and the Spirit of Liberty." *William and Mary Quarterly* 21 4 (October 1964): 561-570.

Burns, Alan. *History of the British West Indies*. London: George Allen & Unwin, 1954.

Butterfield, L. H. *Adams Family Correspondence*. Cambridge, MA: Belknap Press of Harvard University, 1963.

Butterfield, L. H. *The Adams Papers: Diary and Autobiography of John Adams*, 1-4. Cambridge, MA: Belknap Press of Harvard University, 1961.

Canny, Nicholas. "Writing Atlantic History; or, Reconfiguring the History of Colonial British America." *Journal of American History* 86 3 (December 1999): 1093-1114.

Carson, Jane. "The First American Flag Hoisted in Old England." *William and Mary Quarterly* 11 3 (July 1954): 434-440.

Carter, Clarence Edwin. *The Correspondence of General Thomas Gage with the Secretaries of State 1763–1775*, 1-2. New Haven, CT: Yale University Press, 1931.

Channing, Edward and Archibald Cary Coolidge. *The Barrington-Bernard Correspondence and Illustrative Matter 1760–1770*. Cambridge, MA: Harvard University Press, 1912.

Chapin, Bradley. *The American Law of Treason: Revolutionary and Early National Origins*. Seattle: University of Washington Press, 1964.

Chipman, William Pendleton. *In Defense of Liberty: A Story of the Burning Schooner Gaspee in 1772*. New York: A.L. Burt, 1908.

Clark, William Bell. *Naval Documents of the American Revolution*, 1. Washington, DC, 1964.

Clokie, Hugh McDowall and J. William Robinson. *Royal Commissions of Inquiry: The Significance of Investigations in British Politics*. Stanford, CA: Stanford University Press, 1937.

Coan, Marion S. "A Revolutionary Prison Diary: The Journal of Dr. Jonathan Haskins." *New England Quarterly* 17 2 (June 1944): 290-309.

Cole, John N. "Henry Marchant's Journal, 1771–1772." *Rhode Island History* 57 2 (May 1999): 31-55.

Collins, Edward D. "XII. Committees of Correspondence of the American Revolution." *Annual Report of the American Historical Association for the Year 1901*, 1 of 2 (1902): 243-271.

Conforti, Joseph A. *Samuel Hopkins and the New Divinity Movement: Calvinism, the Congregational Ministry, and Reform in New England Between the Great Awakenings*. Grand Rapids, MI: Wm. B. Eerdmans, 1981.

Cook, Elizabeth Christine. *Literary Influences in Colonial Newspapers, 1704-1750*. Port Washington, NY: Kennikat Press, 1912, 1966.

Copeland, David A. *Colonial American Newspapers*. Newark: University of Delaware Press, 1997.

Crane, Verner W. *Benjamin Franklin's Letters to the Press 1758–1775*. Chapel Hill, NC: Institute of Early American History and Culture, 1950.

Cunningham, Anne Rowe. *Letters and Diary of John Rowe, Boston Merchant 1759-1762 1764-1779*. Boston: W. B. Clarke, 1903, 1969.

Cushing, John D. *The Earliest Acts and Laws of the Colony of Rhode Island and Providence Plantations 1647-1719*. Wilmington, DE: Michael Glazier, Inc., 1977.

Dalzell, Frederick. "Prudence and the Golden Egg: Establishing the Federal Government in Providence, Rhode Island." *New England Quarterly* 65 3 (Sept. 1992): 335-388.

Daniels, Bruce C. *Dissent and Conformity on Narragansett Bay: The Colonial Rhode Island Town*. Middletown, CT: Wesleyan University Press, 1983.

Davidson, Philip. *Propaganda and the American Revolution 1763–1783*. Chapel Hill: University of North Carolina Press, 1941.

Davies, K. G. *Documents of the American Revolution 1770–1783*, 1-21. Shannon: Irish University Press, 1974.

DeVaro, Lawrence J. Jr. "The *Gaspee* Affair as Conspiracy." *Rhode Island History* 32 4 (1973): 107-121.

DeVaro, Lawrence Joseph. *The Impact of the Gaspee Affair on the Coming of the Revolution, 1772-1773*. Unpublished Dissertation, 1973.

Dexter, Franklin Bowditch. *The Literary Diary of Ezra Stiles*, 1-3. New York: Charles Scribner's Sons, 1901.

Dickerson, O. M. "Use Made of the Revenue from the Tax on Tea." *New England Quarterly* 31 2 (June 1958): 232-243.

Dickerson, Oliver M. *American Colonial Government, 1696–1765: A Study of the British Board of Trade in Its Relation to the American Colonies, Political, Industrial, Administrative*. New York: Russell & Russell, 1962.

Dickerson, Oliver M. *The Navigation Acts and the American Revolution*. Philadelphia: University of Pennsylvania Press, 1951.

Dickerson, O.M. "The Commissioners of Customs and the 'Boston Massacre.'" *New England Quarterly* 27 3 (September 1954): 307-325.

Donoughue, Bernard. *British Politics and the American Revolution: The Path to War, 1773-75*. London: Macmillan, 1964.

Dukes, Richard Sears. *The* Gaspee *incident as a clash of cultures*. Unpublished Thesis, 1989.

Eaton, Amasa M. "The Development of the Judicial System in Rhode Island." *Yale Law Journal* 14 3 (January 1905): 148-170.

Einstein, Lewis. *Divided Loyalties: Americans in England During the War of Independence*. New York: Russell & Russell, 1933.

Fagerstrom, Dalphy I. "Scottish Opinion and the American Revolution." *William and Mary Quarterly* 11 2 (April 1954): 252-275.

Ferraro, William M. "Localism in Portsmouth and Foster during the Revolutionary and Founding Periods." *Rhode Island History* 54 3 (August 1996): 67-89.

Finestone, Harry. *Bacon's Rebellion: The Contemporary News Sheets.* Charlottesville, VA: University of Virginia Press, 1956.

Fitzpatrick, John C. *The Spirit of the Revolution: New Light from Some of the Original Sources of American History.* Boston: Houghton Mifflin, 1924.

Flournoy, H. W. *Calendar of Virginia State Papers and Other Manuscripts*, VIII, 1890, 1968.

Foner, Eric. *The Story of American Freedom.* New York: W. W. Norton, 1998.

Ford, Paul Leicester. *The Works of Thomas Jefferson*, 1-12. New York: G.P. Putnam's Sons, 1904.

Frantz, John B. *Bacon's Rebellion: Prologue to the Revolution?.* Lexington, MA: D.C. Heath and Company, 1969.

Gage, Thomas. *The Correspondence of General Thomas Gage with the Secretaries of State, and with the War Office and Treasury, 1763-1775*, 2 Vols. New Haven: Yale University Press, 1931-1933.

Gerlach, Larry R., ed. *Legacies of the American Revolution.* Utah State University, 1978.

Gerlach, Larry R. "Charles Dudley and the Customs Quandary in Pre-Revolutionary Rhode Island." *Rhode Island History* 30 2 (1971): 52-59.

Gipson, Lawrence Henry. *The American Revolution as an Aftermath of the Great War for the Empire, 1754-1763.* New York: Academy of Political Science, 1950.

Gipson, Lawrence Henry. *The British Empire Before the American Revolution*, 1-15. New York: Alfred A. Knopf, 1958–1970.

Gipson, Lawrence Henry. *The Coming of the Revolution 1763–1775.* New York: Harper and Row, 1954.

Goldowsky, Seebert J., M.D. "Solomon Drowne and The *Gaspee* Affair: A Premedical Student Views Historic Event." *Rhode Island Medical Journal* 55 9 (September 1972): 287.

Gosnell, Harold F. "British Royal Commissions of Inquiry." *Political Science Quarterly* 49 1 (March 1934): 84-118.

Gravlee, G. Jack and James R. Irvine, eds. *Pamphlets and the American Revolution: Rhetoric, Politics, Literature, and the Popular Press.* Delmar, NY: Scholars' Facsimiles and Reprints, 1976.

Graydon, Alexander. *Memoirs of a Life, Chiefly Passed in Pennsylvania, within the Last Sixty Years; with Occasional Remarks Upon the General Occurrences, Character and Spirit of that Eventful Period.* Harrisburg: Printed by John Wyeth, 1811.

Great Britain Parliament. *The Parliamentary History of England from the earliest period to the year 1803.* London: Longman et al., 1813.

Greene, George Washington. *The Life of Nathanael Greene: Major-General in the Army of the Revolution*, 1-3. New York: G.P. Putnam and Son, 1867.

Greene, Jack P. *Interpreting Early America: Historiographical Essays.* Charlottesville and London: University Press of Virginia, 1996.

Greene, Jack P. *The Reinterpretation of the American Revolution 1763-1789.* New York and Evanston: Harper & Row, 1968.

Greene, Jack P. *Understanding the American Revolution: Issues and Actors.* Charlottesville and London: University Press of Virginia, 1995.

Greene, Jack P. and J. R. Pole. *A Companion to the American Revolution.* Malden, MA: Blackwell, 2000.

Gross, Robert A. *The Minutemen and Their World.* New York: Hill and Wang, 1976.

Gruber, Ira. "The American Revolution as Conspiracy: The British View." *William and Mary Quarterly* XXVI (July, 1969): 360-372.

Haley, John Williams. *Stirring Moments of Rhode Island History: The Great Swamp Fight, the* Gaspee *Affair, the Great Gale of 1815, the Burning of the* Lexington. Providence: 1928.

Hall, David D., John M. Murrin, and Thad W. Tate, eds. *Saints & Revolutionaries: Essays on Early American History.* New York: W. W. Norton, 1984.

Hast, Adele. "State Treason Trials During the Puritan Revolution, 1640-1660." *Historical Journal [Great Britain]* XV I (1972): 37-53.

Hatch, Nathan O. *The Sacred Cause of Liberty: Republican Thought and the Millennium in Revolutionary New England.* New Haven: Yale University Press, 1977.

Headlam, Cecil. *Calendar of State Papers, Colonial Series, America and the West Indies, Preserved in the Public Record Office.* London: Published by His Majesty's Stationery Office, 1924.

Hedges, James B. *The Browns of Providence Plantations: Colonial Years.* Cambridge, MA, 1952.

Hibbert, Christopher. *Redcoats and Rebels: The American Revolution Through British Eyes.* New York: W.W. Norton, 1990.

Hinkhouse, Fred Junkin. *The Preliminaries of the American Revolution as Seen in the English Press, 1763–1775.* New York: Columbia University Press, 1926.

Historical Manuscripts Commission, Eleventh Report, Appendix, Part V. *The Manuscripts of the Earl of Dartmouth: Presented to Both Houses of Parliament by Command of Her Majesty*, 1-3. London: Her Majesty's Stationery Office by Eyre and Spottiswoode, 1887.

Holdsworth, W. E. *A History of English Law*. Boston: Little, Brown, 1924.

Howell, T. B. *A Complete Collection of State Trials*. London: Longman, et. al., 1812.

Hurst, James Willard. *The Law of Treason in the United States*. Westport, CT: Greenwood Publishing Corporation, 1945.

Hutchinson, Peter Orlando. *The Diary and Letters of His Excellency Thomas Hutchinson, Esq.*, 1-2. Boston: Houghton, Mifflin, 1884.

Irvine, James R. and G. Jack Gravlee, eds. *Pamphlets and the American Revolution: Rhetoric, Politics, Literature, and the Popular Press*. Delmar, NY: Scholar's Facsimiles & Reprints, 1976.

Jackson, Donald. *The Diaries of George Washington*, III. Charlottesville: University Press of Virginia, 1978.

James, Sydney V. *Colonial Rhode Island: A History*. New York: Charles Scribner's Sons, 1975.

James, Sydney V. *The Colonial Metamorphoses in Rhode Island: A Study of Institutions in Change*. Hanover and London: University Press of New England, 2000.

James, W. M. *The British Navy in Adversity: A Study of the War of American Independence*. London: Longmans, Green, 1926.

Jameson, J. Franklin. *Privateering and Piracy in the Colonial Period*. New York: Augustus M. Kelley, 1923, 1970.

Jensen, Merrill. *The Founding of a Nation: A History of the American Revolution, 1763-1776*. New York: Oxford University Press, 1968, 2004.

John, Michael. *Face of Revolution*. New York: Macmillan, 1936.

Kaler, James Otis. *When We Destroyed the* Gaspee: *A Story of Narragansett Bay in 1772*. Boston: Dana Estes, 1901.

Kammen, Michael. *A Season of Youth: The American Revolution and the Historical Imagination*. Ithaca and London: Cornell University Press, 1978.

Kegan, Elizabeth Hamer, ed. *The Impact of the American Revolution Abroad*. Washington, DC: Library of Congress, 1976.

Kemmerer, Donald L. *Path to Freedom: The Struggle for Self-Government in Colonial New Jersey 1703-1776*. Princeton, NJ: Princeton University Press, 1940.

Kennedy, John Pendleton. *Journals of the House of Burgesses of Virginia*, 1-2. Richmond, VA: Library Board of the Virginia State Library, MCMV (1905).

Kimball, Gertrude Selwyn. *The Correspondence of the Colonial Governors of Rhode Island 1723–1775*, 1-2. Boston: Houghton, Mifflin, 1903.

Kiracofe, David James. *Treason and the Development of National Identity in Revolutionary America, 1775-1815.* University of Connecticut: Unpublished Dissertation, 1995.

Knox, Horatio B. *The Destruction of the* Gaspee. Providence: Dept. of Education, State of Rhode Island, 1908.

Kukla, Jon. "Order and Chaos in Early America: Political and Social Stability in Pre-Restoration Virginia." *American Historical Review* 90 2 (April 1985): 275-298.

Kurtz, Stephen G. and James H. Hutson. *Essays on the American Revolution.* Williamsburg, VA: Institute of Early American History and Culture, 1973.

Labaree, Benjamin W. *The Atlantic World of Robert G. Albion.* Middletown, CT: Wesleyan University Press, 1975.

Labaree, Benjamin W. *The Boston Tea Party.* New York: Oxford University Press, 1964.

Labaree, Benjamin W. et al. *America and the Sea: A Maritime History.* Mystic, CT: Mystic Seaport, 1998.

Lancaster, Jane. "'By the Pens of Females': Girls' Diaries from Rhode Island, 1788–1821." *Rhode Island History* 57 3 & 4 (August/November 1999): 59-113.

Langford, Paul, ed. *The Writings and Speeches of Edmund Burke.* Oxford: Clarendon Press, 1981.

Lemay, J. A. Leo. *The Canon of Benjamin Franklin 1722-1776.* Newark: University of Delaware Press, 1986.

Lemisch, Jesse. "Jack Tar in the Streets: Merchant Seamen in the Politics of Revolutionary America." *William and Mary Quarterly* 25 3 (July 1968): 371-407.

Lemisch, Jesse. *Jack Tar vs. John Bull: The Role of New York's Seamen in Precipitating the Revolution.* New York: Garland Publishing, 1997.

Lemons, J. Stanley. "Rhode Island and the Slave Trade." *Rhode Island History* 60 4 (Fall 2002): 95-104.

Leslie, William R. "The *Gaspee* Affair: A Study of Its Constitutional Significance." *Mississippi Valley Historical Review* 39 2 (September 1952): 233-256.

Longley, R. S. "Mob Activities in Revolutionary Massachusetts." *New England Quarterly* 6 1 (March 1933): 98-130.

Lovejoy, David S. "Henry Marchant and the Mistress of the World." *William and Mary Quarterly* 12 3 (July 1955): 375-398.

Lovejoy, David S. *Rhode Island Politics and the American Revolution 1760-1776.* Providence, RI: Brown University Press, 1958.

Lucas, Paul R. "Colony or Commonwealth: Massachusetts Bay, 1661-1666." *William and Mary Quarterly* 24 1 (January 1967): 88-107.

Maclay, Edgar Stanton. *Moses Brown Captain U.S.N.* New York: The Baker and Taylor Company, 1904.

Maier, Pauline. "Coming to Terms with Samuel Adams." *American Historical Review* 81 1 (February 1976): 12-37.

Maier, Pauline. "John Wilkes and American Disillusionment with Britain." *William and Mary Quarterly* 3rd ser 20 (1963): 373-395.

Maier, Pauline. "Popular Uprisings and Civil Authority in Eighteenth-Century America." *William and Mary Quarterly* 27 1 (January 1970): 3-35.

Maier, Pauline. *From Resistance to Revolution: Colonial Radicals and the Development of American Opposition to Britain, 1765-1776.* New York: Alfred A. Knopf, 1972.

Malone, Joseph J. *Pine Trees and Politics: the Naval Stores and Forest Policy in Colonial New England 1691-1775.* Seattle: University of Washington Press, 1964.

Marinelli, Mary Mercedes. *The Investigation of the* Gaspee *Attack: A Reappraisal.* Unpublished Thesis, 1962.

Martin, Alfred S. "The King's Customs: Philadelphia, 1763-1774." *William and Mary Quarterly,* 3rd ser. 5 2 (Apr., 1948): 201-216.

Massachusetts Historical Society. *Commerce of Rhode Island 1726-1800.* Norwood, MA: Plimpton Press, 1914.

Massachusetts Historical Society. *Proceedings October, 1916—June, 1917.* Boston: Published by the Society, 1917.

May, W. E. "The *Gaspee* Affair." *Mariner's Mirror [Great Britain]* 63 2 (1977): 129-135.

Mayo, Lawrence Shaw. *The History of the Colony and Province of Massachusetts-Bay by Thomas Hutchinson,* 1-3. Cambridge, MA: Harvard University Press, 1936.

McDonald, Forrest. *Empire and Nation: Letters from a Farmer in Pennsylvania, John Dickinson and Letters from the Federal Farmer, Richard Henry Lee.* Englewood Cliffs, NJ: Prentice-Hall, 1962.

McLoughlin, William G. "Massive Civil Disobedience as a Baptist Tactic in 1773." *American Quarterly* 21 4 (Winter 1969): 710-727.

McLoughlin, William G. *New England Dissent 1630-1833: The Baptists and the Separation of Church and State,* 1-2. Cambridge, MA: Harvard University Press, 1971.

McLoughlin, William G. *Soul Liberty: The Baptists' Struggle in New England, 1630-1833.* Hanover and London: Brown University Press and University Press of New England, 1991.

Meyer, F. V. *Britain's Colonies in World Trade*. London: Oxford University Press, 1948.

Miller, E. I. "The Virginia Committee of Correspondence 1759-1770." *William and Mary College Quarterly Historical Magazine* 22 1 (July 1913): 1-19.

Miller, E. I. "The Virginia Committee of Correspondence of 1773-1775." *William and Mary College Quarterly Historical Magazine* 22 2 (October 1913): 99-113.

Miller, Helen Hill. *The Case for Liberty*. Chapel Hill: University of North Carolina Press, 1965.

Miller, John C. *The Origins of the American Revolution*. Stanford, CA: Stanford University Press, 1943, 1959.

Monahon, Clifford P. "Nathanael Greene's Letters to 'Friend Sammy' Ward." *Rhode Island History* 16 2 (July 1957): 79-89.

Monahon, Clifford. *Correspondence of Governor Samuel Ward May 1775–March 1776*. Providence, RI: Rhode Island Historical Society, 1952.

Moore, W. Harrison. "Executive Commissions of Inquiry." *Columbia Law Review* 13 6 (Jun., 1913): 500-523.

Morgan, Edmund S. "The Puritan Ethic and the American Revolution." *William and Mary Quarterly* 24 1 (January 1967): 3-43.

Morgan, Edmund S. and Helen M. Morgan. *The Stamp Act Crisis: Prologue to Revolution*. Chapel Hill: University of North Carolina Press, 1953.

Morison, Samuel Eliot. *Sources and Documents illustrating the American Revolution 1764-1788 and the formation of the Federal Constitution*. New York: Oxford University Press, 1965.

Morris, Richard B. *The Era of the American Revolution*. New York: Columbia University Press, 1939.

Munro, James. *Acts of the Privy Council of England. Colonial Series*, 1-6. Nendeln, Leichtenstein: Kraus Reprint Ltd., 1908-1912, 1966.

Munro, Wilfred Harold. *Tales of an Old Sea Port: A General Sketch of the History of Bristol, Rhode Island*. Princeton, NJ: Princeton University Press, 1917.

Murphy, Paul L. "Time to Reclaim: The Current Challenge of American Constitutional History." *American Historical Review* 69 1 (October 1963): 64-79.

Neville, John Davenport. *Bacon's Rebellion: Abstract of Materials in the Colonial Records Project*. Not Specified: Jamestown Foundation, 1976.

Nicolson, Colin. *The "Infamas Govener": Francis Bernard and the Origins of the American Revolution*. Boston: Northeastern University Press, 2001.

Norton, Mary Beth. "John Randolph's 'Plan of Accomodations.'" *William and Mary Quarterly* 28 1 (January 1971): 103-120.

Osgood, Herbert L. *The American Colonies in the Eighteenth Century*, 1-3. New York: Columbia University Press, 1924.

Patterson, Stephen E. *A History of Political Parties in Revolutionary Massachusetts 1770–1780*. Dissertation: University of Wisconsin, 1968.

Perry, Richard L., ed. *Sources of Our Liberties: Documentary Origins of Individual Liberties in the United States Constitution and Bill of Rights*. New York: Associated College Presses, 1959.

Polishook, Irwin H. *Rhode Island and the Union 1774-1795*. Evanston, IL: Northwestern University Press, 1969.

Preston, Howard Willis. *Rhode Island and the Sea*. Providence: State Bureau of Information, 1932.

Quincy, Josiah. *Memoir of the Life of Josiah Quincy, Junior, of Massachusetts Bay*. Boston: Little, Brown, 1875.

Rawson, Jonathan A., Jr. "Uncelebrated Burning of H.M.S. *Gaspee*." *New York Times Book Review and Magazine* (June 11, 1922).

Reid, John Phillip. *In a Rebellious Spirit: The Argument of Facts, The Liberty Riot, and the Coming of the American Revolution*. University Park: Pennsylvania State University Press, 1979.

Rodger, N. A. M. *The Command of the Ocean: A Naval History of Britain 1649-1815*. London: National Maritime Museum, 2004.

Rodger, N. A. M. *The Insatiable Earl: A Life of John Montagu, Fourth Earl of Sandwich 1718-1792*. New York and London: W. W. Norton, 1993.

Rude, George. "The London 'Mob' of the Eighteenth Century." *Historical Journal* 2 1 (1959): 1-18.

Rudolph, Lloyd I. "The Eighteenth Century Mob in America and Europe." *American Quarterly* 11 4 (Winter 1959): 447-469.

Schlesinger, Arthur M. "A Note on Songs as Patriot Propaganda 1765-1776." *William and Mary Quarterly* 11 1 (January 1954): 78-88.

Schlesinger, Arthur Meier. "Political Mobs and the American Revolution, 1765-1776." *Proceedings of the American Philosophical Society* 99 4 (August 30, 1955): 244-250.

Schonback, Morris. *Radicals and Visionaries: A History of Dissent in New Jersey*. Princeton, NJ: D. Van Nostrand, 1964.

Shapiro, Alexander H. "Political Theory and the Growth of Defensive Safeguards in Criminal Procedure: The Origins of the Treason Trials Act of 1696." *Law and History Review* 11 2 (Autumn, 1993): 215-255.

Sheidley, Harlow W. *Sectional Nationalism: Massachusetts Conservative Leaders and the Transformation of America, 1815–1836.* Boston: Northeastern University Press, 1998.

Smith, Carl W. *The reexamination of the Gaspee Affair as a cause of the American Revolution.* Unpublished Thesis, 1967.

Smith, Glenn Curtis. "An Era of Non-Importation Associations, 1768-73." *William and Mary College Quarterly Historical Magazine* 20 1 (January 1940): 84-98.

Smith, Lacey Baldwin. *Treason in Tudor England: Politics and Paranoia.* Princeton, NJ: Princeton University Press, 1986.

Snowden, Richard. *The American Revolution: Written in Scriptural, or, Ancient Historical Style.* Baltimore: printed by W. Pechin, 1796.

Sosin, Jack M. *Agents and Merchants: British Colonial Policy and the Origins of the American Revolution, 1763-1775.* Lincoln: University of Nebraska Press, 1965.

Staples, William R. *Rhode Island in the Continental Congress.* Providence: Providence Press Company, Printers to the State, 1870.

Staples, William R. *The Documentary History of the Destruction of the* Gaspee. Providence: Knowles, Vose, and Anthony, 1845, 1990.

Starr, Edward C. *A Baptist Bibliography: Being a Register of Printed Material by and about Baptists: including Works Written Against the Baptists,* Section A. Philadelphia, PA: Judson Press, 1947.

Stayley, Thomas. *The Statue of Truth, in the garden of allegory: addressed to Lord North: containing such remarks as may not be unworthy his Lordship's notice: Useful to the Managers of his Majesty's Revenues, &c. &c. &c.* London: Printed for the Author, 1773.

Stephen, James Fitzjames. *A History of the Criminal Law of England,* II. London: Macmillan, 1883.

Stout, Harry S. *The New England Soul: Preaching and Religious Culture in Colonial New England.* New York: Oxford University Press, 1986.

Stout, Neil R. "The *Gaspee* Affair." *Mankind* 1 1 (1967): 48-51, 89-92.

Stout, Neil R. *The Royal Navy in America 1760-1775.* Annapolis, MD: Naval Institute Press, 1973.

Sutherland, Lucy S. *The Correspondence of Edmund Burke.* Chicago: University of Chicago Press, 1960.

Sypek, Sandra. *An Evaluation of the* Gaspee *commission of inquiry.* Unpublished Thesis, 1969.

Tate, Thad W. "The Coming of the Revolution in Virginia: Britain's Challenge to Virginia's Ruling Class, 1763-1776." *William and Mary Quarterly* 19 3 (July 1962): 323-343.

Thomas, Leslie Joseph. *Partisan Politics in Massachusetts during Governor Bernard's Administration, 1760-1770*. Dissertation: University of Wisconsin, 1960.

Thompson, E. P. "The Moral Economy of the English Crowd in the Eighteenth Century." *Past and Present* 50 (1971): 76-136.

Thompson, Mack E. "The Ward-Hopkins Controversy and the American Revolution in Rhode Island: An Interpretation." *William and Mary Quarterly* 16 3 (July 1959): 363-375.

Thomson, Mark A. *The Secretaries of State 1681-1782*. New York: Frank Cass, 1932, 1968.

Tyler, John W. *Smugglers & Patriots: Boston Merchants and the Advent of the American Revolution*. Boston: Northeastern University Press, 1986.

Ubbelohde, Carl. *The American Colonies and the British Empire, 1607-1763*. New York: Crowell, 1968.

Ubbelohde, Carl. *The Vice-Admiralty Courts and the American Revolution*. Williamsburg, VA: Institute of Early American History and Culture, 1960.

Upton, L. F. S. "Proceedings of Ye Body Respecting the Tea." *William and Mary Quarterly* 22 2 (April 1965): 287-300.

Van Tassel, David D. "Henry Barton Dawson: A Nineteenth-Century Revisionist." *William and Mary Quarterly* 13 3 (July 1956): 319-341.

Warner, Jessica. *John the Painter: Terrorist of the American Revolution*. New York: Thunder's Mouth Press, 2004.

Warren, Mercy Otis. *History of the Rise, Progress and Termination of the American Revolution intersperced with Biographical, Political and Moral Observations*, 1-2. Indianapolis: Liberty Classics, 1805.

Washburn, Wilcomb E. *The Governor and the Rebel: A History of Bacon's Rebellion in Virginia*. New York: W.W. Norton, 1972.

Webb, Stephen Saunders. *1676: The End of American Independence*. New York: Alfred A Knopf, 1984.

West, Stephen. *Sketches of the Life of the Late Rev. Samuel Hopkins, D.D.* Hartford: Hudson and Goodwin, 1805.

Wickwire, Franklin B. "John Pownall and British Colonial Policy." *William and Mary Quarterly* 20 4 (October 1963): 543-554.

Wickwire, Franklin B. *British Subministers and Colonial America 1763-1783*. Princeton, NJ: Princeton University Press, 1966.

Wiener, Frederick B. "The Rhode Island Merchants and the Sugar Act." *New England Quarterly* III (July, 1930): 464-500.

Wiener, Frederick B. "Notes on the Rhode Island Admiralty, 1727-1790." *Harvard Law Review* 46 1 (November 1932): 44-90.

Wilbour, B. O. *The Destruction of the* Gaspee *and the Reasons Therefore*. Providence: 1892.

Wood, Gordon S. "Conspiracy and the Paranoid Style: Causality and Deceit in the Eighteenth Century." *The William and Mary Quarterly* 39 3 (July 1982): 401-441.

Wood, Gordon S. *The Radicalism of the American Revolution*. New York: Vintage Books, 1991.

Wulsin, Eugene. "The Political Consequences of the Burning of the *Gaspee* Part I." *Rhode Island History* III (January 1944): 1-11.

Wulsin, Eugene. "The Political Consequences of the Burning of the *Gaspee* Part II." *Rhode Island History* III (April 1944): 55-64.

York, Neil L. "The Uses of Law and the *Gaspee* Affair." *Rhode Island History* 50 1 (1992): 2-21.

Young, Alfred F. *The American Revolution: Explorations in the History of Radicalism*. DeKalb: Northern Illinois University Press, 1976.

Zobel, Hiller B. *The Boston Massacre*. New York: W.W. Norton, 1970.

ACKNOWLEDGMENTS

I WOULD LIKE TO THANK THE MEMBERS OF MY COMMITTEE: Richard D. Brown, my major advisor, and Lawrence Goodheart and Walter W. Woodward for their helpful support during the preparation of the manuscript. I would also like to thank my wife, Amy Park, for her patience and assistance with this project. Additionally, I would like to thank Todd Andrlik, Bruce H. Franklin, and Don Hagist for all of their patient assistance getting us to publication.

INDEX